Self-Control

Self-Control

Waiting Until Tomorrow for What You Want Today

A. W. Logue

State University of New York at Stony Brook

Prentice Hall
Englewood Cliffs, New Jersey 07632

Library of Congress Cataloging-in-Publication Data

Logue, A. W. (Alexandra W.)
    Self-control : waiting until tomorrow for what you want today /
A.W. Logue.
        p.   cm.
    Includes bibliographical rerferences and indexes.
    ISBN 0-13-803750-7
    1. Self-control.   I. Title.
BF632.L64   1995
153.8—dc20
                                                    94-5478
                                                    CIP

Acquisitions editor: Heidi Freund/Pete Janzow
Cover designer: Bill McClosky
Manufacturing buyer: Tricia Kenny

 © 1995 by Alexandra Woods Logue
A Paramount Communications Company
Englewood Cliffs, NJ 07632

Printed in the United States of America

10 9 8 7 6 5 4 3 2 1

ISBN 0-13-803750-7

Prentice-Hall International (UK) Limited, London
Prentice-Hall of Australia Pty. Limited, Sydney
Prentice-Hall Canada Inc., Toronto
Prentice-Hall Hispanoamericana, S.A., Mexico
Prentice-Hall of India Private Limited, New Delhi
Prentice-Hall of Japan, Inc., Tokyo
Simon & Schuster Asia Pte. Ltd., Singapore
Editora Prentice-Hall do Brasil, Ltda., Rio de Janeiro

To Sam
who showed me that some things
are indeed worth waiting for

Contents

Preface

From the time that I was very small, I was apparently interested in working towards long-term, large goals (that is, I was inclined to show self-control). For example, while in fourth grade, I made an appointment to speak with the principal to discuss what I needed to do to prepare for college. In much more recent times, when this book became unavoidably delayed due to my becoming Chair of the Psychology Department at Stony Brook, I gladly gave up many an immediate pleasure and worked nights and weekends to finish it. (I also realized how badly it would look for someone to be unable to finish a book on self-control.)

Thus, it is not surprising that when Jim Mazur, one of my fellow graduate students at Harvard University, suggested about twenty years ago that we work together on an experiment concerning self-control in pigeons, I was immediately interested. This experiment demonstrated that it was possible to train pigeons to show self-control with regard to food; pigeons could learn to wait for larger amounts of food rather than choosing a smaller amount of food that they could have sooner. Some ten years later, Julie Schweitzer and Beth Sulzer-Azaroff used a similar procedure, derived from Jim's and my work with pigeons, to increase self-control in a group of impulsive children.[1]

During that ten-year period, and continuing to the present day, the research in my laboratory has focused on a multitude of different aspects of self-control. At first the subjects were pigeons. Later, the work was expanded to include adult humans, preschool children, and finally, rats. We have been examining why these subjects do or do not show self-control under a large variety of different conditions. We have sought both to describe the behavior and to find out what causes it.

For someone such as myself who has broad interests within psychology, self-control is a perfect research topic. Research on self-control is relevant to many basic research issues, such as how animals (including human animals) make choices and, more specifically, how the sizes and delays of rewards affect those choices. Research on self-control is also relevant to a large variety of clinical problems involving people such as overeaters, who are unable to show self-control. Finally, research on self-control is also relevant to many applied issues, including the writing of a book. Prentice Hall, the publisher of this book, writes in its author's guide:

"Two of the chief causes of manuscript elephantiasis are lack of self-control in sticking to the original plan for the book, and mere wordiness. Often the original plan is a good one, but in the actual writing the author goes off at tangents to the main purpose; or, though keeping in general to the plan, overwhelms it with detail."[2]

I made sure to keep these points in mind while writing this book!

Clearly, the topic of self-control is an important one in that it is of much concern to basic research, clinical applications, and our daily lives. Self-control, and the lack of it, is an integral part of our everyday existence.

Many areas of psychology have something to say about self-control. As just a few examples, psychologists who study clinical psychology, cognitive psychology, developmental psychology, learning, motivation, personality theory, physiological psychology, and social psychology have conducted research on self-control. Thus, studying self-control offers an unusual opportunity to focus on a particular aspect of behavior and to see how different areas within psychology try to understand that behavior. Studying self-control can help to show how the different pieces of psychology fit together—how they complement each other and even overlap. Studying self-control can help psychologists, their students, and educated laypeople to see psychology as a unified whole consisting of a collection of somewhat different methods whose sole purpose is to understand a particular behavior. Research on self-control from a large variety of areas of psychology is included in this book, and even some research from outside of psychology.

However, for someone who is interested in understanding self-control, learning about the field is difficult. Until now, there has been no book that has synthesized the basic research on self-control along with its clinical applications. This book provides just such a synthesis. Part I introduces the main issues relevant to the study of self-control, including definitions of self-control and techniques involved in studying self-control. Part II provides information regarding general determinants of self-control, including evolutionary processes, development, and general methods for changing self-control. Part III uses the information from Parts I and II as a base to examine various specific areas of concern with regard to self-control: eating, drug abuse, and other health-related behaviors; education, management, and money; and topics concerning how people get along with themselves and others including cooperation, lying, depression, suicide, and aggression. At the end of the book is a concluding section focused on the nature of self-control in our current environment. This conclusion is followed by a list of places to contact for further information regarding some of the clinical problems raised in the book.

Two caveats are in order. First, as with any topic that relates to so many different research areas, it is not possible to include all research on self-control within one book. However, the extensive reference notes at the end of each chapter list a great many additional resources that can be examined. Second, this is not a self-help book. It will not tell you how to solve your own or someone else's self-control problems. What it hopefully will do is to give you some insight with regard to what might be responsible for your or someone else's self-control problems, and it will help you to find out where further information and help may be located; practical problem solving requires professional help. The list of organizations at the end of the book should be useful in finding this additional information and assistance.

This book is intended for readers with or without previous courses in psychology; for those with little psychology background, essential research strategies are described in detail. This book may be used as a supplementary or a main text in classes. It can also serve as an introduction to the study of self-control for psychologists, including clinical psychologists who are interested in how basic research might help them to understand certain clinical problems. Finally, this book is also intended for educated laypeople, who may never enroll in another course but would like to learn something more about self-control and what causes it. The only requirement for being able to read and understand this book is a commitment to a scientific approach to the study of behavior—a commitment to studying behavior such as self-control using the same scientific methods that are used in biology, chemistry, and physics. As with my previous book, *The Psychology of Eating and Drinking*,[3] one of my goals in writing this book on self-control has been to bring scientific psychological research to a broad audience in order to show just how much can be learned about the nature and causes of behavior by using a scientific approach.

References

1. Schweitzer, J. B., and Sulzer-Azaroff, B. (1988). "Self-control: Teaching Tolerance for Delay in Impulsive Children." *Journal of the Experimental Analysis of Behavior*, 50, 173–186.
2. Prentice Hall (1978). *Prentice Hall Author's Guide*. Englewood Cliffs, NJ: Prentice Hall, p. 2.
3. Logue, A. W. (1991). *The Psychology of Eating and Drinking: An Introduction* (2nd ed.). New York: Freeman.

Acknowledgments

Many people and organizations assisted me in preparing this book. Two colleagues have stimulated my work on self-control enormously. They are James Mazur, a perfect collaborator, with whom I began my work on self-control when we were both graduate students at Harvard; and Howard Rachlin, my colleague at Stony Brook, whose work inspired me even before we first met. My students over the past 16 years have been a notable influence in my ideas about self-control. In particular, I should mention my senior thesis and graduate student coauthors (Adolfo Chavarro, John Chelonis, Lori Forzano, Elise Kabela, Benjamin Mauro, Telmo Peña-Correal, George King, Monica Rodriguez, Michael Smith, Henry Tobin, and Joseph Volpe). Without their continued stimulation and assistance, much of my work on self-control would never have been done. My administrative positions (first as Associate Dean of the Division of Social and Behavioral Sciences, appointed by Dean Andrew Policano, and second as Chair of the Psychology Department, elected by the Psychology Department Faculty and appointed by Dean Bryce Hool and Provost Tilden Edelstein) provided me with much material for the sections on self-control and management in Chapter 9, as well as with much practical experience with self-control issues.

Two editors who did not sign the book, but who were nonetheless very influential in shaping it, are Susan Arellano and Jonathan Cobb. Walter Mischel arranged for me to have library privileges at Columbia University so that I could work on my book during my sabbatical. A number of people graciously provided me with the detailed answers that I requested regarding specific issues related to self-control. These people include: William Arens, Daniel Klein, Curtis Marean, Lawrence Martin, and Elizabeth Stone. Others, including Susan Brennan, Dana C. Dawes, William Dawes, and the REU/

MRAP students of the summer of 1991, contributed to the quotes and apho-
risms spread throughout the book. A conversation with Paul Wortman about
self-control in people of advanced age was extremely useful. A number of
people gave me excellent, constructive comments concerning specific parts of
the manuscript. They are: Robert Boice, Robert Eisenberger, David Glass,
Robert Hoff, Joseph Pear, Howard Rachlin, Ian Shrank, and Michael Zeiler.
Jeffrey Kirk proved a wonder at getting the manuscript into shape, including
doing the initial drafts of the figures and constructing the author index. Both
he and John Chelonis produced for me from the library a seemingly endless
stream of computer searches and research articles. Catherine Sexton showed
herself to be a perfectionist in drafting the final versions of the figures.

I also want to acknowledge the editorial staff of Prentice Hall. Susan
Brennan signed the book and has continued to support it enthusiastically and
to follow the manuscript's progress despite her migration to W. H. Freeman
(where, coincidentally, she is responsible for my book *The Psychology of Eating and Drinking*[1]). Peter Janzow and Heidi Freund took up the reins from Susan, and their enthusiasm about the book has been infectious. Maureen
Richardson's steady efforts as the Production Editor brought the book into its
published form.

Twentieth Century Fox provided the photograph of Marilyn Monroe
from the movie *Monkey Business* for Figure 4.1 and Columbia Pictures provided the photograph of Jamie Lee Curtis from the movie *Perfect* for Figure
4.2. Phototeque, in New York City, was of great assistance in locating these
two photographs.

Throughout it all, for the past 16 years, the Long Island Railroad has provided many, many hours of uninterrupted work time. Harvard University,
the National Institute of Mental Health, the National Science Foundation,
Sigma Xi, and the State University of New York have all provided funds for
research conducted in my laboratory that is reported here.

As always, I owe my deepest thanks to Ian Shrank and Samuel Shrank,
whose never-ending support of my work, and whose encouragement, keep
me working towards those big rewards, no matter what.

Reference

1.   Logue, A. W. (1991). *The Psychology of Eating and Drinking: An Introduction* (2nd
     ed.). New York: Freeman.

Self-Control

Part I

Introduction

1

Overview

People often do things that result in some immediate gratification, but which in the long run are not very beneficial. They:

- steal, even though they could go to jail.
- splurge on dessert rather than sticking to a diet.
- smoke despite the possibility of cancer and emphysema.
- drink alcohol despite long-term damage to brain and liver.
- use their credit cards without having money to pay the credit-card bill.
- buy a fancy car instead of saving for retirement.
- have sex without using condoms.
- party instead of studying for a test.

Many other examples can be found. Engaging in such behaviors, those that result in some immediate gratification at the expense of long-term, greater benefits, can be termed *impulsiveness*. The converse, engaging in behaviors that result in delayed (but more) reward, can be termed *self-control*.[1] Much of human behavior is impulsive. In fact, some clinical psychologists state that many clinical problems are impulsiveness problems—that many clients seek therapy because they keep performing a behavior (such as yelling at their spouses) which may have some immediate rewards, but which is probably not the best strategy in the long run.[2]

   In an age in which we can cure some people of cancer and can send astronauts to the moon—actions that require a great deal of effort for a very distant payoff—why is so much of our behavior impulsive? Why are we sometimes able to wait for delayed rewards but unable to wait at other times? In order to best increase self-control, we need to understand what causes impulsiveness and why it is present in our society.

This book offers a new explanation of impulsiveness based on research results with humans and other animals. The book will contend that impulsiveness is caused by our tendency to discount, or value less, events that are delayed as compared with events that are immediate. A good grade received in three months is worth less to a student than is a good grade received immediately. That is why many students choose, at the beginning of a term, to go to a movie instead of to study. The book will further contend that this discounting is a result of evolution. People, as well as other animals, have evolved so as to discount delayed events because in nature delayed events may not always occur. For example, a hunter-gatherer waiting for some berries to ripen on a bush may never get the chance to eat the berries—birds may eat them first, the berries may be destroyed in a rainstorm, the hunter-gatherer may be eaten by a lion, or the hunter-gatherer may die of starvation before the berries have ripened. In such situations, an animal should choose between immediately available outcomes; it will not pay to wait for delayed outcomes.

However, in our present environment, there is sometimes great certainty that particular delayed events will indeed occur. Most students, if they work hard, will receive better grades; money saved in a bank is very likely to be there for a rainy day ten years from now; and repeated shoplifting is very likely to result in a jail sentence.

The evolutionary analysis shows that self-control should not be labeled as good and impulsiveness as bad. Self-control is not a goal to be reached as part of normal development (even though children do tend to be more impulsive than adults). There are situations in which the best overall strategy is impulsiveness.

This book will maintain that people need to evaluate carefully the choices they make, with less emotional baggage and with more consideration of the overall benefits of making a particular choice. We need to understand that not only is impulsiveness sometimes the best strategy, but when someone is impulsive that person is not inherently bad; impulsiveness is part of our evolutionary heritage. What we should do is identify those situations in which self-control is more advantageous than impulsiveness, and then engage in whatever actions are necessary to ensure that self-control does indeed occur.

In order to increase self-control, it is necessary to understand precisely what physiological mechanisms and behavioral situations are responsible for people making self-control or impulsive choices. Although some factors responsible for impulsiveness and self-control are fairly general and apply to most situations, others can differ depending on the particular situation. Although evolution may have shaped people and other animals so that they discount delayed events, different mechanisms may be responsible for this discounting in different situations,[3] and a thorough understanding of all of these mechanisms will assist in our being able to modify self-control and impulsive behavior.

The remainder of Part I of this book further defines self-control and impulsiveness and provides some general background for these phenomena. Part II describes the evolutionary, developmental, learning, and cultural determinants of self-control and impulsiveness, as well as general methods for changing these behaviors. Evidence from research conducted with nonhuman, as well as human, subjects is presented. Part III describes particular situations in which self-control and impulsiveness are of concern. For each of these situations, the book explains what causes self-control or impulsiveness, and then how that behavior might be modified. The chapters in this part of the book provide examples concerning eating behavior; drug abuse; other health-related behaviors; education, management, and money; and getting along with yourself and others. The concluding section following Parts I, II, and III summarizes the mismatch between our evolutionary heritage and our current environment, as well as summarizing the major methods available for meliorating this mismatch. Finally, at the end of the book is a list of organizations to contact regarding self-help and other information regarding unwanted impulsive behaviors.

REFERENCES

1. Ainslie, G. W. (1974). "Impulse Control in Pigeons." *Journal of the Experimental Analysis of Behavior*, 21, 485–489.

    Logue, A. W. (1988). "Research on self-control: An integrating framework." *Behavioral and Brain Sciences*, 11, 665–709.

    Rachlin, H., and Green, L. (1972). "Commitment, Choice and Self-control." *Journal of the Experimental Analysis of Behavior*, 17, 15–22.

2. Goldfried, M. R., and Merbaum, M. (Eds.), (1973). *Behavior Change Through Self-control*. New York: Holt, Rinehart and Winston.

    Wilson, G. T., and O'Leary, K. D. (1980). *"Principles of Behavior Therapy."* Englewood, Cliffs, NJ: Prentice Hall.

3. Cosmides, L., and Tooby, J. (1987). "From Evolution to Behavior: Evolutionary Psychology as the Missing Link." In J. Dupré (Ed.), *The Latest on the Best: Essays on Evolution and Optimality* (pp. 277–306). Cambridge: MIT Press.

    Zeiler, M. D. (1991, May). *Behavior as Evolutionary Biology*. Paper presented at the Association for Behavior Analysis, Atlanta, Georgia.

2

Background
and Definitions

We are constantly faced with choices—what to eat, where to go, when to sleep, and a myriad of others. At the very least, we must choose between doing something and doing nothing. All of these choices are between outcomes of varying degrees of pleasantness and aversiveness. We could describe this variation as that in which some outcomes are larger (i.e., more pleasant or less aversive) than others. The outcomes also vary in terms of when they will occur. Some occur immediately after they are chosen, others occur much later.

Suppose there is a choice between two outcomes that are of equal size, but one outcome will occur much later than the other (see Figure 2.1a). For example, suppose you are hungry and go to a restaurant and order soup, and the waiter says that you can have tomato soup that is ready right now or pumpkin soup that is still being made and will be ready in half an hour. Suppose further that you like tomato soup and pumpkin soup about the same. In this case, you will almost certainly choose the sooner outcome, the tomato soup.

Now suppose there is a choice between two outcomes that will occur after an equal amount of time, but one outcome is larger than the other (Figure 2.1b). For example, suppose the waiter says that both tomato soup and pumpkin soup are available now, and that you like pumpkin soup much more than tomato soup. In this case, you will almost certainly choose the larger outcome, the pumpkin soup.

However, suppose there is a choice in which one outcome is larger but also more delayed than the other (Figure 2.1c). For example, suppose the waiter says that you may have the tomato soup that is ready now, or the pumpkin soup (which you prefer) in half an hour. What will you choose then? This last type of choice, one between a larger but more delayed outcome and a smaller but less delayed outcome, is the subject of this book. In such a situ-

(a) Choice Between Two Outcomes of Different Delays

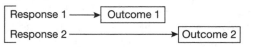

(b) Choice Between Two Outcomes of Different Sizes

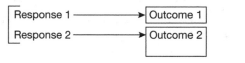

(c) Self-Control Choice

Figure 2.1. Three types of choices. A bracket indicates that a choice is available between the two responses. The length of the line between a response and its outcome indicates the amount of time after the response that the outcome occurs. The size of the outcome box indicates the size of an outcome. (a) Choice between two outcomes of different delays but equal sizes. (b) Choice between two equally delayed outcomes of unequal sizes. (c) Choice between a less delayed, smaller outcome and a more delayed, larger outcome.

ation, the book defines *self-control* as the choice of the larger, more delayed outcome (the pumpkin soup), and *impulsiveness* as the choice of the smaller, less delayed outcome (the tomato soup).[1] Similar terms for these types of choices are *delay of gratification* and *immediate gratification*.

This type of choice situation is very common for humans as well as for other animals (for an example, see Box 2.1). Self-control and impulsiveness are of concern to individuals for their own and their friends' and families' well-being. In addition, health, managerial, and law professionals want to know why people sometimes behave in ways that in the long run are not best for themselves, for their families, for their employers, or for society, as well as wanting to know how self-control can be increased.

ADVANTAGES AND DISADVANTAGES OF THE PRESENT DEFINITIONS

One seeming disadvantage of the present definitions of self-control and impulsiveness might be that these definitions are for very specific kinds of

How to decide between a palm reading or tarot? . . . The cards tend to deal more with the immediate future . . . and palms are more long-term. Most people tend to go for the cards. For some reason, everyone wants to know the immediate future.[2]

Box 2.1

choice behavior, and elsewhere the terms self-control and impulsiveness are often used to describe many different sorts of behaviors. In other words, perhaps there are many behavioral phenomena thought of as self-control and impulsiveness to which the present definitions do not apply, thus limiting the applicability of research using these definitions.

For example, self-control has been used to describe situations in which someone (a) persists with a repetitive task although faced with distraction,[3] (b) changes his or her own behavior through changing the influences that regulate that behavior (e.g., through the use of self-reward),[4] (c) does not engage in behavior motivated by anger,[5] or (d) tolerates aversive stimuli in return for a large reward.[6] Impulsiveness has been used to describe situations in which someone responds quickly, and inaccurately, when several solutions to a problem are available.[7] However, in each of these cases, the kind of behavior termed self-control or impulsiveness can be described as choice behavior between larger, more delayed outcomes and smaller, less delayed outcomes.

For instance, someone changing his or her own behavior through changing the influences that regulate that behavior can be described as someone choosing between doing behavior A (the behavior to be changed), a behavior that will result in a smaller, sooner reward; or doing behavior B, a behavior that will prevent behavior A and will result in the subject behaving so as to obtain a larger reward later.

An example of this type of self-control would be someone putting a finger under his or her own nose to stop a sneeze. In this case, sneezing is the impulsive choice, and putting a finger under the nose so that sneezes are suppressed is the self-control choice.

All of the above behaviors labeled as self-control and impulsiveness fit well within the present book's own definitions. Therefore, research using these definitions is not of limited applicability.

Another possible disadvantage of the present definitions of self-control and impulsiveness is not that they encompass too few behaviors, but that they encompass too many. Using the terms self-control and impulsiveness for this particular type of choice behavior (choices between larger, delayed outcomes and smaller, less delayed outcomes) adds all kinds of implications about what is being studied—implications about such concepts as willpower that may not be intended. Therefore, why label the behavior of concern by the terms self-control and impulsiveness? Why use these terms at all? Why not just write a book about choices between larger, more delayed outcomes and smaller, less delayed outcomes? The reason that the terms self-control and impulsiveness should be retained is because they are short, easy to understand, and, through their use in our culture, help to suggest ideas for experiments.

The definitions of self-control and impulsiveness given here also have a distinct advantage in that they are operational definitions. They describe what self-control and impulsiveness are in terms of certain observable operations, certain environmental events. As a result, it is possible to program self-control choices in the laboratory. Operational definitions enable laboratory investigation of the phenomena they define. Although some may see such laboratory investigations as overly simplistic, laboratory experiments of operationally defined phenomena in simplified situations are a central characteristic of productive scientific research, and such experiments can have practical applications.

Finally, the definitions of self-control and impulsiveness given here describe self-control and impulsiveness as being a function of two factors: the size of a specific outcome and the length of delay to that outcome. Therefore, defined in this way, self-control and impulsiveness research can have implications for understanding the general effects on behavior of the size of an outcome and the delay to an outcome. Similarly, any research on these two factors may be useful in understanding self-control and impulsiveness. In general, research has shown that (1) as the delay to the larger reward increases, self-control decreases;[8] and (2) subjects are more likely to wait for a larger, rather than a smaller, reward.[9] As with any scientific approach, breaking down a phenomenon into its component parts can be extremely helpful in understanding the causes and effects of that phenomenon.

SELF-CONTROL AND IMPULSIVENESS IN CONTEXT

Whether a particular behavior should be classified as self-control or impulsiveness or neither depends on the context in which the choice is made. First, note that the definitions of self-control and impulsiveness given in this book state that whether a choice consists of self-control or impulsiveness depends on the *relative* size of and the *relative* delay of the outcome. A self-control response is one which results in a *larger, more* delayed outcome, and an impulsive response is the reverse. This means that a choice that would be classified as self-control in one context (such as a choice of pumpkin soup that would not be ready for thirty minutes over immediately available tomato soup) could be classified as impulsiveness in another context in which an even larger, more delayed response alternative was available (such as leek soup that would not be ready for an hour). The present definitions of self-control and impulsiveness are relative, not absolute, definitions.

The context can also affect whether or not a response is classified as self-control or impulsiveness by affecting the degree to which an individual values a particular reward. For example, suppose a mail carrier with only a pay telephone available was choosing between spending her change now to get a candy bar from a vending machine versus using that change to call a friend who would be home later. The amount of time since the mail carrier had eaten and the amount of time since the mail carrier had spoken with her friend would affect the value of each outcome, and therefore whether calling the friend would or would not be classified as self-control (as well as what choice was made).

Context affects the classification of behaviors as self-control and impulsiveness in still another way. Some choices, such as the choice to smoke a single cigarette, result in the loss of few long-term positive consequences if just made once. Therefore it is difficult to classify such choices as impulsiveness. However, smoking a large number of cigarettes can result in the loss of some very large long-term positive consequences (such as one's life). In this case, smoking is impulsive. Some behaviors can be classified as impulsiveness (or self-control) only within the context of other behaviors that the subject is emitting.

These many effects of context on self-control help to explain why it is that an individual's self-control can differ so markedly in different situations. For example, someone may have no difficulty in showing self-control with regard to saving money, but have significant difficulty showing self-control with regard to food.[10] Such context effects will be discussed in more detail in Chapter 6: Eating.

POSITIVE VERSUS NEGATIVE CONSEQUENCES

If a particular outcome is a positive one, then not having it is a negative outcome. The reverse is also true; if a particular outcome is negative, then not having it is positive. Therefore, any choice between a larger, more delayed outcome and a smaller, less delayed outcome is also a choice between a relatively small, less delayed loss and a relatively large, more delayed loss.

For example, students often have the choice between going to a movie (resulting in the immediate, but relatively small positive outcome of a night's fun) or studying (resulting in the large positive outcome of good grades later; see Figure 2.2a). This choice could also be equivalently described as one between not studying (resulting in the large negative outcome of failing grades later) or not going to a movie (resulting in the immediate, but relatively small negative outcome of the loss of a night's fun; Figure 2.2b). No matter how this choice is described, to maximize the actual overall positive consequences and

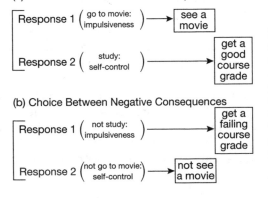

(a) Choice Between Positive Consequences

Response 1 (go to movie: impulsiveness) ⟶ see a movie

Response 2 (study: self-control) ⟶ get a good course grade

(b) Choice Between Negative Consequences

Response 1 (not study: impulsiveness) ⟶ get a failing course grade

Response 2 (not go to movie: self-control) ⟶ not see a movie

Figure 2.2. A self-control choice described both in terms of positive consequences (a), and negative consequences (b). In either case, the self-control choice is Response 2 (study, not go to movie) and the impulsive choice is Response 1 (go to movie, not study). A bracket indicates that a choice is available between the two responses.

minimize actual overall negative consequences, students should choose to study (i.e., not to go to the movie).

Consider an alternative example involving the choice of whether or not to go to the dentist. Framed as a choice between positive consequences, someone has a choice between avoiding the pain of being treated by the dentist now versus avoiding the pain of a very diseased mouth later. Framed as a choice between negative consequences, someone has a choice between the pain of being treated by the dentist now versus the pain of a very diseased mouth later. Once again, no matter how this choice is described, to maximize actual overall positive consequences and minimize actual overall negative consequences, people should choose to go to the dentist (i.e., they should choose to avoid the pain of a very diseased mouth). Note that when a self-control choice is described in terms of negative rather than positive consequences, choosing the smaller, less delayed consequence (e.g., not seeing a movie, experiencing pain at the dentist) over the larger, more delayed consequence (e.g., getting a failing course grade, having a diseased mouth) is now a self-control choice. (see Box 2.2).

> Don't put off until tomorrow
> what you can do today.

Box 2.2

As a final example of a self-control choice that can be described as a choice between an immediate, small negative outcome and a delayed, large negative outcome, consider the choice faced by someone sunbathing on a Maine beach on an uncomfortably hot day. The sunbather can either cool off by taking a dip in the water, whose cold temperature will not be at all pleasant, or the sunbather can continue to sweat and swelter on the beach. In this case, taking an unpleasant dip in order to cool off is the self-control choice, and continuing to sweat and swelter on the beach is the impulsive choice.

In summary, every self-control choice can be described either in terms of positive or negative consequences. Sometimes this book may appear to contradict its own definition of self-control in that it may define the sooner, smaller outcome as self-control. However, this will only occur if that outcome is actually aversive and its choice results in actual greater, but more delayed, net positive benefits for the subject.

RESEARCH TECHNIQUES
FOR INVESTIGATING SELF-CONTROL

The Experimental Method

This book focuses on laboratory research in which self-control is examined under controlled conditions. In the laboratory, experimenters attempt to hold everything constant except for one variable (the *independent variable*), which the experimenter manipulates. Then any observed changes in the subject's behavior (the *dependent variable*) can fairly confidently be ascribed to the changes in the independent variable. This type of research employs what is known as the *experimental method*, and it is used to determine cause and effect. The ability to determine cause and effect is a distinct advantage of the experimental method. Because it is hard for any person to behave in a precisely prescribed manner, using the experimental method in self-control experiments often means removing the experimenter from contact with the subject, and using a computer to measure the subject's responses and to deliver outcomes.

However, paying attention only to data collected using the experimental method can have disadvantages. First, by definition, controlling all aspects of conditions during an experiment except for one variable means that laboratory conditions are unlike those experienced in the world outside of the laboratory. It is true that animals' bodies are no different outside and inside the laboratory, and therefore to a large degree the behavior shown by animals in the laboratory will reflect rules of behavior outside of the laboratory. However, the only way to observe the actual nonlaboratory behavior of an animal is outside of a laboratory. To at least some degree, behavior in the laboratory is artificial.

A second disadvantage to relying solely on data collected using the experimental method is that there are many aspects of self-control and impulsive behavior about which no controlled experiments have yet been performed, or perhaps could be performed. For example, no one has yet tested self-control in a large sample of children at one-year intervals from infancy to adulthood. Laboratory investigation is expensive—both in terms of money and time. Further, as indicated above, certain aspects of the environment, such as social interactions, may be extremely difficult to investigate using the experimental method because they cannot be precisely controlled.

Therefore, recognizing that research using the experimental method is sometimes inadequate or incomplete, this book, though focusing on controlled, laboratory research, will sometimes include discussion of other types of research. For example, Chapter 4 will include material on cultural differences in self-control, and Part III (Applications) will contain speculations concerning possible implications of laboratory self-control research for nonlaboratory situations.

Human and Nonhuman Subjects

Some of the laboratory research conducted so far on self-control and impulsiveness has used nonhuman subjects, primarily pigeons and rats. Therefore, research using nonhuman subjects will play a role in this book.

Laboratory research with nonhuman subjects has several distinct benefits. First, it is possible to control environmental conditions and genetic composition to a much greater extent for nonhuman than for human subjects. Laboratory animals are bred for many generations to ensure genetic homogeneity, and each member of a species can be raised from birth under virtually identical conditions. Thus, with laboratory animals (as opposed to humans), any differences between treatment groups are more likely to be due to the different treatments, rather than differences in the genes and previous experiences of the animals in different groups. This makes it easier for researchers to determine whether or not a particular treatment does or does not have an effect. Second, it is possible to conduct experiments with nonhuman subjects that might not be considered ethical to conduct with humans. For example, experiments with nonhuman subjects working for food rewards frequently deprive the subjects of food until they reach 80 percent of their free-feeding weights, a procedure that would usually not be considered ethical if used with humans. Third, it may be extremely difficult to conduct long-term studies (including developmental studies) with human subjects. Few humans have the time available for repeatedly participating in an experiment. Fourth, experiments with nonhuman subjects are usually less expensive to conduct, because human subjects generally command a high hourly rate (although the care and feeding of nonhuman subjects can be fairly expensive). Finally, because nonhuman and human animals share a common evolutionary history, results from experiments with nonhuman subjects can be expected to have some implications for human behavior.

However, if an important goal is to understand human behavior, conducting experiments primarily with nonhuman subjects also has several disadvantages. First, although we share an evolutionary history with other animals, each species evolved in its own particular ecological niche. Therefore, to the degree to which evolution can shape behavior for particular environments (see Chapter 3), different species may have evolved different behavioral rules, and results from one species will not necessarily apply to other species. Second, nonhuman and human species simply are not identical with respect to language, perceptual, and other cognitive abilities. Therefore, to at least some degree, results from nonhuman species cannot apply to human behavior.

This book will attempt to take advantage of the information provided by nonhuman research on self-control while at the same time remaining cautious regarding cross-species generalizations.

Experimental Design

There are many ways to program events in an experiment so as to investigate self-control and impulsiveness as defined earlier in this chapter. All of these methods include an explicit choice between a larger, more delayed outcome and a smaller, less delayed outcome. However, there are still many ways in which experiments can vary. It will be helpful to describe here some of these experimental methods and their similarities and differences so that when they are mentioned in subsequent chapters, the essential aspects and usefulness of their procedures will be clear. The references also provide some examples of each of the methodological variations discussed in this section.

One way that experiments on self-control and impulsiveness vary is in the large variety of outcomes that have been used. In order to induce subjects to make choices between these outcomes, they are usually highly desirable ones such as access to food (for hungry human and nonhuman subjects), toys (for children), money, removal of loud noise, or pleasurable slides (these last three types have been used for human adults).[11] Some experiments only occasionally deliver *primary rewards* (outcomes such as food that are rewarding even though they have never been associated with any other rewards), and at other times deliver *conditioned rewards* (such as a light or a tone that are rewarding due to having been previously associated with primary rewards). Points exchangeable for money at the end of the session can also be considered in the category of conditioned rewards, and several self-control experiments with adult humans have used these as the outcomes.[12] In other experiments with humans, the subjects are given booklets describing several choices and are told that they will receive one of their choices at the end of the experiment.[13] Finally, in some experiments with humans, outcomes are given that have no contact with primary rewards as part of the experiment. This type of experiment includes giving subjects written questions about specific hypothetical choices or about more general self-control behavior.[14] For example, someone may be asked to imagine a choice between an immediate small amount of money and a delayed large amount of money. Clearly, the more direct contact that a subject has with an outcome in an experiment, the more confident an experimenter can be that the subject had an accurate perception of the outcome and was not making choices randomly. However, using hypothetical, imagined outcomes does have the advantage of permitting the use of outcomes such as larger amounts of money delayed months or years, outcomes that would be impractical for use in the laboratory.

Another way in which the design of experiments on self-control differs is that subjects may be presented with many choices, or many sessions of many choices each, or with just one choice.[15] Once again, particularly if the choices are similar, the more choices with which a subject is presented, the more confident an experimenter can be that the subject's choices are based on accurate perceptions of the available outcomes. In addition, certain types of mathematical analyses of results are impossible without multiple choices.[16] However, it should also be pointed out that outside of the laboratory, the exact same choice is rarely repeatedly available. People must often choose between two outcomes without direct knowledge of those outcomes. Instead, they base their choices on past related experience, including information they have obtained from other apparently knowledgeable persons or from the media.

An example of a one-time self-control choice that many people must make without direct knowledge of the outcomes is the choice between putting some money into a retirement fund versus spending that money on

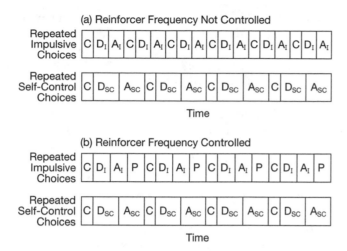

Figure 2.3. Repeated impulsive and self-control choices as a function of time (a) when reinforcer frequency is not controlled, and (b) when reinforcer frequency is controlled. C represents the period during which the subject chooses, D_I and A_I represent the delay and outcome-access periods for the impulsive alternative, D_{SC} and A_{SC} represent the delay and outcome-access periods for the self-control alternative, and P represents a post-outcome delay period.

a new stereo. The person faced with such a choice has never retired, has no idea of how long his or her retirement will last, and has never owned that particular stereo before. However, that person will probably have had some experience with other people who have retired and with other stereo systems, and will perhaps have read about the importance of preparing for retirement and the virtues of this specific stereo system.

When an experiment involves repeated choices, it may be possible for subjects to obtain the smaller, less delayed outcomes at a higher rate than the larger, more delayed outcomes (see Figure 2.3a). Such a situation will occur if a subject has another opportunity to choose as soon as an outcome has been received—there will then be less time between choice opportunities, assuming that the subject chooses smaller, less delayed outcomes rather than larger, more delayed outcomes. Because it is possible for the outcome rate to affect choice preference, experiments that are not interested in the effects of the outcome rate on preference will usually impose some sort of delay period following the receipt of the smaller, less delayed outcome so that choice opportunities occur at the same rate no matter which outcome is chosen (see Figure 2.3b).

Still another way in which the design of experiments on self-control differs concerns the way in which the outcome delays are programmed. In many experiments with both human and nonhuman subjects, the delay is a fixed time interval between when the choice response is made and when access to the outcome begins. The dependent variable is how many choices are made of the more preferred, more delayed outcome. However, in other experiments, the delay lasts for as long as the subject will wait before choosing the less preferred, less delayed outcome. This procedure has been used often with children.[17] In a typical experiment of this sort, children are told that they can have two pretzels if they wait to ring a bell until the experimenter returns, and only one pretzel if they ring the bell sooner. The dependent variable for this type of procedure is the length of time that a child will wait before ringing the bell. Still another way of programming the delay is to have a fixed interval, but allow the subject, while waiting for the larger outcome, to change his or her choice to the smaller, less delayed outcome.[18] Lastly, in a few experiments, subjects have been required to make repeated responses while waiting for the larger, more delayed outcome.[19]

A final aspect of experimental design that can differ in self-control experiments concerns what the subject has to do in order to make a choice. Often, the subject has only to make a single response—a mark on a piece of paper, a push of a button, a rod push, etc.[20] However, in many experiments, a *schedule of reinforcement* is employed, in which certain rules set by the experimenter determine which responses will be effective choice responses, in other words, which responses will receive *reinforcers* (known popularly as rewards). The most commonly used schedule of reinforcement for self-control experiments consists of two *concurrent variable-interval schedules*.[21] In this type of schedule, there are two, independently operating, variable-interval schedules, one for each of the two choice alternatives. For each of these variable-interval schedules, after varying intervals of time, the next response will be effective, resulting in the receipt of the reinforcer (similar to finally seeing a subway coming after numerous glaces down the subway tunnel). For example, suppose choice responses were effective according to concurrent variable-interval 15-second schedules. This means that on the average, every 15 seconds a particular response (such as a push of a left button) will result in an outcome of a specific delay and size (such as a 10-second delay followed by 10 seconds of access to food); and also, on the average, every 15 seconds a different response (such as a push of a right button) will result in a different outcome of a specific delay and size (such as a 2-second delay followed by 2 seconds of access to food). Variable-interval schedules tend to generate moderate, steady response rates.[22]

CONCLUSION

Humans and other animals must often choose between a larger, but more delayed outcome (self-control) and a smaller, but less delayed outcome (impulsiveness). This type of choice behavior is of much importance in our daily lives and can be investigated in a variety of ways in the laboratory. Animals are often impulsive, indicating that delaying the larger outcome makes it in some way less valuable. The next chapter will describe the evolutionary basis of impulsiveness and self-control, paying particular attention to the possible impact of evolution on animals' valuation of delayed outcomes.

REFERENCES

1. Ainslie, G. W. (1974). "Impulse Control in Pigeons." *Journal of the Experimental Analysis of Behavior*, 21, 485–489.

    Logue, A. W. (1988). "Research on Self-control: An Integrating Framework." *Behavioral and Brain Sciences*, 11, 665–709.

    Rachlin, H., and Green, L. (1972). "Commitment, Choice and Self-control." *Journal of the Experimental Analysis of Behavior*, 17, 15–22.

2. From "I See a Taco in Your Future" by Leslie Brenner. Copyright (c) 1991 by Leslie Brenner. Originally published in *New York Magazine*, December 2, 1991. Reprinted by arrangement with Virginia Barber Literary Agency. All rights reserved.

3. Patterson, C. J., and Mischel, W. (1975). "Plans to Resist Distraction." *Developmental Psychology*, 11, 369–378.

4. Goldfried, M. R., and Merbaum, M. (Eds.), (1973). *Behavior Change Through Self-control*. New York: Holt, Rinehart and Winston.

    Skinner, B. F. (1953). *Science and human behavior*. New York: The Free Press.

5. Kagan, J. (1984). *The Nature of the Child*. New York: Basic Books.

6. Kanfer, F. H., and Goldfoot, D. A. (1966). "Self-control and Tolerance of Noxious Stimulation." *Psychological Reports*, 18, 79–85.

7. Kagan, J., and Kogan, N. (1970). "Individual Variation in Cognitive Processes." In P. H. Mussen (Ed.), *Carmichael's Manual of Child Psychology* (3rd ed., pp. 1273–1365). New York: Wiley.

    Kagan, J., Rosman, B. L., Day, D., Albert, J., and Phillips, W. (1964). "Information Processing in the Child: Significance of Analytic and Reflective Attitudes." *Psychological Monographs*, 78 (Whole No. 578), 1–37.

8. Mischel, W., and Metzner, R. (1962). "Preference for Delayed Reward as a Function of Age, Intelligence, and Length of Delay Interval." *Journal of Abnormal and Social Psychology*, 64, 425–431.

    Schwarz, J. C., Schrager, J. B., and Lyons, A. E. (1983). "Delay of Gratification by Preschoolers: Evidence for the Validity of the Choice Paradigm." *Child Development*, 54, 620–625.

9. Herzberger, S. D., and Dweck, C. S. (1978). "Attraction and Delay of Gratification." *Journal of Personality*, 46, 214–227.

    Maitland, S. D. P. (1967). "Time Perspective, Frustration-failure and Delay of Gratification in Middle-class and Lower-class Children from Organized and Disorganized Families." *Dissertation Abstracts*, 27, 3676–B.

10. Logue, A. W., and King, G. R. (1991). "Self-control and Impulsiveness in Adult Humans when Food Is the Reinforcer." *Appetite*, 17, 105–120.

    Logue, A. W., King, G. R., Chavarro, A., and Volpe, J. S. (1990). "Matching and Maximizing in a Self-control Paradigm Using Human Subjects." *Learning and Motivation*, 21, 340–368.

11. Davids, A. (1969). "Ego Functions in Disturbed and Normal Children: Aspiration, Inhibition, Time estimation, and Delayed Gratification." *Journal of Consulting and Clinical Psychology*, 33, 61–70.

    Logue and King, "Self-control and Impulsiveness," 105–120.

Logue, A. W., Rodriguez, M. L., Peña-Correal, T. E., and Mauro, B. C. (1984). "Choice in a Self-control Paradigm: Quantification of Experience-based Differences." *Journal of the Experimental Analysis of Behavior*, 41, 53–67.

Mischel, W., and Moore, B. (1973). "Effects of Attention to Symbolically Presented Rewards on Self-control." *Journal of Personality and Social Psychology*, 28, 172–179.

Navarick, D. J. (1987). "Reinforcement Probability and Delay as Determinants of Human Impulsiveness." *The Psychological Record*, 37, 219–226.

Solnick, J. V., Kannenberg, C. H., Eckerman, D. A., and Waller, M. B. (1980). "An Experimental Analysis of Impulsivity and Impulse Control in Humans." *Learning and Motivation*, 11, 61–77.

Yates, J. F., and Revelle, G. L. (1979). "Processes Operative During Delay of Gratification." *Motivation and Emotion*, 3, 103–115.

12. Logue, A. W., Peña-Correal, T. E., Rodriguez, M. L., and Kabela, E. (1986). "Self-control in Adult Humans: Variation in Positive Reinforcer Amount and Delay." *Journal of the Experimental Analysis of Behavior*, 46, 159–173.

13. Mischel, W., and Grusec, J. (1967). "Waiting for Rewards and Punishments: Effects of Time and Probability on Choice." *Journal of Personality and Social Psychology*, 5, 24–31.

14. Loewenstein, G., and Thaler, R. H. (1989). "Anomalies: Intertemporal choice." *Journal of Economics Perspectives*, 3, 181–193.

Rosenbaum, M. (1980). "A Schedule for Assessing Self-control Behaviors: Preliminary Findings." *Behavior Therapy*, 11, 109–121.

15. Logue, A. W. (1988). "Research on Self-control: An Integrating Framework." *Behavioral and Brain Sciences*, 11, 665–709.

16. Ibid.

17. Ibid.

18. Logue, A. W., and Peña-Correal, T. E. (1984). "Responding During Reinforcement Delay in a Self-control Paradigm." *Journal of the Experimental Analysis of Behavior*, 41, 267–277.

19. Patterson and Mischel (1975). "Plans to Resist Distraction," 369–378.

20. Logue, A. W., and Chavarro, A. (1992). "Self-control and Impulsiveness in Preschool Children." *Psychological Record*, 42, 189–204.

Logue, Peña-Correal, Rodriguez, and Kabela, "Self-control in Adult Humans," 159–173.

Mischel and Grusec, "Waiting for Rewards and Punishments," 24–31.

21. Logue, "Research on Self-control," 665–709.

22. Reynolds, G. S. (1975). *A Primer of Operant Conditioning* (rev. ed.). Glenview, Illinois: Scott, Foresman and Company.

Part II

Determinants
of
Self-Control

3

Our Evolutionary Heritage

In addition to limbs and sensory organs, the brains of all animals, including humans, have evolved. This means that certain aspects of animals' behavior, those aspects that are dependent on the structure of an animal's brain and other body parts, have also evolved. Since 1970, psychology has increasingly focused on the evolution of cognition, learning, motivation, and perception— different aspects of the behavior of animals when they are in contact with the environment.[1]

This chapter will propose that humans and other animals evolved a particular behavioral trait: a tendency to discount, that is, value less, delayed outcomes, a tendency that causes impulsiveness. The proposition that the tendency to discount delayed events evolved just as did other traits cannot be proved or disproved because it is based on events that happened in the very distant past. However, it is possible to show that discounting delayed outcomes would often have been adaptive for evolving animals, and that this trait is no longer as adaptive for human animals. In addition, the present chapter will discuss the degree to which an evolutionary contribution to a particular behavior predetermines that behavior, and how evolution may or may not determine the physiological mechanisms directly responsible for the behavior.

DISCOUNTING OF DELAYED EVENTS

Humans as well as other animals discount delayed events. In other words, events that are delayed are not worth as much to an animal as events that are immediate. Most people will agree with this statement based on experiences that they have had in their daily lives. There is also ample laboratory evidence supporting this statement. In fact, through laboratory research, psychologists know not only that most species discount delayed events but the degree to which they discount them. Psychologists have been able to show that the discounting is not linear.[2] In other words, a graph of outcome value as a function of outcome delay does not follow a straight line.

Figure 3.1a shows the effect of delay on outcome value if there is no discounting, in other words, if delay has no effect. The solid vertical line shows the value of the outcome at the time it is received, the value of the outcome if the choice resulted in the outcome with no delay. The horizontal line, at the same height as the vertical line, indicates that the value of the outcome does not decrease as the time at which the choice is made moves to the left, backwards in time, away from the time at which the outcome would be received, so that there is an increasing delay between a choice and receipt of the outcome. Figure 3.1b shows a linear relationship between outcome value and delay. Figure 3.1c shows the type of nonlinear function that is actually obtained in the laboratory—a hyperbola. Depending on the species and the situation, sometimes this curve falls off very steeply, and sometimes the curve is very shallow, but in all cases if there is any discounting at all, the data are consistent with a hyperbolic function.[3]

Several characteristic aspects of self-control and impulsive behavior can be explained on the basis that the function between outcome value and delay is a hyperbola. For example, the hyperbolic function is consistent with the fact that if an outcome is very near in time, an increase in the delay of that outcome can have a large impact on your value of that outcome. However, if an

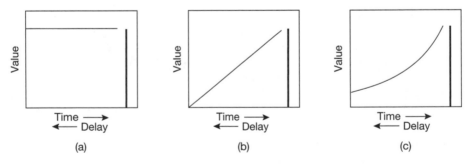

(a)   (b)   (c)

Figure 3.1. Hypothetical value of an outcome as a function of time. The solid vertical line shows the value of the outcome at the time it is received, the value of the outcome if the choice resulted in the outcome with no delay. The function to the left of the solid vertical line indicates the value of the outcome as one moves backwards in time, away from the time at which the outcome would be received. In other words, the function to the left of the solid vertical line indicates the value of the outcome as the delay to receipt of the outcome increases. (a) No change in the value of the outcome as a function of time to receipt of the outcome. (b) A linear change in the value of the outcome as a function of time to receipt of the outcome. (c) A hyperbolic change in the value of the outcome as a function of time to receipt of the outcome.

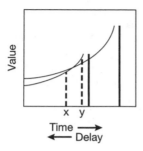

Figure 3.2. Hypothetical gradients of the value of two outcomes as a function of time—a larger, more delayed outcome and a smaller, less delayed outcome. The letters x and y indicate two points at which choices between the two outcomes might be made.

outcome is very distant in time, a little more delay does not make much of a difference.

Figure 3.2 shows the hyperbolas for two outcomes—a smaller, less delayed outcome and a larger, more delayed outcome—on the same graph. Note that these particular hyperbolas cross. As a result, if you were to choose between the two outcomes at time x, you would choose the larger, more delayed outcome. However, if you were to choose between the two outcomes at time y, you would choose the smaller, less delayed outcome. In other words, your choice between the two outcomes would reverse depending on how distant in time the two outcomes were. This type of choice reversal is often found in self-control paradigms. For example, consider the situation in which you have a choice between getting a little extra sleep in the morning (the smaller, less delayed outcome) and getting to work on time (the larger, more delayed outcome). The night before (point x), you indicate a choice of getting to work on time by setting an alarm clock. However, the next morning (point y), your choice is likely to be to get some additional sleep.

The hyperbolas shown in Figures 3.1c and 3.2 come from a particular mathematical function, a power function, indicating the relationship between outcome value and outcome delay:

$$V = 1/D^s, \tag{1}$$

in which V is outcome value, D is outcome delay, and s is an exponent that describes how sensitive V is to the effect of delay. In general, in Equation 1, as outcome delay increases, outcome value decreases, however, this also depends on the size of s (see Table 3.1). If s is relatively large, small changes in outcome delay result in large changes in outcome value; the subject is very sensitive to the effects of outcome delay and the functions in Figures 3.1c and 3.2 are very steep. If s is relatively small, large changes in outcome delay result in small changes in outcome value; the subject is not very sensitive to the effects of outcome delay and the functions in Figures 3.1c and 3.2 are very shallow. In the extreme case, if s is equal to 0, then D^s is always equal to 1.0, no matter what the value of D (outcome delay), so that varying outcome delay has no effect on outcome value and the function shown in Figure 3.1a is obtained.[4]

Power functions are useful in describing more than the effects of delay

TABLE 3.1   Effects on V of Different Values of s in the Equation $V = 1/D^s$

D	Value of V			
	$s = 0$	$s = 0.5$	$s = 1.0$	$s = 2.0$
0.50	1.00	1.41	2.00	4.00
1.00	1.00	1.00	1.00	1.00
5.00	1.00	0.45	0.20	0.04

size on outcome value. The effect on perceived magnitude of the physical size of many perceptual qualities, such as loudness, brightness, line length, and many others, are best described by power functions. These power functions are thought to represent a basic characteristic about our perceptual systems, about the way that our bodies perceive the external world.[5] As equal units of magnitude are added to external stimuli, our perceptual systems do not perceive these additions as equal units. Our perceptual systems perceive the sizes of these additions as varying in size consistent with power functions, not the linear functions that describe the actual physical changes in the external stimuli.

THE ENVIRONMENT IN WHICH HUMANS AND OTHER ANIMALS EVOLVED

An analysis of the environment in which humans and other animals evolved suggests that animals may have evolved a tendency to discount delayed events. Humans used to live in an environment more similar to that of other animals, one in which future food sources and, in fact, any future events were highly unpredictable.[6] Approximately 1.4 million years ago, hominids were hunter-gatherers in Africa.[7] They took what they could from their environment, sometimes hunting other animals and sometimes gathering roots, seeds, fruits, nuts, etc. from the forests and fields. Food access at this time was actually fairly adequate and stable; the climate was fairly constant, natural disasters such as droughts or fires did not much affect the food supply, there was a low population density, and the hunter-gathers moved around a great deal to take optimal advantage of available food sources.[8] However, even though food access was fairly stable, life was not. Life expectancy was much shorter than it is now due to increased death from disease and accidents.

Approximately one million years ago, hunter-gatherers began to migrate out of Africa and away from the equator.[9] As they did so, the weather became more variable and access to food sources became more unstable. Therefore, in addition to the reasons listed above for the African hunter-gatherers, these humans had a shorter life expectancy than we do as a result of occasional starvation.[10]

Don't count your chickens before they hatch.

Box 3.1

It was only about ten thousand years ago, relatively recently in humans' evolutionary history, that some hunter-gatherer societies began to settle in particular locations and to engage in agriculture. Natural disasters of various sorts could and often did wipe out a crop, and although these people learned how to store food and to trade, they still frequently lived on the edge of starvation.[11] Further, medical knowledge was very limited in most of these societies. Life expectancy was even shorter than it was for hunter- gatherers.[12] Many early agricultural societies worshipped omnipotent nature gods, thus expressing their perceived inability to control future events.[13]

In these kinds of early human environments, specific delayed events were not very likely to occur. If delayed events are not very likely to occur, then waiting for them is not likely to result in any benefit[14] (see Box 3.1). In other words, impulsiveness, not self-control, is likely to maximize overall benefits in an environment in which future events are uncertain. For example, if, as a result of frequent plagues, individuals are unlikely to live to the completion or even the beginning of their reproductive years, there will be little point to those individuals showing self-control with regard to sexual behavior and pregnancy; sexual behavior resulting in pregnancy should be engaged in at every opportunity. The present discussion makes it clear that, if self-control is defined simply as the choice of larger, more delayed outcomes over smaller, less delayed outcomes, then self-control is not necessarily equal to overall maximization of positive outcome. To determine what response maximizes overall positive outcome, it may be useful also to take into account outcome probability. (For a discussion concerning how making an event improbable may be equivalent to delaying it, see Chapter 9.)

Impulsiveness involves decreased valuation of delayed outcomes. We know that impulsiveness is more likely than self-control to maximize overall benefits in an uncertain environment. We also know that humans and other animals were exposed to an uncertain environment over many, many generations during their evolutionary histories. Therefore, it is probable that during evolution, people and other animals that tended to value delayed outcomes less than immediate outcomes were more likely to survive in at least some situations. Further, in the environment in which our ancestors and the ancestors of other species evolved, genes that contributed to impulsiveness probably increased an individual's *inclusive fitness*—the survival of that individual's biological relatives (the survival of the most likely carriers of that individual's genes).[15] This greater inclusive fitness of animals that discounted delayed events would have resulted in an increased proportion of future animals possessing genes that tended in some way to contribute to this delayed outcome discounting. Thus it is likely that humans and other animals possess genes for delayed outcome discounting.

There are situation and species differences in discounting and impulsiveness;[16] at least some of these differences may have an evolutionary basis. For example, in laboratory experimental sessions, hungry humans are more impulsive for food rewards than for points exchangeable for money at the end of each laboratory session.[17] This situation-specific difference in self-control is apparently due to a difference in the immediate utility of the two types of rewards. For a hungry animal, an immediate food reward ensures that the animal has enough energy to obtain food in the future (see also Chapter 6). However, there is no immediate use for points obtained in laboratory sessions when those points are only exchangeable for money after the session is over; the way to maximize benefits in such sessions is simply to maximize the number of points obtained over the whole session (for further discussion of self-control and money see Chapter 9).

Laboratory investigations also show that humans, although impulsive under some conditions, demonstrate significantly more self-control in the laboratory than do rats or pigeons.[18] Some researchers have argued that these species differences are due, not to differences in the environments in which these species evolved, but to differences in the cognitive abilities of the different species.[19] In explaining the relatively great self-control of humans, one researcher, Richard D. Alexander, has even argued that "the central evolved function of the human psyche . . . is to yield an ability to anticipate or predict the future and to manipulate it in the (evolutionary, reproductive) interests of self's genetic success."[20] Further, he has stated that human consciousness "is the capacity to over-ride immediate rewards and punishments in the interests of securing greater rewards visualized in the future."[21] Nevertheless, as the next chapter will demonstrate, humans are not the only species that can show self-control. In addition, although humans may be more likely to show self-control in some situations than are other species, they certainly are still impulsive much of the time in ways that are not the overall best strategy. Humans' consciousness apparently still requires additional evolution. More immediate solutions to our problems with impulsiveness will be discussed in subsequent chapters.

OUR CURRENT ENVIRONMENT

The current environment of the majority of the people in the United States is quite different from that of hunter-gatherers or early agricultural societies. First, for most people today, food of some sort is always available. Even if someone has no money for food, our culture has instituted food-stamp programs and soup kitchens. Second, our expected life span is considerably longer than that of evolving humans. Many diseases have been eradicated. Others, such as all sorts of bacterial infections, are usually curable. It is not unusual to rid someone of cancer. At the same time, the chances of someone dying from a flood or a wild animal attack are quite small. Most people can expect to live long, relatively healthy lives. Third, in our culture, we have formalized the rules by which people must live. In other words, we have created laws, along with ways in which those laws are enforced (tax collectors, police officers, lawyers, etc.). Through printed and audiovisual media, as well as by word of mouth, there is extensive communication regarding the existence of these laws and the consequences for breaking them. Fourth, we simply have more knowledge now about the probability of the occurrence of certain future events such as particular kinds of weather, demographic trends, and the usable life of a machine. Finally, even when someone does not know for sure what the consequences for a particular action might be, that person may be able to influence events to ensure that a particular outcome occurs. That might also have been true during, for example, hunter-gatherer times, but only if the person could expect to live long enough to exert the necessary and desirable influence, not as likely then as now. All together, these characteristics of our current society indicate that in our society the consequences for certain behaviors are often (although certainly not always) quite specific and quite certain.

> Nothing is certain except death and taxes.

Box 3.2

Given that many future events in our current environment are now highly predictable, discounting of those events can be unadaptive.[22] Discounting of delayed events that are virtually certain to occur can result in people making choices that are not the best overall strategy. Some small positive outcome may be obtained in the short term, but in the long term, benefits will

> *Carpe diem* (seize the day; the enjoyment of the pleasures of the moment without concern for the future).[23]

Box 3.3

not be maximized. For example, someone may choose to smoke despite the possibility of severe long-term health risks. Yet despite the lack of overall, long-term, maximum benefit, people persist in behaving as if many events almost certain to occur are unlikely or nonexistent, and therefore engage in unadaptive impulsiveness (see Boxes 3.2, 3.3, and 3.4).

> A bird in the hand is worth two in the bush.

Box 3.4

ROLE OF EVOLUTION IN DETERMINING BEHAVIOR

If we assume that to at least some degree, the discounting of delayed outcomes by humans and other animals has been shaped by evolution, does this mean that this discounting is inevitable? No, it does not.

Suppose that some aspect of humans' physiology results in delayed outcomes being valued less than immediate outcomes. In other words, assume that some aspect of humans' physiology is responsible for ensuring that the value of s in Equation 1 is not equal to 0. Physiology is not fixed. It may be changed. Some aspects of physiology are easier to change than others, but all aspects of physiology may be changed.

Further, even if physiology conducive to the discounting of delayed outcomes is present, this does not mean that the animal will behave as if a particular delayed outcome is discounted. First, in order to be impulsive someone must be aware that the impulsive choice exists. Second, the person must be physically capable of performing a response that indicates that discounting has occurred. Finally, no behavior can be exhibited without the presence of an appropriate environment, one that permits the expression of the impulsive behavior. For example, a student cannot go to a movie instead of studying unless that student knows that the movie is being shown, feels well enough to go, and has the money to pay for it. Someone cannot behave impulsively, thus indicating discounting of delayed events, unless certain conditions (such as the easy availability of the impulsive choice) are present. Behavioral, as well as perceptual, constraints can affect discounting.[24]

In summary, evolutionary contributions to a particular behavior do not spell behavioral determinism. Both the hardware (the physiology), the software (the knowledge and learning), as well as the environment conducive to expression of the behavior must be present in order for a particular behavior to be emitted. Without any of these factors, the behavior will not occur. Knowledge of the factors necessary for the expression of a particular behavior will become useful in Chapter 5 which discusses general methods for modifying self-control and impulsive behavior.

ROLE OF EVOLUTION IN DETERMINING MECHANISMS OF BEHAVIOR

As discussed in the previous section, the expression of a particular behavior is dependent on a specific physiology. However, evolution acts at the interface between the body and the environment. Natural selection acts on the function of a behavior, not the physiological mechanism responsible for that behavior.[25] For example, if students who studied were more likely to have relatives who survived, the genes that contributed to studying would be expected to increase in future populations. However, this would not necessarily mean that a particular neurological system for studying would also become more frequent in future populations. This could happen if the studying of all of the students who studied was controlled by this particular system. However, for every behavior there is always more than one physiological mechanism that can be responsible for that behavior.[26] This is similar to computer programming. Ultimately, the person using the program is interested in what the program does, not how it does it, and there is always more than one way to write the program so that it functions in a certain way. Figure 3.1c, Figure 3.2, and Equation 1 describe self-control and impulsive behavior as shaped by evolution, not mechanisms of self-control and impulsive behavior.

Particularly given that the degree of discounting may differ in different species and in different situations, evolution may have resulted in the existence of different physiological mechanisms responsible for the discounting across these different species and situations. Knowledge of the particular physiological mechanism responsible for self-control and impulsiveness in a particular situation can be useful in planning any interventions to increase or decrease self-control. Examples of such knowledge will be presented in the chapters in Part III.

Some researchers have tried to identify a particular part of the brain that is responsible for impulsiveness and self-control. The area that has received the most attention is the *septum* (a part of the *limbic* system). Researchers have contended that this area of the brain is involved in the perception of relationships between stimuli that are not temporally contiguous.[27] Other researchers have suggested that the *prefrontal cortex* (the frontal parts of the cerebral cortex of the brain)[28] is involved in self-control in the form of the ability to alternate responses when there are long delays between the responses, the ability to inhibit inappropriate responses, and the ability to plan for the future (possibly due to the relationship between the prefrontal cortex and the limbic system).[29] However, there has not yet been research conducted of sufficient diversity to establish the septum, the limbic system, and the prefrontal cortex as the central players in the physiological determination of general self-control and impulsive behavior.

CONCLUSION

Humans and other animals tend to discount delayed events, and this discounting can be described by power functions. The tendency to discount delayed events may have an evolutionary basis. However, an evolutionary contribution to discounting does not mean that a particular physiological mechanism is always responsible for this discounting, nor does it mean that the discounting is inevitable. Many different physiological mechanisms may be responsible for discounting, and the responsible mechanism may differ depending on the species and situation under consideration. In addition, a

> Good things come to those who
> wait.

Box 3.5

physiological mechanism is not immutable—it can be changed. Further, a demonstration of impulsiveness depends on an awareness of and an ability to choose the impulsive option. For all of these reasons, discounting, even discounting to which evolution has contributed, is not inevitable.

This chapter has attempted to show that evolution may have con-

> Haste makes waste.

Box 3.6

tributed to the tendency to show impulsiveness or self-control. This chapter has also demonstrated that impulsiveness is adaptive under some circumstances. Therefore the moral standards that our society sometimes applies to self-control, wherein self-control is "good" and impulsiveness is "bad" (see Boxes 3.5, 3.6, 3.7, and 3.8), may be misdirected. People are sometimes better off being impulsive. Further, even when self-control is clearly the best over-

> Patience is a virtue.

Box 3.7

all strategy, it is not clear that impulsiveness should be seen as a moral, rather than an evolutionary, issue. People are not somehow lacking in character or moral fiber if they are impulsive. The impulsiveness may reflect evolutionary tendencies rather that have been shaped over many generations. Energy would be better spent determining how to get around these tendencies rather than agonizing about their sometimes unfortunate consequences.

> It is better to have a hen tomor-
> row than an egg today.[30]

Box 3.8

REFERENCES

1.   Church, R. M. (1989). "Theories of Timing Behavior." In S. B. Klein and R. R. Mowrer (Ed.), *Contemporary Learning Theories: Instrumental Conditioning Theory and the Impact of Biological Constraints on Learning* (pp. 41–71). Hillsdale, NJ: Erlbaum.

Collier, G. H. (1983). "Life in a Closed Economy: The Ecology of Learning and Motivation." In M. D. Zeiler and P. Harzem (Ed.), *Advances in Analysis of Behavior: Vol. 3. Biological Factors in Learning* (pp. 223–274). New York: Wiley.

Logue, A. W. (1979). "Taste Aversion and the Generality of the Laws of Learning." *Behavioral and Brain Sciences*, 86, 276–296.

Real, L. A. (1991). "Animal Choice Behavior and the Evolution of Cognitive Architecture." *Science*, 253, 980–986.

2. Ainslie, G., and Herrnstein, R. J. (1981). "Preference Reversal and Delayed Reinforcement." *Animal Learning and Behavior*, 9, 476–482.

3. Logue, A. W. "Research on Self-control: An Integrating Framework." *Behavioral and Brain Sciences*, 11, 665–709.

Rachlin, H., and Raineri, A. (1992). "Irrationality, Impulsiveness, and Selfishness as Discount Reversal Effects." In G. Lowenstein and J. Elster (Eds.), *Choice Over Time* (pp. 93–118). New York: Russell Sage Foundation.

4. Logue, "Research on Self-control," 665–709.

5. Stevens, S. S. (1975). *Psychophysics*. New York: Wiley.

6. Kagel, J. H., Green, L., and Caraco, T. (1986). "When Foragers Discount the Future: Constraint or Adaptation?" *Animal Behaviour*, 36, 271–283.

7. Zihlman, A. L. (1982). *The Human Evolution Coloring Book*. Oakville, CA: Coloring Concepts, Inc.

8. Harlan, J. R. (1975). *Crops and Man*. Madison, WI: American Society of Agronomy.

9. Zihlman, *The Human Evolution Coloring Book*.

10. Harlan, *Crops and Man*.

11. Ibid.

12. Cohen, M. N. (1987). "The Significance of Long-term Changes in Human Diet and Food Economy." In M. Harris and E. B. Ross (Eds.), *Food and Evolution: Toward a Theory of Human Food Habits* (pp. 261–283). Philadelphia: Temple University Press.

13. Harlan, *Crops and Man*.

14. Kagel, Green, and Caraco, "When Foragers Discount the Future," 271–283.

Logue, "Research on Self-control," 665–709.

15. Barash, D. P. (1977). *Sociobiology and Behavior*. New York: Elsevier.

Hamilton, W. D. (1964). "The Genetical Evolution of Social Behaviour. I." *Journal of Theoretical Biology*, 7, 1–16.

Hamilton, W. D. (1964). "The Genetical Evolution of Social Behaviour. II." *Journal of Theoretical Biology*, 7, 17–52.

Maynard Smith, J. (1978). "Optimization Theory in Evolution." *Annual Review of Ecology and Systematics*, 9, 31–56.

16. Ainslie and Herrnstein, "Preference Reversal and Delayed Reinforcement," 476–482.

Lejeune, H., and Wearden, J. H. (1991). "The Comparative Psychology of Fixed-interval Responding: Some Quantitative Analyses." *Learning and Motivation*, 22, 84–111.

Real, "Animal Choice Behavior," 980–986.

Richelle, M., and Lejeune, H. (1984). "Timing Competence and Timing Performance: A Cross-species Approach." In J. Gibbon, and L. Allan (Eds.), *Timing and Time Perception* (pp. 254–268). New York: The New York Academy of Sciences.

Timberlake, W., Gawley, D. J., and Lucas, G. A. (1987). "Time Horizons in Rats Foraging for Food in Temporally Separated Patches." *Journal of Experimental Psychology: Animal Behavior Processes*, 13, 302–309.

Zeiler, M. D. (1991, May). *Behavior as Evolutionary Biology*. Paper presented at the Association for Behavior Analysis, Atlanta, Georgia.

17. Flora, S. R., and Pavlik, W. P. (1992). "Human Self-control and the Density of Reinforcement." *Journal of the Experimental Analysis of Behavior*, 57, 201–208.

Logue, A. W., and King, G. R. (1991). "Self-control and Impulsiveness in Adult Humans When Food Is the Reinforcer." *Appetite*, 17, 105–120.

Logue, A. W., Peña-Correal, T. E., Rodriguez, M. L., and Kabela, E. (1986). "Self-control in Adult Humans: Variation in Positive Reinforcer Amount and Delay." *Journal of the Experimental Analysis of Behavior*, 46, 159–173.

18. Logue, A. W., King, G. R., Chavarro, A., and Volpe, J. S. (1990). "Matching and Maximizing in a Self-control Paradigm Using Human Subjects." *Learning and Motivation*, 21, 340–368.

Logue, A. W., Rodriguez, M. L., Peña-Correal, T. E., and Mauro, B. C. (1984). "Choice in a Self-control Paradigm: Quantification of Experience-based Differences." *Journal of the Experimental Analysis of Behavior*, 41, 53–67.

Tobin, H., Chelonis, J. J., and Logue, A. W. (1993). "Choice in Self-control Paradigms Using Rats." *Psychological Record*, 43, 441–454.

Tobin, H., and Logue, A. W. (in press). "Self-control Across Species (*Columba livia, Homo sapiens*, and *Rattus norvegicus*)." *Journal of Comparative Psychology*.

19. Real, "Animal Choice Behavior," 980–986.

20. Alexander, R. D. (1989). "Evolution of the Human Psyche." In P. Mellars, and C. Stringer (Eds.), *The Human Revolution: Behavioural and Biological Perspectives on the Origins of Modern Humans* (pp. 455–513). Princeton: Princeton University Press (p. 459).

21. Ibid., p. 477.

22. Ainslie, G. (1992). *Picoeconomics: The Strategic Interaction of Successive Motivational States within the Person*. Cambridge, United Kingdom: Cambridge University Press.

23. Horace. *Odes*, Book 1, Ode 11, line 8.

24. Kagel, Green, and Caraco, "When Foragers Discount the Future," 271–283.

Real, "Animal Choice Behavior," 980–986.

Stephens, D. W., and Krebs, J. R. (1986). *Foraging Theory*. Princeton: Princeton University Press.

25. Cosmides, L., and Tooby, J. (1987). "From Evolution to Behavior: Evolutionary Psychology as the Missing Link." In J. Dupré (Ed.), *The Latest on the Best: Essays on Evolution and Optimality* (pp. 277–306). Cambridge: MIT Press.

Zeiler, *Behavior as Evolutionary Biology*.

26. Anderson, J. R. (1978). "Arguments Concerning Representations for Mental Imagery." *Psychological Review*, 85, 249–277.

27. Gorenstein, E. E., and Newman, J. P. (1980). "Disinhibitory Psychopathology: A New Perspective and a Model for Research." *Psychological Review*, 87, 301–315.

Newman, J. P., Gorenstein, E. E., and Kelsey, J. E. (1983). "Failure to Delay Gratification Following Septal Lesions in Rats: Implications for an Animal Model of Disinhibitory Psychopathology." *Personality and Individual Differences*, 4, 147–156.

28. Grossman, S. P. (1967). *A Textbook of Physiological Psychology*. New York: Wiley.

29. Flekkoy, K. (1983). "The Neuropsychological Basis for the `Dopamine Hypothesis' in Schizophrenia." *Nordisk-Psychiatrisk-Tidsskrift*, 37, 283–289. (From *Psychological Abstracts*, 1983, 74, Abstract No. 25165.)

Masterton, B., and Skeen, L. C. (1972). "Origins of Anthropoid Intelligence: Prefrontal System and Delayed Alternation in Hedgehog, Tree Shrew, and Bush Baby." *Journal of Comparative and Physiological Psychology*, 81, 423–433.

Nauta, W. J. H., and Feirtag, M. (1986). *Fundamental Neuroanatomy*. New York: W. H. Freeman.

30. Fortune from a fortune cookie sold by Pacific Fortune Cookie, Inc., New York, NY.

4

The Development
of Self-Control

Infant and adult humans differ in many ways. How infants and adults respond in self-control situations is one such difference. This chapter describes how self-control changes during development, and the factors that appear to be responsible for these changes. This description will include a discussion of gender and cultural differences concerning self-control.

A wide variety of factors is responsible for the development of self-control. Some of these factors might be classified as genetic factors and some as environmental factors. However, no factor is entirely genetic or environmental. For example, a genetic predisposition for a certain characteristic cannot be expressed without a suitable environment. People will only have genetically determined brown hair if their environment does not include blond hair dye. Similarly, the environment can only affect a characteristic if there is a suitable genetically determined physiology. For example, people can only learn how to sing the latest song if they have genetically determined vocal cords with which to sing. Thus, although some factors that affect the development of self-control might be primarily genetic factors and others primarily environmental factors, in all cases, both genes and environment play a role.

This chapter's description of the factors that may contribute to the development of self-control will overlap to some degree with topics covered in the next chapter, General Methods for Changing Self-Control. However, here the focus will be on the factors that are present during the development of most individuals, whereas in the next chapter, the focus will be on interventions that have been used to increase or decrease self-control in a wide variety of situations. Thus this chapter will focus on differences in self-control between different age groups, whereas the next chapter will be more concerned with individual differences in self-control within an age group. Subsequent chapters will consider interventions for specific situations. Together, all of the chapters will demonstrate that in addition to general developmental trends, there are sometimes large individual and situational differences in self-control.[1]

SELF-CONTROL AS A DEVELOPMENTAL GOAL

Self-control has been a major concern among all sorts of professionals concerned with development (see Box 4.1). Almost by definition, studying the

It's very, very, very hard to wait,
Especially when you're waiting for something very nice.
It's very, very, very hard to wait.
[A song from *Mister Rogers' Neighborhood*[2]]

Box 4.1

development of self-control seems to assume that self-control is more desirable than impulsiveness. In fact, some developmental psychologists have indeed seen self-control as a goal, an end point, of normal development. Infants are described as behaving only to obtain pleasure, with no ability whatsoever to delay gratification. Then, as the child ages, there is an increasing tendency to demonstrate self-control.[3] This description of development is compatible with the view that impulsiveness is always bad (immature) and self-control is always good (mature). Such an orientation toward the development of self-control is unfortunate, given that, as discussed in the previous chapter, in some situations, impulsiveness and not self-control is the most adaptive response.

More recently, some developmental psychologists have described the development of self-control in a more complex way that takes into account the fact that impulsiveness is sometimes the more adaptive response. According to this view, the end result of normal development is individuals who have the capacity to demonstrate either impulsiveness or self-control, depending on which is the adaptive response.[4]

Thus, in examining the development of self-control and the factors responsible for that development, it is important not only to assess whether self-control is more likely at certain ages, but also whether the adaptiveness of a particular choice plays an increasing role as individuals age. Unfortunately, almost all of the research that has been conducted on the development of self-control has employed situations in which self-control, and not impulsiveness, is the adaptive response. These data need to be supplemented by future research concerning the behavior of individuals of different ages in situations in which impulsiveness is the adaptive response. Until such future research is conducted, discussions of the development of self-control, including this chapter, will of necessity emphasize research in which self-control is the adaptive response.

CHANGES IN SELF-CONTROL AS A FUNCTION OF AGE

In order to examine what factors play a role in the development of self-control, it is necessary to first establish how self-control changes as a function of age. In general, self-control does tend to increase with age. Younger children show relatively more impulsiveness and older children show relatively more self-control. However, these changes have been demonstrated primarily by comparing younger and older preschoolers. Self-control has not been measured in infants, nor have there been direct comparisons of self-control in adults and children. One study with preschool children, using laboratory procedures that were fairly comparable to those that have been used with adults, does seem to indicate that children show less self-control than do adults.[5] In addition, the majority of studies have shown greater self-control in older children when children have been compared within the range of 18 months to six years of age.[6] However, most studies do not appear to find any differences in self-control between 6 and 12 years of age.[7]

These results are consistent with the view that as children age they have a longer future-time perspective.[8] Older children are less affected by outcome delays and are able to take into account events that are in the distant future. This age-related change can be described as an increase in children's *time horizon*, the time period over which individuals integrate a series of events.[9]

Although there have not been direct comparisons of self-control in children and adults, the results of self-control experiments with adults are strikingly different than those with children. Among adults, in the laboratory it has proved impossible to obtain consistent impulsiveness for rewards unless being impulsive also resulted in a higher rate of reward (and thus a greater amount of total obtained reward). In other words, consistent impulsiveness has only been obtained in human adults in the laboratory when impulsiveness, and not self-control, was the adaptive response.[10]

Edmund J. S. Sonuga-Barke has suggested that children progress through two stages in developing the adult pattern of laboratory self-control behavior. He has suggested that first they learn to wait for the more preferred outcome; they learn that it can be advantageous to wait for something rather than always choosing the immediate outcome. Then they learn when they should wait for the more preferred outcome; they learn that it is not always advantageous to wait for the more preferred outcome (similar to the behavior of the adults described above). According to Sonuga-Barke's research, children reach the first stage around the age of 6 years, and the second stage around the age of 9 to 12 years.[11]

Sonuga-Barke's contention that there is a change in self-control behavior around 9 to 12 years of age may seem contradictory to the findings cited above indicating that self-control does not appear to change between the ages of 6 and 12 years. However, Sonuga-Barke's postulated second stage in the development of self-control behavior is only evident if the subjects are given a self-control choice in which choosing the impulsive outcome actually results in the most total benefit. The studies described above demonstrating no increase in self-control in children between the ages of 6 and 12 years did not have this characteristic. In all of those studies, self-control was the adaptive response.

Sonuga-Barke's description of the development of self-control may also seem contradictory to the evolutionary basis for impulsiveness described in Chapter 3. However, Chapter 3 postulates only that there is an evolutionary basis for the discounting of delayed outcomes. Sonuga-Barke's description of the development of self-control does not preclude discounting of delayed outcomes by people at any developmental level. People can learn techniques to decrease or remove the effects of discounting of delayed outcomes (see Chapter 5).

POSSIBLE BASES OF AGE-RELATED CHANGES IN SELF-CONTROL

There are many characteristics that distinguish younger children, older children, and adults, and that could be responsible for self-control increasing with age. A great deal of research has examined the relationships between age-related changes in self-control and age-related changes in specific abilities, including both cognitive and motor abilities. Additional research has examined the effect on self-control of experiences with long outcome delays and experience with effort to obtain outcomes, experiences which many children have during their early years.

Perceptual Abilities

Before any choice can be made, including a self-control choice, an individual must perceive that the choice exists; the individual's brain must somehow indicate the presence of a choice. This perception may include more or less accurate information about the actual, physical characteristics of the particular choice. The degree to which the perception is complete and accurate will be a function of the abilities of the individual's sensory systems, and these abilities change with age. Using the most extreme example, very young animals, including humans, due to the immaturity of their sensory systems, are unable to detect certain aspects of the environment.

The two primary aspects of perceptual ability that have been studied with regard to their possible contribution to the development of self-control choices are the ability to estimate time and the ability to direct attention to and away from certain events. Data on the relationship between time estimation ability and self-control are not extensive. However, the ability to estimate time intervals does appear to improve with age, and is greater in normal, as opposed to emotionally disturbed, children.[12] In addition, greater self-control does appear to be associated with greater time estimation ability.[13] For example, one study using adolescent emotionally disturbed boys gave the boys a time estimation test in which they had to estimate the time that a stopwatch was running. Boys who would only work for a delayed, valuable outcome if there were some immediate benefit for doing so tended to estimate the stopwatch times as too short. However, boys who would work for a delayed, valuable outcome without any immediate benefit for doing so tended to estimate these times more accurately.[14] In another experiment, one which used children who were approximately 6 years of age, children who tended to show self-control also tended to show good time discrimination. The good time discrimination was evidenced by these children responding primarily when reinforcers were available on a *fixed-interval* schedule of reinforcement, a schedule in which reinforcers were available only after fixed intervals of time had passed.[15]

The ability to direct attention, particularly to certain aspects of the self-control situation, has also been examined. Some researchers feel that the ability to control attention is an essential aspect of self-control.[16] In an extremely clever and time-consuming experiment, Monica L. Rodriguez and her colleagues examined in detail the relationship between attention deployment and self-control.[17] The subjects were 6- to 12-year-old boys who had been characterized as having a variety of emotional and adjustment problems and who were attending a special summer residential camp program. Each boy was told that he would receive one of two piles of food items: the larger pile if he did not ring a bell and waited until the experimenter returned, and the smaller pile if he rang the bell (thus bringing back the experimenter to deliver the smaller pile immediately). The experimenters continuously monitored each boy's attention during the waiting period. They determined when each boy's gaze was directed at the food or bell versus away from those tempting items. Boys who tended to look at the food or the bell tended to wait for a shorter time before ringing the bell than did boys who tended to look away from the food or the bell. Further, older boys were more likely to look away from the food or the bell than were younger boys.

Additional research using children ranging between 24 and 36 months of age has obtained results similar to those of Rodriguez and her colleagues. In this additional, very young sample, age was significantly correlated with directing attention away from the rewards during the delay periods. Further, children who tended to wait a long time for the rewards also tended to look away from the rewards for longer periods.[18]

Finally, research conducted by Walter Mischel and his colleagues has suggested that in addition to the ability to direct attention that may predict self-control, self-control may predict the ability to direct attention. These researchers found a significant positive relationship between the amount of time that a child would wait for a larger reward when that child was 4 or 5 years of age, and the degree to which that child was rated as attentive by the child's parents when the child was an adolescent.[19]

The research on perceptual abilities and self-control demonstrates that time estimation ability and the ability to direct attention are both related to the ability to show self-control, and that all of these abilities increase with age. However, because much of this research is correlational, it does not always tell us what the causal relationships between age, directed attention, and self-control are, or whether or not some fourth variable is responsible for the relationships among the other three.

Experience with Long Delays

Everyone experiences long delays for some outcomes at some times. Several researchers have contended that such experiences contribute to the general tendency of an individual to show self-control.[20] As people grow and mature, they experience an increasing number of long delays, and to the degree that these delays are followed by positive outcomes, the general willingness to wait for outcomes is presumed to increase.

Robert Eisenberger and Michael Adornetto conducted a laboratory experiment on the effect on self-control of experience with long delays. The subjects in their experiment were second- and third-grade children. Those children who were given experience with delayed rewards for easy tasks and then tested for self-control were more likely to show self-control than were children who were given experience with immediate rewards for easy tasks. Eisenberger and Adornetto attributed this result to a decrease in the aversiveness of delay periods through habituation to long delays.[21] Another way to describe the results of this study is that the children learned that long delays were sometimes followed by large rewards in this experiment, and therefore it was to their advantage to wait, at least sometimes.

Intelligence

It would not be surprising if self-control were also related to the development of intelligence. In order to demonstrate self-control, it may be helpful not only to be able to perceive the physical characteristics of the outcomes, but to be able to compare them, to remember past relevant information (such as experience with long delays and techniques for increasing self-control), to apply that information to the present choice problem, and perhaps to be able to describe the available alternatives, all characteristics measured by intelligence tests.

A very large number of experiments have investigated the relationships between intelligence and self-control. These experiments are more diverse than they might at first seem, because there are many different aspects to intelligence. Intelligence involves verbal, mathematical, spatial, and other abilities. One or more of these might be related to the development of self-control. This section is concerned with intelligence as measured by formal intelligence tests. The next section will describe the possible relationships between language behavior and self-control.

Many experiments, using a variety of different subject populations, as well as a variety of measures of self-control and of intelligence, have obtained significant correlations between degree of self-control and intelligence.[22] In addition, mentally retarded adolescents appear to demonstrate less self-control than do normal adults.[23] Unfortunately, there has been almost no systematic investigation of the relationship between specific aspects of intelligence and self-control. One example of a recent, careful experiment that used a widely accepted, specific measure of intelligence is the experiment by Rodriguez and her colleagues described earlier.[24] These researchers administered the Peabody Picture Vocabulary Test (PPVT), a measure of verbal intelligence, to each of their subjects, and found a significant positive relationship between the tendency of a subject to delay and scores on the PPVT. Scores on the PPVT were, however, not significantly correlated with the subjects' ability to describe techniques useful for increasing self-control. Therefore, being able to describe useful self-control techniques is apparently not an essential aspect of any contribution that intelligence might make to the demonstration of self-control.

Other aspects of the research literature are also indicative of a relationship between self-control and general intellectual aptitude. For example, in an intriguing and difficult study, Walter Mischel and his colleagues found that self-control in 4- to 5-year-olds predicted SAT scores in high school.[25] In another experiment, kindergarten children stated that they believed that smart children would delay more than other children.[26] Finally, there is some indication in experiments with human adults that those subjects who are mathematically skilled are better able to respond so as to maximize total received reward in experiments involving delay of reward.[27]

Language Behavior

One definition of self-control in children is that a child's behavior can be controlled by the parents' use of language.[28] According to this definition, language behavior is critical to a demonstration of self-control. However, the question remains as to whether or not language behavior contributes to the development of self-control when self-control is defined as it is in this book—

choice of larger, more delayed outcomes over smaller, less delayed outcomes.

In considering the issue of whether or not the development of language behavior assists humans in showing self-control, it may be useful to consider species differences in addition to age differences concerning self-control. Humans have much more complex language behavior than do other species. Therefore, if self-control differs between humans and other species, complex language behavior may be responsible and may contribute to the observed increase in self-control in humans as a function of age.

In fact, when self-control has been examined in either pigeons or rats, unless special training or precommitment procedures are used, these species are consistently impulsive with regard to food rewards in the laboratory. This is so even when the subjects' impulsiveness results in their receiving less food than is necessary to maintain their body weights, and when they are studied using naturalistic procedures.[29] The self-control behavior of nonhumans contrasts with that of adult humans, who have consistently shown self-control in the laboratory.[30]

In addition to human adults simply tending to show more self-control in the laboratory than nonhumans, other aspects of adult human behavior in the laboratory tend to suggest that language contributes to adult humans' self-control. Consider a series of experiments by Alexandra W. Logue and her colleagues.[31] These experiments gave adult female humans the same choices between rewards of varying amounts and delays as had been given previously to pigeons. Rewards for the humans consisted of points exchangeable for money at the end of each session. The subjects tended to choose the alternative that resulted in the most total received reward, in other words, the self-control alternative. In postsession questionnaires, they reported following maximization strategies. They stated that they attempted to estimate the durations of the events occurring during the experiments through various counting techniques, and then, based on that information, to follow the strategy that would obtain the most total points during a session. The data, as well as the subjects' own reports, suggested that the subjects were following a maximization strategy during the experiments and that this behavior was dependent on their verbal abilities and histories.

Several other laboratory experiments examining behavior on various schedules of reinforcement suggest that the presence or absence of covert or overt verbal behavior can have an effect on performance. In general, the performance of nonverbal children and of nonverbal adults is more similar to the behavior of nonhumans than to the behavior of verbal children and verbal adults.[32] For example, with fixed-interval schedules, the pattern of responses of young, preverbal children, as compared with that of older children and adults, is similar to the pattern of responses of pigeons, and instructions can increase the similarity of the response pattern of verbal children to that of adults.[33] C. Fergus Lowe and Pauline J. Horne have suggested that what human subjects say to themselves is critical to how they behave on schedules of reinforcement. According to Lowe and Horne, this verbal behavior, including verbal behavior about the programmed contingencies of reinforcement (i.e., verbal behavior about the rules governing the delivery of reinforcers[34]), affects behavior just as do the programmed contingencies of reinforcement.[35]

In contrast to all of these data suggesting that language behavior must have some effect on self-control, the data directly examining the role of language behavior in self-control in children are mixed. Some studies have found that language capacity or vocabulary are positively related to self-control,[36] but others have not.[37] There appears to be disagreement as to whether or not language is important in the development of self-control. As will be discussed further in the section below concerning the acquisition of techniques for increasing self-control, it is possible that what assists self-control is the ability to make certain kinds of verbalizations during delay periods, not language ability in general.

Activity Level

Sometimes showing self-control involves withholding a response. For example, suppose child A takes child B's cookie. Child B could strike the thief, and such an action might result in the immediate return of the cookie. But in the long term, if child B strikes child A, child B could be labeled a bully, or could be punished by an adult, or could cause the thief to hit back with a blow even harder than that struck by child B. A number of responses, all involving not hitting, might be most successful in the long term in allowing child B to keep his cookie; withholding hitting can be an example of a self-control response. However, these alternative responses would probably all involve child B withholding the hitting response.

Several researchers, including Alexander R. Luria and Lev S. Vygotsky, have defined self-control specifically as learning to control responding. For these researchers, self-control is control (particularly verbal control) of motor behavior; self-control is the ability of a child to make a particular, desirable response at a specific time according to an external or internal command, while not making a nondesirable response. They contend that this ability develops over time, and data have been collected supporting this position.[38] Consistent with the concept that response control and self-control are related, the ability of delinquents to inhibit motor behavior has been shown to be positively correlated with the amount of time that the delinquents think will pass before the occurrence of certain events in their future[39] (a measure of a subject's time horizon, which is related to self-control). However, there is apparently no significant relationship between motor inhibition and self-control in nondelinquents or in emotionally disturbed boys.[40]

Given that self-control can involve someone withholding a response, it is possible that general activity level might be related to the development of self-control. Children (or other subject populations with relatively high innate activity levels) might have particular difficulties in controlling their responses within self-control situations. Younger children do have trouble responding at a slow rate to obtain a reward.[41] Further, pigeons, which are notoriously difficult to discourage from pecking, have difficulty showing self-control when the self-control response consists of not pecking. Elicited (nonvoluntary) pecks can apparently interfere with a pigeon showing self-control.[42] The section on hyperactivity in Chapter 9 will provide additional evidence regarding the relationship between a high general-activity level and self-control.

Experience with Effort

Outcomes differing in the amount of effort necessary to obtain them may be similar to outcomes differing in delay, because a greater effort usually requires more time to expend than does a lesser effort. Thus, choice of a larger reward that requires more effort to expend, over a smaller reward that requires less effort to expend, can be described as self-control.

From the time of birth we are exposed, to at least some degree, to outcomes that are delivered only after we have expended some effort. Robert Eisenberger and his colleagues have contended that such experiences are critical to the development of self-control when choosing the self-control alternative involves expending greater effort than choosing the impulsive alternative. These researchers have conducted experiments using both preadolescent children and rats, and have obtained similar results with both species. In each of their experiments, in comparison with control subjects, subjects previously given experience with rewards following a substantial expended effort were more likely to choose a larger reward requiring more effort over a smaller reward requiring less effort. Eisenberger and his colleagues believe that experience with large rewards requiring substantial effort for delivery can result in a generalized increased tendency to choose such rewards in comparison to subjects without this experience.[43]

In addition to effort experience, additional research suggests that certain subject characteristics can modify the degree to which a subject will choose a larger reward that requires substantial effort for delivery. In particular, there has been research conducted concerning the relationship between effortful self-control and individuals' locus of control. Locus of control measures to what degree someone believes that external events are caused by other external events (an external locus of control) or by something to do with the person himself or herself (an internal locus of control). One experiment showed that if a high school student has an internal locus of control, that student is not as likely to choose a larger reward requiring perhaps an impossible degree of effort as is a student who has an external locus of control.[44]

Acquisition of General Self-Control Strategies

As children age, they acquire general strategies for increasing self-control. This section will describe some of these strategies and how they change with age. There will be more detailed discussion of techniques for increasing self-control in the next chapter.

The majority of the work on age-related changes in general strategies for increasing self-control has been conducted by Harriet N. Mischel and Walter Mischel.[45] These researchers studied children whose year in school ranged from preschool through grade six. Mischel and Mischel found that at age four few of the children seemed to be aware of what sorts of strategies would be useful for demonstrating self-control. To the contrary, children at this age appeared to engage in behaviors, such as attending to the larger reward during the delay period, that actually make it more difficult to wait for that reward. However, by the end of the fifth year, children begin to learn what sorts of behaviors will make it easier to wait. For example, they learn that distracting themselves (such as by singing a song, playing a game, or falling asleep) or instructing themselves (such as by repeating to themselves that waiting will result in the larger reward) can help in the demonstration of self-control. In addition, somewhere between the third and sixth grades, children are able to report that thinking abstractly about the rewards and the task (such as thoughts about the shape of the rewards) rather than about the consummatory properties of the rewards (such as their taste) will also help in their demonstrating self-control.

The self-control strategies that are acquired during the development of most normal children can all be seen as ways of decreasing the discounting that occurs when outcomes are delayed.[46] Reminding oneself of the contingency or of the abstract qualities of the outcome may help to make the outcome seem to be here now, rather than distant in time. In contrast, attending to the consummatory properties of the outcomes can make the delay period seem longer than its actual physical length. Some researchers might describe such an increased effect of the outcome delay as resulting from an increase in the frustration caused by the delay period.[47] For cases in which the outcomes consist of food, Chapter 6 provides a possible physiological explanation of the decrease in self-control resulting from attention to the consummatory properties of the outcomes.

SELF-CONTROL IN PEOPLE OF ADVANCED AGE

Although there is as yet no research on this topic, it is possible that people of advanced years may show a decrease in some self-control behaviors in their daily lives. If someone believes that he or she may not have many years to live, such a person would be very unlikely to choose an outcome that will not occur until some years into the future. Thus people of advanced age may be less likely to save money, to stop smoking, or to eat low cholesterol foods. Research needs to be conducted to determine whether or not this hypothesis is correct.

GENDER DIFFERENCES

Given that males and females differ somewhat in their development,[48] males and females may also differ with regard to self-control in different ways at different ages. In other words, there may be an interaction between age and gender with respect to self-control.

There has been only one experiment examining gender differences in self-control in human adults.[49] That study found no difference between men and women pushing a rod left or right to choose between a larger, more delayed food reward and a smaller, less delayed food reward. However, these results do not mean that all gender differences in human adults' self-control are lacking. Only this one type of self-control laboratory procedure has been employed to date with adults of different genders; use of a different self-control procedure might yet reveal a gender difference in self-control performance. One study has shown that people describe men and women who are low in self-control as differing in other key respects. People believe that men who are low in self-control tend to be assertive in a negative way; they try to overcontrol their environment. In contrast, people believe that women who are low in self-control tend to be yielding in a negative way; they do not try to control their environment enough.[50] It is not known whether or not these popularly held beliefs concerning personality differences between low self-control men and women are accurate descriptions of behavior. However, if they are accurate, there might be gender differences in performance within a self-control laboratory paradigm in which self-control is defined as inhibition of aggression (assuming that aggression could be described as extreme assertiveness involving negative overcontrol of the environment). Such an experiment might reveal less self-control in men than in women.

The question as to whether men and women differ concerning self-control must remain open until there is further research (but see also the sections on anorexia nervosa and bulimia nervosa in Chapter 6). However, greater self-control in girls than in boys appears to be a firmly established fact.[51] The studies on which this conclusion is based used a variety of different self-control paradigms and children in school ranging from preschool to high school. For children, the most important issue is not whether or not there are gender differences, but what might be the cause of these differences. One factor that appears not to be responsible is differences in the language ability of boys and girls. Although, as indicated earlier in this chapter, language skills do appear to be positively related to self-control, and although some researchers have reported that girls, on the average, have greater language skills than boys, these differences are typically small enough so as to be considered essentially nonexistent.[52] Gender differences in language ability are an insufficient explanation of the gender differences in self-control.

Many other possible explanations regarding why boys would be more impulsive than girls have been suggested by the research literature. For example, it has been suggested that boys are socialized to act independently and

assertively, which can be inconsistent with self-control, and girls are socialized to control their impulses and to conform with society's norms, which can
be consistent with self-control.[53] Gender differences in activity level[54] could
also make it more difficult for the relatively more active boys to wait for delayed reinforcers.[55] Finally, if there are gender differences in some of the factors already discussed as important in the development of self-control, factors such as experience with long delays and knowledge and use of
distraction techniques, these gender differences could help to explain the
gender differences obtained in children's self-control. Many more experiments are needed before researchers will know the precise determinants of
greater self-control in girls than in boys.

CULTURE

One way to examine how development of self-control might differ for
different people is to examine self-control as a function of culture. By definition, cultures vary in terms of the experiences provided the people who are a
part of those cultures. It is possible, therefore, that during development, people in different cultures acquire different degrees or types of self-control. An
examination of self-control as a function of culture can also be useful in revealing the degree to which self-control and impulsiveness can vary among
groups of people despite humans' common evolutionary heritage. This section on culture will first examine self-control within the United States culture,
including how self-control in the United States may have changed over time
and how self-control may differ among different groups within the United
States. This section will then examine the role that self-control plays in Japanese culture.

United States

There appear to be strong cultural tendencies in the United States for
both self-control and impulsiveness. On the one hand, one of the major principles on which the United States was founded appears to have been self-control. Self-control and resistance to temptation have been part of Americans'
Judeo-Christian heritage (see Boxes 4.2, 4.3, 4.4, and 4.5). However, in recent
decades, there has been concern that this early emphasis on self-control may
be dissipating.[58] The 1970s and the 1980s were the decades of the *me* genera-
tion; many young adults wanted rewards without undergoing the sometimes
necessary wait. It is not clear that the 1990s are any different. Further, the baby
boom children are now in their thirties and forties and are not saving as much
money as their parents did when they were their age. It is not known why
this is so. Possible reasons include the fact that the baby boomers never experienced the depression, and people now past the age of retirement are not
as poor as previously, so that baby boomers do not worry as much about sav-

O beautiful for pilgrim feet
  Whose stern, impassioned
    stress
A thoroughfare for freedom beat
  Across the wilderness!
America! America!
  God mend thine every flaw,
Confirm thy soul in self-control,
  Thy liberty in law!
[From "America the Beauti-ful"[56]]

Box 4.2

Blessed is the man that en-dureth temptation: for when he is tried, he shall receive the crown of life, which the Lord hath promised to them that love him. [James, 1:12]

Box 4.3

Get thee behind me, Satan.

Box 4.4

If a man is allured by the things of this world and is estranged from his Creator, it is not he alone who is corrupted, but the whole world is corrupted with him. But if he exercises self-control, cleaves to his Creator and makes use of this world only insofar as it helps him to serve his Creator, he himself rises to a higher order of being and he carries the world along with him. [*Mesillat Yesharim*][57]

Box 4.5

ing for their own retirement years.[59] Robert Eisenberger has written a book, *Blue Monday: The Loss of the Work Ethic in America,* regarding what he sees as disastrous trends in the United States toward impulsiveness. According to Eisenberger:

The American vision involved not simply economic betterment but a willingness to work diligently toward that more prosperous future. As America became affluent, a preoccupation with leisure and sensual pleasure began to replace traditional work values, making managers, workers, and students less willing to undergo the self-denial required to achieve long-term goals. Society's emphasis on getting ahead by hard work disappeared before most of today's Americans were born. More than ever before, Americans view school and work as an unpleasant interlude in their relaxation and entertainment, to be gotten out of the way with a minimum of effort.[60]

Nevertheless, it is not clear that all aspects of self-control behavior are decreasing in our society. Kelly D. Brownell has described our current obsessive focus on inappropriate (thin) body size and general physical fitness as a form of self-control[61] (for a comparison of the degree to which a trim body was important in the 1950s versus the degree to which it has become important in the past ten years, see Figures 4.1 and 4.2). According to Brownell, in our present society self-control is considered a laudable goal, and the degree to which someone is judged as possessing self-control is significantly affected by the degree to which the person has a fit, thin body. Brownell sees this increase in focus on self-control as detrimental to our society because body size and shape are largely determined by physiological factors beyond a person's control (for additional information regarding self-control and eating see Chapter 6). Brownell's and Eisenberger's views illustrate that a culture's expectations with regard to self-control can vary as a function of the situation.

Figure 4.1.   A "perfect" figure from the 1950s: Marilyn Monroe (with Cary Grant).

Another way to examine self-control as a function of different situations within a particular culture is to examine self-control as a function of socioeconomic status (SES). There have been many studies conducted which have examined self-control in different socioeconomic groups. All of these studies have used children (through high school age). Most,[62] but not all,[63] of the studies have found less self-control in low SES groups as compared with higher SES groups.

The studies demonstrating a significant relationship between SES and self-control are all correlational studies. Therefore it is not possible to determine what is responsible for the observed relationship. For example, some researchers feel that deprivation level can affect self-control, with more deprived subjects demonstrating less self-control[64] (see also Chapter 6). If people of low SES can be conceived of as having a high general deprivation level due to their poverty, then it is possible that the low SES causes their low self-control. On the other hand, suppose that people who have low self-control have difficulty obtaining and keeping well-paying jobs. Then low self-control could cause low SES. As still a third possibility, suppose people with a limited time horizon have difficulty in both showing self-control and in obtaining and keeping well-paying jobs. Then an individual's time horizon could affect both self-control and SES and would be responsible for the correlation between self-control and SES. Consistent with this hypothesis, one study with children has shown that SES is related to temporal span as well as to self-control. (Temporal span was measured by asking the subjects, chil-

Figure 4.2.   A "perfect" figure from the 1980s: Jamie Lee Curtis.

dren, to draw lines whose length corresponded to the lengths of different time intervals presented by the experimenters.)[65] However, once again, these are correlational data. Therefore there could be still a fourth variable that determines temporal span, SES, and self-control, and is responsible for the correlations between them. Additional experiments are needed to determine the causal relationships between temporal span, SES, and self-control, if any.

Japan

Much has been written about self-control in Eastern as compared with Western cultures. Some of this material has been concerned with apparent differences in the definition of self-control in Western and Eastern societies. In Western societies, self-control has been described as "goal-oriented productivity, assertiveness, and instrumental doing," whereas in Eastern societies it has been described as "yielding, letting go, acceptance, and nonattachment."[66] However, this difference between Eastern and Western self-control behavior is not due to a difference in the definition of self-control, but instead to a difference in what is considered a large outcome worth waiting for in these two cultures. In Western society, such outcomes often consist of concrete, discrete outcomes such as money, food, or a good grade; but in Eastern society they tend to be less concrete, more spiritual outcomes—outcomes such as harmony.[67] After taking into account the difference in the nature of the large outcomes, both Eastern and Western self-control styles can be defined as responding so as to obtain larger, more delayed outcomes.

Some researchers have been concerned, not with differences between Eastern and Western self-control styles, but with the relative emphasis put on self-control in each of these two societies. For example, many people consider the Japanese culture to be virtually synonymous with self-control. Perhaps related to their high population density, from early in childhood the Japanese stress consensus and cooperation. Individual gratification is valued much less than is advancement of the fortunes of the group, something that requires that each individual member of the group put aside personal desires in order to work for long-term societal goals.[68] An example of such societal values can be seen in the samurai, the former warrior aristocracy of Japan: "The *samurai* lived by `The Code of the Warriors,' called *bushido*. *Bushido* instructed them in religion and martial arts, and taught them about loyalty, self-control, and noble behavior."[69] Societal values stressing self-control have also been present in Japanese-Chinese folklore:

> In ancient times, a Chinese man once said to his pet monkeys that he would give them three pieces of fruit in the morning and four in the evening. As the monkeys got very angry, he told them instead that they would be given four pieces of fruit in the morning and three in the evening. Then the monkeys were very satisfied. This story teaches us that, unless we use our brains, we, too, can be tricked as easily as the monkeys. . . . In Japan, we have a saying: `An impatient

beggar will be given less alms.' This, of course, means: 'Wait and you will be given more.'[70]

Today, Japanese businesses and managers are known for taking a much more long-term view in their planning than their Western counterparts. The Japanese are also noted for their high rate of savings. Around 1980, the average Japanese was putting about 20 percent of disposable income into savings.[71] The comparable figure in the United States at that time was around 5 percent.[72] The high rate of savings among the Japanese may be due to a combination of the Japanese feeling that good times do not last long and that their children's education will be expensive. In addition, until recently in Japan, many businesses required their employees to retire at age 55, years before social security payments could begin, thus making retirement savings a necessity.[73]

However, self-control does not completely dominate Japanese society. Just as there is concern that self-control in the United States is decreasing, there is also concern that self-control in Japan is decreasing. This concern is based on such findings as a recent decrease in the rate of savings.[74] This recent decrease in the savings rate could be linked to the fact that the Japanese retirement age is now more usually 60 than 55.

In addition, Japanese young adults now seem more inclined to feel that working hard should result in immediate, rather than delayed rewards. A Japanese government survey taken in 1980 indicated that since 1960, there had been a large decrease in the percentage of people between 15 and 19 who stated that they were working toward future large rewards, and a large increase in the percentage who stated that they wished to have an individual, rather than a group-oriented life-style.

Students' behavior as shaped by the Japanese educational system exemplifies both the extreme self-control and the impulsiveness that have been associated with Japanese youth. In high school, many Japanese students spend countless hours preparing for the examinations for college. Consequently, they forego many immediate pleasures considered essential by American teenagers. In other words, when preparing for college entrance examinations, Japanese students show extreme self-control. However, once admitted to college, it is extremely difficult for Japanese students to earn grades warranting dismissal. Further, in hiring college graduates, many Japanese organizations put more emphasis on the college examination score rather than on performance during college. Thus, once a student has been admitted to college, for the next four years there is very little incentive to focus on studying as a means to a large future reward. At this time, obtaining immediate pleasures seems to best characterize Japanese students' behavior.[75]

In summary, although the Japanese and American cultures have sometimes appeared to be significantly different with respect to self-control, impulsiveness, as well as self-control, is present in each culture. In addition, previous differences between the two cultures with respect to self-control may be disappearing. Whether this trend will, in the end, be more or less beneficial for human survival and well-being remains to be seen.

CONCLUSION

This chapter has described a large number of possible influences on the development of self-control. Self-control does increase with age, and it apparently does so more quickly in girls than in boys. A number of factors may be responsible for these findings. The development of perceptual abilities, intelligence, and language behavior, as well as experience with long delays and effort, age-related changes in activity level, and learning of general self-control strategies may all play a role. There are also sometimes striking differences in self-control as a function of culture, although the responsible factors are not yet precisely known.

The research described in this chapter helps to identify some possible causes of individual differences in self-control that may be stable over time. For example, if someone is relatively high in language ability over time, that person may also be relatively high in self-control over time. Stable individual differences in self-control do, in fact, appear to exist. At the same time, self-control can vary a great deal as a function of the particular situation,[76] as subsequent chapters will demonstrate.

REFERENCES

1. Mischel, W. (1984). "Convergences and Challenges in the Search for Consistency." *American Psychologist*, 39, 351–364.

Mischel, W., Shoda, Y., and Peake, P. K. (1988). "The Nature of Adolescent Competencies Predicted by Preschool Delay of Gratification." *Journal of Personality and Social Psychology*, 54, 687–696.

2. Rogers, F. (Executive Producer), and Martin, H. (Producer and Director). (1986, December 14). *Mister Rogers' Neighborhood* [Television Series]. Family Communications, Inc.

3. Kopp, C. B. (1982). "Antecedents of Self-regulation: A Developmental Perspective." *Developmental Psychology*, 18, 199–214.

Mischel, W., Shoda, Y., and Rodriguez, M. L. (1989). "Delay of Gratification in Children." *Science*, 244, 933–938.

4. Ibid.

Sonuga-Barke, E. J. S., Lea, S. E. G., and Webley, P. (1989). "The Development of Adaptive Choice in a Self-control Paradigm." *Journal of the Experimental Analysis of Behavior*, 51, 77–85.

5. Logue, A. W., and Chavarro, A. (1992). "Self-control and Impulsiveness in Preschool Children." *Psychological Record*, 42, 189–204.

6. Inouye, A., Sato, S., and Sato, Y. (1979). "Developmental Study in Delayed Preference Behavior." *The Japanese Journal of Psychology*, 50, 82–88.

Miller, D. T., Weinstein, S. M., and Karniol, R. (1978). "Effects of Age and Self-verbalization on Children's Ability to Delay Gratification." *Developmental Psychology*, 14, 569–570.

Mischel, W., and Metzner, R. (1962). "Preference for Delayed Reward as a Function of Age, Intelligence, and Length of Delay Interval." *Journal of Abnormal and Social Psychology*, 64, 425–431.

Sarafino, E. P., Russo, A., Barker, J., Consentino, A. M., and Titus, D. (1982). "The Effect of Rewards on Intrinsic Interest: Developmental Changes in the Underlying Processes." *The Journal of Genetic Psychology*, 141, 29–39.

Vaughn, B. E., Kopp, C. B., and Krakow, J. B. (1984). "The Emergence and Consolidation of Self-control from Eighteen to Thirty Months of Age: Normative Trends and Individual Differences." *Child Development*, 55, 990–1004.

7. Crooks, R. C. (1977). "Magnitude of Reward and Preference in a Delayed-reward Situation." *Psychological Reports*, 40, 1215–1219.

Walsh, R. P. (1967). "Sex, Age, and Temptation." *Psychological Reports*, 21, 625–629.

8. Wilson, J. Q., and Herrnstein, R. J. (1985). *Crime and Human Nature*. New York: Simon & Schuster.

9. Krebs, J. R., and Kacelnik, A. (1984). "Time Horizons of Foraging Animals." In J. Gibbon, and L. Allan (Ed.), *Timing and Time Perception* (pp. 278–291). New York: New York Academy of Sciences.

10. Logue, A. W., Forzano, L. B., and Tobin, H. (1992). "Independence of Reinforcer Amount and Delay: The Generalized Matching Law and Self-control in Humans." *Learning and Motivation*, 23, 326–342.

Logue, A. W., Peña-Correal, T. E., Rodriguez, M. L., and Kabela, E. (1986). "Self-control in Adult Humans: Variation in Positive Reinforcer Amount and Delay." *Journal of the Experimental Analysis of Behavior*, 46, 159–173.

Millar, A., and Navarick, D. J. (1984). "Self-control and Choice in Humans: Effects of Video Game Playing as a Positive Reinforcer." *Learning and Motivation*, 15, 203–218.

11. Sonuga-Barke, E. J. S., Lea, S. E. G., and Webley, P. (1989). "Children's Choice: Sensitivity to Changes in Reinforcer Density." *Journal of the Experimental Analysis of Behavior*, 51, 185–197.

Sonuga-Barke, Lea, and Webley, "The Development of Adaptive Choice," 77–85.

12. Davids, A. (1969). "Ego Functions in Disturbed and Normal Children: Aspiration, Inhibition, Time Estimation, and Delayed Gratification." *Journal of Consulting and Clinical Psychology*, 33, 61–70.

Mischel, and Metzner, "Preference for Delayed Reward," 425–431.

13. Levine, M., and Spivak, G. (1959). "Incentive, Time Conception and Self Control in a Group of Emotionally Disturbed Boys." *Journal of Clinical Psychology*, 15, 110–113.

Siegman, A. W. (1961). "The Relationship between Future Time Perspective, Time Estimation, and Impulse Control in a Group of Young Offenders and in a Control Group." *Journal of Consulting Psychology*, 25, 470–475.

14. Levine, and Spivak, " Incentive Time Conception and Self-control," 110–113.
15. Darcheville, J. C., Rivière, V., and Wearden, J. H. (1992). "Fixed-interval Performance and Self-control in Children." *Journal of the Experimental Analysis of Behavior*, 57, 187–199.
16. Kendall, P. C., and Finch, A. J. (1979). "Developing Nonimpulsive Behavior in Children: Cognitive-behavioral Strategies for Self-control." In P. C. Kendall, and S. D. Hollon (Eds.), *Cognitive-behavioral Interventions* (pp. 37–79). New York: Academic Press.
17. Rodriguez, M. L., Mischel, W., and Shoda, Y. (1989). "Cognitive Person Variables in the Delay of Gratification of Older Children at Risk." *Journal of Personality and Social Psychology*, 57, 358–367.
18. Vaughn, B. E., Kopp, C. B., Krakow, J. B., Johnson, K., and Schwartz, S. S. (1986). "Process Analyses of the Behavior of Very Young Children in Delay Tasks." *Developmental Psychology*, 22, 752–759.
19. Mischel, Shoda, and Peake, "The Nature of Adolescent Competencies," 687–696.
20. Eisenberger, R., and Adornetto, M. (1986). "Generalized Self-control of Delay and Effort." *Journal of Personality and Social Psychology*, 51, 1020–1031.
    Litrownik, A. J., Franzini, L. R., Geller, S., and Geller, M. (1977). "Delay of Gratification: Decisional Self-control and Experience with Delay Intervals." *American Journal of Deficiency*, 82, 149–154.
    Wilson, and Herrnstein, *Crime and Human Nature*.
21. Eisenberger, and Adornetto, "Generalized Self-control," 1020–1031.
22. Funder, D. C., and Block, J. (1989). "The Role of Ego-control, Ego-resiliency, and IQ in Delay of Gratification in Adolescence." *Journal of Personality and Social Psychology*, 57, 1041–1050.
    Golden, M., Montare, A., and Bridger, W. (1977). "Verbal Control of Delay Behavior in Two-year-old Boys as a Function of Social Class." *Child Development*, 48, 1107–1111.
    Mischel, and Metzner, "Preference for Delayed Reward," 425–431.
    Rodriguez, Mischel, and Shoda, "Cognitive Person Variables," 358–367.
23. Ragotzy, S. P., Blakely, E., and Poling, A. (1988). "Self-control in Mentally Retarded Adolescents: Choice as a Function of Amount and Delay of Reinforcement." *Journal of the Experimental Analysis of Behavior*, 49, 191–199.
24. Rodriguez, Mischel, and Shoda, "Cognitive Person Variables," 358–367.
25. Mischel, Shoda, and Rodriguez, "Delay of Gratification," 933–938.
26. Nisan, M., and Koriat, A. (1977). "Children's Actual Choices and Their Conception of the Wise Choice in a Delay-of-gratification Situation." *Child Development*, 48, 488–494.
27. Mawhinney, T. C. (1982). "Maximizing Versus Matching in People Versus Pigeons." *Psychological Reports*, 50, 267–281.
    Rodriguez, M. L., and Logue, A. W. (1988). "Adjusting Delay to Reinforcement: Comparing Choice in Pigeons and Humans." *Journal of Experimental Psychology: Animal Behavior Processes*, 14, 105–117.
28. Golden, Montare, and Bridger, "Verbal Control of Delay Behavior," 1107–1111.
29. Ainslie, G. W. (1974). "Impulse Control in Pigeons." *Journal of the Experimental Analysis of Behavior*, 21, 485–489.

Green, L., Fisher, E. B., Perlow, S., and Sherman, L. (1981). "Preference Reversal and Self-control: Choice as a Function of Reward Amount and Delay." *Behaviour Analysis Letters*, 1, 43–51.

Grosch, J., and Neuringer, A. (1981). "Self-control in Pigeons under the Mischel Paradigm." *Journal of the Experimental Analysis of Behavior*, 35, 3–21.

Logue, A. W., Chavarro, A., Rachlin, H., and Reeder, R. W. (1988). "Impulsiveness in Pigeons Living in the Experimental Chamber." *Animal Learning and Behavior*, 16, 31–39.

Logue, A. W., and Peña-Correal, T. E. (1984). "Responding During Reinforcement Delay in a Self-control Paradigm." *Journal of the Experimental Analysis of Behavior*, 41, 267–277.

Logue, A. W., and Peña-Correal, T. E. (1985). "The Effect of Food Deprivation on Self-control." *Behavioural Processes*, 10, 355–368.

Logue, A. W., Rodriguez, M. L., Peña-Correal, T. E., and Mauro, B. C. (1984). "Choice in a Self-control Paradigm: Quantification of Experience-based Differences." *Journal of the Experimental Analysis of Behavior*, 41, 53–67.

Rachlin, H., and Green, L. (1972). "Commitment, Choice and Self-control." *Journal of the Experimental Analysis of Behavior*, 17, 15–22.

Tobin, H., Chelonis, J. J., and Logue, A. W. (1993). "Choice in Self-control Paradigms Using Rats." *Psychological Record*, 43, 441–454.

30. Logue, A. W. (1988). "Research on Self-control: An Integrating Framework." *Behavioral and Brain Sciences*, 11, 665–709.

    Tobin, H., and Logue, A. W. (in press). "Self-control Across Species (*Columba livia, Homo sapiens*, and *Ratus norvegicus*)." *Journal of Comparative Psychology*.

31. Logue, Peña-Correal, Rodriguez, and Kabela, "Self-control in Adult Humans," 159–173.

32. Logue, "Research on Self-control," 665–709.

33. Bentall, R. P., and Lowe, C. F. (1987). "The Role of Verbal Behavior in Human Learning: III. Instructional Effects in Children." *Journal of the Experimental Analysis of Behavior*, 47, 177–190.

    Bentall, R. P., Lowe, C. F., and Beasty, A. (1985). "The Role of Verbal Behavior in Human Learning: II. Developmental Differences." *Journal of the Experimental Analysis of Behavior*, 43, 165–181.

    Lowe, C. F., Beasty, A., and Bentall, R. P. (1983). "The Role of Verbal Behavior in Human Learning: Infant Performance on Fixed-interval Schedules." *Journal of the Experimental Analysis of Behavior*, 39, 157–164.

34. Skinner, B. F. (1974). *About Behaviorism*. New York: Knopf.

35. Lowe, C. F., and Horne, P. J. (1988). "On the Origins of Selves and Self-control." *Behavioral and Brain Sciences*, 11, 689–690.

36. Kopp, (1982). "Antecedents of Self-regulation," 199–214.

    Vaughn, Kopp, Krakow, Johnson, and Schwartz, "Process Analyses," 752–759.

37. Kopp, "Antecedents of Self-regulation," 199–214.

    Maitland, S. D. P. (1967). "Time Perspective, Frustration-failure and Delay of Gratification in Middle-class and Lower-class Children from Organized and Disorganized Families." *Dissertation Abstracts*, 27, 3676-B.

38. Kopp, "Antecedents of Self-regulation" 199–214.

39. Siegman, "The Relationship Between Future Time Perspective," 470–475.

40. Levine, and Spivak, "Incentive, Time Conception and Self Control," 110–113.

Siegman, "The Relationship Between Future Time Perspective," 470–475.

41. Bentall, and Lowe, "The Role of Verbal Behavior in Human Learning," 177–190.

42. Lopatto, D., and Lewis, P. (1985). "Contributions of Elicitation to Measures of Self-control." *Journal of the Experimental Analysis of Behavior*, 44, 69–77.

43. Eisenberger, and Adornetto, "Generalized Self-control," 1020–1031.

Eisenberger, R., Mitchell, M., and Masterson, F. A. (1985). "Effort Training Increases Generalized Self-control." *Journal of Personality and Social Psychology*, 49, 1294–1301.

Eisenberger, R., Weier, F., Masterson, F. A., and Theis, L. Y. (1989). "Fixed-ratio Schedules Increase Generalized Self-control: Preference for Large Rewards Despite High Effort or Punishment." *Journal of Experimental Psychology: Animal Behavior Processes*, 15, 383–392.

44. Trommsdorff, G., and Schmidt-Rinke, M. (1980). "Individual Situational Characteristics as Determinants of Delay of Gratification." *Archiv für Psychologie*, 133, 263–275.

45. Mischel, H. N., and Mischel, W. (1983). "The Development of Children's Knowledge of Self-control Strategies." *Child Development*, 54, 603–619.

Mischel, Shoda, and Rodriguez, "Delay of Gratification," 933–938.

46. Karniol, R., and Miller, D. T. (1981). "The Development of Self-control in Children." In S. S. Brehm, S. M. Kassin, and F. X. Gibbons (Eds.), *Developmental Social Psychology* (pp. 32–50). Oxford: Oxford University Press.

47. Mischel, W., and Ebbesen, E. B. (1970). "Attention in Delay of Gratification." *Journal of Personality and Social Psychology*, 16, 329–337.

48. Maccoby, E. E., and Jacklin, C. N. (1974). *The Psychology of Sex Differences*. Stanford: Stanford University Press.

49. Forzano, L. B., and Logue, A. W. (1992). "Predictors of Adult Humans' Self-control and Impulsiveness for Food Reinforcers." *Appetite*, 19, 33–47.

50. Shapiro, D. H. (1983). "Self-control: Refinement of a Construct." *Biofeedback and Self-Regulation*, 8, 443–460.

51. Kanfer, F. H., and Zich, J. (1974). "Self-control Training: The Effects of External Control on Children's Resistance to Temptation." *Developmental Psychology*, 10, 108–115.

Logue, and Chavarro, "Self-control and Impulsiveness," 189–204.

Maccoby, and Jacklin, *The Psychology of Sex Differences*.

Sonuga-Barke, Lea, and Webley, "Children's Choice," 185–197.

Trommsdorff, and Schmidt-Rinke, "Individual Situational Characteristics," 263–275.

Walsh, "Sex, Age, and Temptation," 625–629.

52. Hyde, J. S., and Linn, M. C. (1988). "Gender Differences in Verbal Ability: A Meta-analysis." *Psychological Bulletin*, 104, 53–69.

Jacklin, C. N. (1989). "Female and Male: Issues of Gender." *American Psychologist*, 44, 127–133.

Rutter, M. (1977). "Speech Delay." In M. Rutter and L. Herso (Eds.), *Child Psychiatry: Modern Approaches* (pp. 688–716). Philadelphia: Lippincott.

53. Funder, D. C., Block, J. H., and Block, J. (1983). "Delay of Gratification: Some Longitudinal Personality Correlates." *Journal of Personality and Social Psychology*, 44, 1198–1213.

    Low, B. S. (1989). "Cross-cultural Patterns in the Training of Children: An Evolutionary Perspective." *Journal of Comparative Psychology*, 103, 311–319.

54. American Psychiatric Association. (1987). *"Diagnostic and Statistical Manual of Mental Disorders* (3rd ed. rev.)." Washington, DC: Author.

55. Campbell, S. B., Szumowski, E. K., Ewing, L. J., Gluck, D. S., and Breaux, A. M. (1982). "A Multidimensional Assessment of Parent-identified Behavior Problem Toddlers." *Journal of Abnormal Child Psychology*, 10, 569–592.

    Schweitzer, J. B., and Sulzer-Azaroff, B. (1988). "Self-control: Teaching Tolerance for Delay in Impulsive Children." *Journal of the Experimental Analysis of Behavior*, 50, 173–186.

56. Bates, K. L. (1987). "America the Beautiful." In P. C. Beall and S. H. Nipp (Eds.), *Wee Sing America*. Los Angeles: Price Stern Sloan, p. 17. (Original work written in 1893.)

57. Quoted in: Goldman, A. L. (1991). *The Search for God at Harvard*. New York: Ballantine Books, pp. 74–75.

58. Eisenberger, R. (1989). *Blue Monday: The Loss of the Work Ethic in America*. New York: Paragon House.

59. Nasar, S. (1991, September 24). "Baby Boomers Fail as Born-again Savers." *The New York Times*, pp. A1, D5.

60. Eisenberger, *Blue Monday*, p. ix.

61. Brownell, K. D. (1991). "Dieting and the Search for the Perfect Body: Where Physiology and Culture Collide." *Behavior Therapy*, 22, 1–12.

62. Freire, E., Gorman, B., and Wessman, A. E. (1980). "Temporal Span, Delay of Gratification, and Children's Socioeconomic Status." *The Journal of Genetic Psychology*, 137, 247–255.

    Golden, Montare, and Bridger, "Verbal Control of Delay Behavior," 1107–1111.

    Maitland, "Time Perspective," 3676-B.

    Walls, R. T., and Smith, T. S. (1970). "Development of Preference for Delayed Reinforcement in Disadvantaged Children." *Journal of Educational Psychology*, 61, 118–123.

63. Herzberger, S. D., and Dweck, C. S. (1978). "Attraction and Delay of Gratification." *Journal of Personality*, 46, 214–227.

    Straus, M. A. (1962). "Deferred Gratification, Social Class, and the Achievement Syndrome." *American Sociological Review*, 27, 326–335.

64. Snyderman, M. (1983). "Optimal Prey Selection: The Effects of Food Deprivation." *Behaviour Analysis Letters*, 3, 359–369.

    Stephens, D. W., and Krebs, J. R. (1986). *Foraging Theory*. Princeton, NJ: Princeton University Press.

65. Freire, Gorman, and Wessman, "Temporal Span," 247–255.

66. Shapiro, "Self-control," 443–460 (p. 444).

67. Imada, S., and Imada, H. (1988). "Self-restraint: A Type of Self-control in an Approach-avoidance Situation." *Behavioral and Brain Sciences*, 11, 687–688.

68. Christopher, R. C. (1983). *The Japanese Mind*. New York: Fawcett Columbine.

69. Kalman, B. (1989). *Japan, the Land*. New York: Crabtree, p. 14.

70. Imada, and Imada, "Self-restraint," 687–688.

71. Christopher, *The Japanese Mind*.

72. Nasar, "Baby Boomers Fail," pp. A1, D5.

73. Christopher, *The Japanese Mind*.

74. Nasar, "Baby Boomers Fail," pp. A1, D5.

75. Christopher, *The Japanese Mind*.

76. Mischel, W. (1990). "Personality Dispositions Revisited and Revised: A View after Three Decades." In L. A. Pervin (Ed.), *Handbook of Personality: Theory and Research* (pp. 111–134). New York: Guilford.

5

General Methods
for Changing
Self-Control

How to increase self-control is an issue that permeates our society. This chapter describes some general methods for changing self-control. However, the methods described here may not be quite as general as the chapter title implies.

THE GENERALITY OF METHODS
FOR CHANGING SELF-CONTROL

Virtually all of the interventions to be discussed in this chapter were originally designed only for the purpose of increasing, and not decreasing, self-control. The preponderance of studies designed to increase self-control may indicate our society's perception that instances in which self-control occurs but is unadaptive are few and far between. This perception may be due either to our believing that people have a strong tendency to behave impulsively, so that increasing impulsiveness is usually not difficult; or to our usually considering self-control, and not impulsiveness, to be a desirable outcome (see Chapter 3); or to both. However, as discussed in Chapter 3 and more specifically in Chapter 6, self-control does sometimes occur in a way that is very unadaptive. When and if our society becomes aware of the occurrence of sometimes unadaptive self-control, research may be conducted on general methods for increasing impulsiveness. Until then, it is possible to speculate that doing the opposite of the strategies described below for increasing self-control should in many cases increase impulsiveness.

Two other characteristics of the general methods for changing self-control discussed in this chapter suggest that these methods may not actually be that general. One of these characteristics is that most of these methods have been developed for and tested in children. There are some experiments that have used human adults or nonhumans, but they are in the minority. This characteristic of the research may have resulted from our general perception (and empirical fact, see Chapter 4) that children are generally more impulsive than adults. Therefore increases in self-control may be easier to demonstrate in the laboratory with children, and we may perceive the need for an increase in self-control as being greatest in this group. Another possible reason for the focus on children with regard to investigations of general self-control interventions may be that when human adults are used, the experiments tend to be directed at solving particular self-control problems present in adults. Such experiments focus on, for example, overeating, drug abuse, or crime. Subsequent chapters will be devoted to these particular kinds of self-control problems.

The second way in which the material in this chapter may not be as general as the chapter title implies, or even as general as intended by the experimenters who conducted the experiments, is that the results may be rather situation specific. For example, results obtained from experiments designed to increase self-control when the outcomes consist of food may not apply to situations in which the outcomes do not consist of food (see Chapter 6). However, for most of the research in this chapter, the researchers perceived their experiments as investigating general methods for increasing self-control, and the results of these experiments do not contain any obvious indication of situation specificity (although it should be kept in mind that the experiments may not have been designed for this purpose). Subsequent chapters, concerned with particular self-control problems, will provide some indications regarding the situation specificity of self-control mechanisms and interventions.

CHAPTER ORGANIZATION AND CONTENTS

The methods for changing self-control that are discussed in this chapter have been organized in terms of the different aspects of the self-control choice paradigm (see Chapter 2). Recall that making a choice within a self-control paradigm depends on the delays of the outcomes, the sizes of the outcomes, and what particular outcome contingencies are present (for example, whether or not a subject can change its choice during the delay period). Therefore this chapter is organized according to these three elements of a self-control choice: outcome delay, outcome size, and outcome contingencies.

In organizing the interventions described in this chapter according to these three aspects of the self-control paradigm, the material presented will include more than just manipulations of these three aspects' physical state in the external environment. Manipulations of solely these three aspects' *perceived* physical state will also be included. The external physical state of these three aspects influences behavior only to the extent that the external physical state affects the subjects' perception of this external physical state. Our behavior is not a function of what is present in our environment, but of what we *think* is present in our environment. Sometimes our perceptions reflect the external physical environment rather closely, but sometimes they do not. One example of a lack of a one-to-one correspondence between the external physical environment and our internal representation (that is, perception) of that environment is given by Equation 1 in Chapter 3; choice in a self-control paradigm (and, apparently, our perception of the available choices) occurs according to power functions, not linear functions, of the external physical values of outcome delays and sizes. Given that our behavior is ultimately a function of our perceived, not external physical, environment (although the two may be closely related), within a self-control paradigm anything that affects the perceived delays or sizes of the outcomes, or the perceived outcome contingencies, will affect self-control. Therefore this chapter includes research on manipulations of perceived outcome values and outcome contingencies without concurrent manipulation of their external physical states.

Given that behavior is a function of the perceived, and not external, physical environment, an argument might be made that the research described here should consist only of research concerning the effects of perceived outcome values and outcome contingencies. However, such a focus would have several unfortunate limitations. First, although there may not be a one-to-one correspondence between units of external physical magnitude and units of perceived magnitude, perceived magnitude does tend to increase with external physical magnitude (for example, see Equation 1 in Chapter 3, which shows how outcome value increases as outcome immediacy—the inverse of outcome delay—increases). Therefore, in considering what sorts of interventions might influence self-control, interventions that focus on changing the external physical state of the outcomes, or on changing the external physical nature of the outcome contingencies, and not just those that focus on changes in the perceived outcome state and perceived outcome contingencies, should be considered. Second, interventions involving manipulation of the external physical state of the outcome or the external physical nature of the outcome contingencies may have an advantage over interventions involving manipulation solely of the perceived value of the outcomes or of the perceived outcome contingencies. In manipulating solely the perception of physical value it is difficult to specify precisely what has been manipulated (if anything). Manipulation of physical value is much easier to describe and quantify.

However, both experiments designed to manipulate only perceived outcome values and outcome contingencies, and those designed to manipulate external physical, as well as perceived, outcome values and outcome contingencies, share a methodological difficulty. A manipulation may fail to affect self-control because the sort of factor being examined (such as outcome delay) has no effect on self-control or because the manipulation failed to change the perception of the choice situation. Techniques involving concurrent recording of physiological measures may help to resolve such interpretation problems (see, for example, Chapter 6). Positive findings, in which a manipulation does affect self-control, and which constitute the majority of published research, are easier to interpret: When a manipulation involving outcome delay, outcome size, and/or outcome contingencies does affect self-control, then the manipulation did affect some aspect of the perceived self-control paradigm as well as affecting self-control behavior.

OUTCOME DELAY

Outcome delays appear to affect outcome value by discounting the physical value of an outcome; outcomes that are delayed are valued less. According to Figure 3.2, impulsiveness occurs when delay discounts the physical value of a larger outcome to a degree that the perceived value of that outcome is less than that of a smaller, less delayed outcome. Clearly, anything that can be done to bring the larger outcome effectively closer in time relative to the smaller outcome should increase self-control and vice versa. As an example, consider a situation in which someone, who highly desires new clothes but does not have much money, and who can take only one day off for the next few weeks, perceives that he or she has available a choice between taking the day off today and buying one outfit, or waiting to take the day off until after tomorrow's payday so as to be able to buy three outfits. In an extreme case, changing to a perceived choice between one outfit now and three outfits now will ensure choice of the three outfits. Similarly, changing to a perceived choice between one outfit tomorrow and three outfits tomorrow will also ensure choice of the three outfits. Making the perceived relative delays of the two alternatives appear more similar should result in greater choice of the larger outcome and vice versa.

A large number of experiments have manipulated the relative delays of the two outcomes in a large variety of ways. The simplest way is simply to change the relative physical values of the delays to the two outcomes. As expected, greater relative delay to the larger outcome results in less self-control.[1]

Another way to change the perceived relative values of the delays to the self-control alternatives is to give subjects exposure to particular delays prior to giving them the self-control choice.[2] Some researchers have argued that prior exposure to delays results in habituation to the frustration or aversiveness caused by delay.[3] Such a view predicts that prior exposure to any length of delay should always result in at least some subsequent increased self-control. An alternative view is that prior exposure should affect subsequent self-control behavior by causing contrast effects—that delays in a self-control paradigm seem shorter or longer than they really are due to previously exposing subjects to extremely long or short delays, respectively. A final view is that delay preexposure affects outcome expectancy.[4] Both of the latter two views predict that delay preexposure should either increase or decrease self-control depending on the relative lengths of the preexposed delays and the delays within the self-control choice, a prediction that is supported by the available data.[5]

One particular kind of delay preexposure involves a fading procedure (see Figure 5.1). In this procedure, subjects are first given a choice between equally delayed large and small outcomes. Then the delay to the small outcome is very gradually decreased, that is, faded, until eventually the subject is choosing between a larger, more delayed outcome and a smaller, immediate outcome (alternatively, the delay to the large outcome can be very gradually increased). Both nonhuman (pigeon) and human (impulsive children) subjects exposed to this procedure have subsequently shown increased self-control.[6]

Perhaps because of its relationship to preexposure to outcome delay, preexposure to response effort can also increase self-control. This research has been conducted by psychologists who have defined self-control as a choice between a smaller, easily available outcome and a larger, less easily available outcome. According to these researchers, demonstrating self-con-

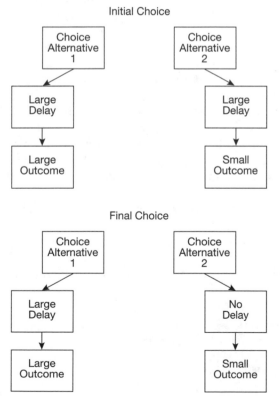

Figure 5.1. Diagram of the fading procedure used to increase self-control (see text for additional explanation of this procedure).

trol involves actively maintaining a choice for a larger outcome over some period of time, through some continued type of effort. Although at first glance
it might not appear so, this definition of self-control is very similar to the definition presented in Chapter 2, because greater effort often requires more
time to exert than does less effort. Similarly, some researchers have stated that
enduring a long delay is more effortful than enduring a short delay. Whatever the underlying mechanism, in children, rats, and pigeons preexposure
to effortful responding increases subsequent choices of a larger outcome requiring more effort.[7] More generally, past association of rewards with physical or cognitive effort can make the sensation of effort itself rewarding, resulting in the phenomenon that Robert Eisenberger has aptly named *learned
industriousness*.[8]

One of the most commonly used methods for increasing self-control
through manipulations of outcome delays involves manipulations of the perceived speed of the passage of time. Consider again the choice between one
outfit available now and three outfits available tomorrow. If time is perceived
as passing very quickly, then the perceived delay to the three outfits will be
shorter, and self-control should increase. On the other hand, if time is perceived as passing very slowly, then the perceived delay to the three outfits
will be longer, and self-control should decrease. A large number of experiments have been directed at determining what sorts of manipulations affect
the perceived speed of the passage of time. Unfortunately, many of these experiments have looked only at the manipulations' effects on self-control, and
have not taken any concurrent measures of the speed of the passage of time.
Therefore we have no way of knowing whether or not a change in the perceived speed of the passage of time is indeed the mechanism by which these
manipulations affect self-control. Although the mechanism may not yet have
been firmly identified, in general, experiments do appear to show that certain activities that seem to make time pass more quickly also increase self-
control. For example, during the delay to the larger outcome, doing enjoyable
activities, thinking enjoyable thoughts, or even having stimuli previously
associated with rewards being present increase self-control, and vice versa[9]
(see Boxes 5.1 and 5.2 and Figure 5.2). Further, research has shown that a decrease in subjects' attention to the delay period also increases self-control,
possibly by means of a concurrent increase in the perceived speed of the passage of time. For example, one of the best ways for a subject to ensure that her
self-control choice is maintained while waiting for the larger outcome is for
the subject to completely remove any attention to the larger outcome's delay
period by falling asleep.[11] Time seems to pass very quickly in such a situation.

> By the mass, 'tis morning;
> Pleasure and action make the
> hours seem short.
> [William Shakespeare[10]]

Box 5.1

A watched pot never boils.

Box 5.2

OUTCOME SIZE

Whether we show self-control or not is a function of the relative number of clothing outfits available, in addition to their relative delay. In Figure 3.2, if the height of the larger, more delayed outcome were made very tall, in other words, if the perceived size of the larger outcome were made even larger, there might never be a crossover point and self-control would always be shown. On the other hand, in the same figure, if the height of the smaller, less delayed outcome were made taller, in other words, if the perceived size of the smaller outcome were made larger, the crossover point would shift to the left, earlier in time, and there would be a much greater time period over which impulsiveness would be shown. Manipulations that change the perceived relative sizes of the outcomes can affect self-control.

" Conversely, time slows down when your'e not having fun."

Figure 5.2. *Drawing by Nick Downes.* Reprinted by permission from *Science*, 1990, 247, 696.

Presence of Outcomes

An obvious way to influence the relative sizes of the outcomes is to manipulate the perception that the outcomes are present. An outcome that is not present and can never be present has no size, and will always be preferred less than an outcome that is or will be present, no matter what the size of the latter outcome.

Experiments on the influence of the presence of the outcomes on self-control have attempted to manipulate outcome presence both by physical manipulations of the outcomes themselves and by manipulation of attention to the outcomes. Researchers have shown that in general, it is more difficult to wait for a larger outcome if the outcomes are physically present. Such results have been obtained using pigeons and children.[12] Other researchers have found that by directly instructing children not to attend to the outcomes, self-control has been increased.[13] Still other researchers have postulated that people will be less impulsive if they control their attention so as to not think about the tempting situation.[14] In general, any distracting activity that takes attention away from the outcomes should increase self-control. Further, it is possible that some of the distracting activities described above with regard to making time seem to pass more quickly or slowly may exert their effect partially or wholly through manipulating subjects' attention to the outcomes.

Long before there was any empirical work on the effects of distraction on self-control, there was at least some awareness in psychology that such techniques ought to be effective. B. F. Skinner, in his 1948 novel about a utopian community, *Walden Two*, describes his idea of one way to teach children self-control, using the technique of removing the presence of the smaller, less delayed outcome:

> We give each child a lollipop which has been dipped in powdered sugar so that a single touch of the tongue can be detected. We tell him he may eat the lollipop later in the day, provided it hasn't already been licked. . . . A simple principle like putting temptation out of sight would be acquired before four. . . . First of all, the children are urged to examine their own behavior while looking at the lollipops. This helps them to recognize the need for self-control. Then the lollipops are concealed, and the children are asked to notice any gain in happiness or any reduction in tension. Then a strong distraction is arranged—say, an interesting game. Later the children are reminded of the candy and encouraged to examine their reaction. The value of the distraction is generally obvious.[15]

Note that in Skinner's description, frustration appears to function as an intervening variable: The presence of the lollipop causes frustration which then decreases self-control; the absence of the lollipop decreases frustration and increases self-control. Distraction decreases the frustration and increases self-control without necessitating physical manipulation of the outcomes. Nevertheless, despite Skinner's clear and confident (but hypothetical) 1948 description of the influence of frustration on self-control, we do not yet know whether frustration is influenced by reward presence, or whether frustration directly influences self-control. However, we do know that learning how to use distraction to increase self-control can be very useful. In situations in which people are not able to physically manipulate the outcomes of a self-control choice, psychological manipulation of the perceived presence and other physical characteristics of the outcomes may be possible.

Several other techniques may help people to increase self-control by increasing their awareness of the presence of the larger, more delayed outcome. An example of such a technique involves teaching people how to think about self-control situations in terms of cost-benefit rules. According to this method, people are taught to analyze a choice situation in terms of all of the possible costs and benefits associated with each possible choice, including what opportunities may be lost through making a particular choice (a type of cost). They are also taught to weigh carefully the relative net value of each outcome before making a decision. Instruction regarding this type of decision making does appear to increase choices of the alternative that provides the most benefit in the long term.[16] Some people may not attend to valuable, distant outcomes without this type of instruction.

Another way of helping people to increase self-control through increasing their awareness of the larger, more delayed outcome is the modeling of self-control. Watching someone else make a self-control choice and benefit by that choice can help to emphasize the presence and availability of the larger, more delayed outcome. Modeling may also make the perceived time to the more delayed outcome seem shorter. Although research does appear to indicate that modeling can help increase self-control,[17] the precise mechanism by which this occurs is not yet known.

Relative Size of Outcomes

Changes in relative outcome size can be used to change self-control without going to the extreme of removing the presence of one or both of the outcomes. Simply making the relative size of the larger, more delayed outcome even larger will increase self-control. This can be done by increasing the physical or perceived size of the larger outcome, decreasing the physical or perceived size of the smaller outcome, or both. The relative size of an outcome can be manipulated by changing the volume of the outcome, the amount of timed access to the outcome, or the quality of the outcome. A number of experiments have demonstrated the usefulness of such strategies using both pigeons and humans.[18] In one experiment, pigeons, notoriously impulsive, were more likely to show self-control if the self-control alternative consisted of the same duration of access to a more, rather than a less, preferred grain.[19] In another variation on this theme, human subjects were more likely to choose an alternative requiring more work (the self-control alternative) if that alternative yielded a reward of increased size.[20]

The experiments described so far all used external physical manipulation in order to change perceived relative outcome size. However, it also appears possible to use certain types of thoughts and emotions to manipulate perceived relative reinforcer size. Material presented earlier in this chapter has already indicated that in general, a positive mood increases self-control, possibly because such emotions generally increase the perceived speed of the passage of time. Such emotions may also generally influence the perceived relative size of outcomes. We simply do not have enough information to assess the validity of these hypotheses. However, the possibility that specific types of emotions can affect the relative size of specific types of outcomes appears a bit more certain (although as yet largely unsupported by laboratory evidence). For example, suppose someone has a choice between going out with friends now or studying to get a better grade later. If the person has had a difficult day in which the entire human race appeared to be irrational and irritating, then the resulting anger toward humans may prevent enjoyment of going out, increasing the relative value of studying as well as the probability of choosing studying. Emotions may change the relative value of specific, available outcomes, and may thus change self-control.[21]

The ways in which someone appears to think about the outcomes can also affect self-control, perhaps by influencing the perceived relative size of the outcomes. Walter Mischel and his colleagues have shown in repeated experiments that if someone is told to think, or reports thinking, about the consummatory, motivational properties of outcomes (what he calls "hot thoughts"), self-control decreases. However, if someone is told to think, or reports thinking, about the nonconsummatory, nonmotivational properties of outcomes (what he calls "cool thoughts"), self-control increases.[22] His experiments have all been conducted with children. In a typical experiment, he gives children a choice between one pretzel available now and three pretzels available later (if the child does not ring a bell until after a waiting period). Instructing the children to think about the taste of the pretzels and how crunchy they are decreases self-control. However, instructing the child to think about the shape and color of the pretzels increases self-control.[23] Although we are even less sure of a pigeon's than a child's thoughts, some comparable data appear to have been obtained in pigeons exposed to a self-control paradigm. Pigeons are less likely to wait for a larger amount of grain if the light in the hopper that delivers the grain is illuminated while they wait. This light could serve the same stimulus function as Mischel's hot thoughts, having been associated with the motivational properties of the grain.[24] Mischel has speculated that hot and cool thoughts influence self-control by means of their effects on frustration, rather than by directly influencing perceived relative reinforcer size; hot thoughts increase frustration whereas cool thoughts do not.[25] However, there is as yet no direct evidence of frustration or of its usefulness in explaining self-control.

Combining Outcomes

A final way to increase the relative size of the self-control outcome in a self-control choice paradigm is to combine that outcome with another positive or negative outcome, thus increasing or decreasing the net value of the self-control alternative, respectively. This can be done in a variety of ways. One of the ways is through reward or punishment for the self-control choice; each time the self-control choice is made, a reward or a punisher is given.[26] The most obvious way to do this may be for an experimenter or a friend to simply deliver the additional reward or punisher. For example, parents can give their children cookies each time they display self-control. More generally, socialization resulting in self-control (or impulsiveness) involves multiple members of a child's social group delivering rewards (or punishers) for children's self-control behavior.

Self-reward and self-punishment can also be used.[27] In *self-reward*, someone engages in a pleasurable activity (a reward) whenever that person has engaged in another specified activity. In *self-punishment*, someone engages in an unpleasurable activity (a punisher) whenever that person has engaged in another specified activity. There are no obvious, current, external contingencies present with regard to the performance of the pleasurable or unpleasurable activity; the person seems to be solely responsible for the implementation of the reward or punisher. Thus, it is not always possible to know when self-reward and self-punishment are occurring, nor what influences them. It is also not clear to what extent the concepts of self-reward and self-punishment are useful above and beyond knowing the subject's history with the external environment. Much more work needs to be done on these issues with respect to the usefulness of self-reward and self-punishment in self-control.

Related to the concept of self-reward are the concepts of *alliances between rewards* and of *side bets*, both described in detail by George Ainslie.[28] Both of these concepts are somewhat speculative as a means for increasing self-control. As of yet, there is not a great deal of empirical research to support them. Nevertheless, they are intriguing concepts deserving of additional research.

The technique of making alliances between rewards relies on the principle that an outcome (which we will call Outcome B), defined as a self-control choice with regard to a smaller, less delayed outcome (Outcome A), can also be defined as an impulsive choice with regard to a still larger, more delayed outcome (Outcome C; see Chapter 2). If the choice of Outcome C can be combined with the choice of Outcome A (that is, if these two outcomes can be allied), their total value may be large enough to prevent the choice of Outcome B. For example, suppose a state employee in charge of a large account and with no current necessary expenditures is faced with the following alternatives for Outcomes A, B, and C: spend some money now on somewhat inexpensive frivolous items, spend the money during the remainder of the fiscal year on moderately expensive items whose necessity becomes apparent during that time, and save the money for large emergencies that may occur in the distant future. By perceiving the choice as between either Outcome B or Outcomes A + C, the state employee may be able to save some money for emergencies at distant times. However, saving for the distant future may prove impossible if the choice is perceived as being between Outcomes A and C, or B and C.

Side bets are similar to alliances between rewards in that they also take advantage of available choices other than those that are strictly part of the self-control choice. Side bets are useful when someone perceives that there is a long series of similar choices to be made. For example, suppose someone who enjoys coming home at the end of the day to a neat house decides to make his or her bed each day. This person then knows that for the rest of his or her working life, there will be a choice each morning as to whether or not to make the bed. Making the bed will result in the greatly desired neat house in the evening. Not making the bed will result in some moderately desired additional leisure time in the morning. In using a side bet to improve the probability that the bed will be made, the person decides (privately and perhaps publicly) that all of the larger, more delayed outcomes will be lost if that person *just once* does not make the bed. In the particular example here, the person might state that if just once the bed is not made, the bed will never get made again, the house will never be neat again, and society will permanently brand this person as messy. By thus combining many of the larger, more delayed outcomes, their total value can be sufficient to prevent even a single choice of the smaller, less delayed outcome.

OUTCOME CONTINGENCIES

Someone can be aware that various outcomes exist which have specific delays and sizes, but be unaware of what responses will or will not result in those outcomes. The relationships between responses and outcomes are called the *outcome contingencies*. Certain response contingencies and the perceived presence of those contingencies can be used to increase self-control.

Choice Change Option

One of the simplest outcome contingencies that can affect the degree to which self-control is or is not shown concerns whether or not the subject has the option to change his or her choice while waiting for the larger, more delayed outcome. Laboratory research has shown that pigeons are less likely to end up actually receiving the larger, more delayed outcome if such a choice change is available.[29] This may be because, as in the description of the side-bet situation above, subjects in this situation have essentially repeated choices between an immediate, smaller outcome and a delayed, larger outcome, and so the probability of an eventual impulsive choice is simply higher than if only one such choice were available.

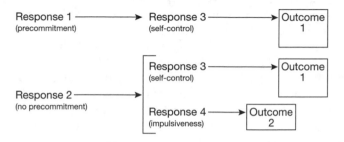

Figure 5.3.   Diagram of precommitment (Response 1) and no precommitment (Response 2) choice alternatives.

Precommitment

A related type of contingency that can also affect self-control is a *pre-commitment* contingency[30] (see Figure 5.3). In this situation, prior to having to make a choice between a self-control outcome (Response 3 in Figure 5.3) and an impulsive outcome (Response 4 in Figure 5.3), someone can make a re-sponse that will prevent that person from subsequently making the impul-sive response. This prior response is the precommitment response (Response 1 in Figure 5.3). In contrast, not making the precommitment response (Re-sponse 2) results in the presentation of the usual self-control choice.

Precommitment techniques have been used since ancient times to in-crease self-control. George Ainslie describes one of the first recorded in-stances of the use of precommitment in the following way:

> The first analysis of precommitment appeared in the *Odyssey*, in which Odysseus had to sail past the Sirens. Because the sound of their voices was more alluring than any other motivation, his problem was to keep himself and his crew from rowing toward it and onto the rocks. He found two devices: Because he wanted to be able to hear the Sirens, he had his crew tie him to the mast and ordered them not to untie him until they had reached their goal. His crew, how-ever, had to be left free to row, so he stopped their ears with wax.[31]

Odysseus used precommitment to protect both himself and his crew from the impulsive response of going to the Sirens. He prevented himself from going to the Sirens by preventing his own movement, and he prevented his crew from going to the Sirens by preventing their ability to hear. In both cases, Odysseus essentially eliminated the impulsive response, and made only the self-control response of sailing past the Sirens possible.

A more modern example of precommitment is our use of the alarm clock. In the morning, someone has a choice between the larger, more delayed outcome of getting to school (or work) on time and the smaller, less delayed outcome of some extra sleep. The night before, that person will precommit to making the self-control response the next morning by setting an alarm clock. When that alarm clock rings the next morning, it will essentially remove the response of continued sleep, and will make the only possible response that of getting to school (or work) on time (in some cases it may be necessary to use a very loud alarm clock located far from the bed).

Precommitment has been shown in human as well as nonhuman subjects, although there seem to be large individual differences in the ability to precommit.[32] Precommitment responses are interesting to psychologists because they indicate that people and other animals' preferences between the self-control and impulsive outcomes change as a function of time. Consider the example of the alarm clock. In setting the alarm clock the night before, someone is indicating that at that point in time he or she prefers the larger, more delayed outcome of getting to school (or work) on time. However, the next morning, this preference reverses. Such preference reversals are implicit in Figure 3.2. At point x in that figure, the larger, more delayed outcome has a higher value and the subject should be able to make a precommitment response. At point y, the smaller, less delayed outcome has a higher value and the subject will not be able to make a precommitment response. Precommitment strategies are an extremely useful, general self-control technique widely recognized in the popular culture (see Box 5.3).

A stitch in time saves nine.

Box 5.3

Contingency Perception

In addition to having available certain responses that can affect self-control, being aware of or learning to what outcomes different responses will lead can also affect self-control. Someone will not show self-control unless that person has somehow learned that the self-control response will eventually lead to a larger outcome. Several aspects of self-control procedures contribute to such learning. First is simply experience with the self-control situation. Experimenters ensure such experience for pigeons in self-control experiments by using multiple trials and occasionally making only one response available. Such a procedure forces the pigeon to make that response in order to continue to the next trial in the experiment. In this way the pigeons learn the consequences for each alternative choice response.[33] Humans gain experience with the consequences for the choices in a self-control paradigm by making the responses and receiving the consequences, or by learning about the consequences through watching or speaking with other people who are either involved in a similar choice or who have some knowledge about such a choice.[34] *Monitoring*, keeping careful track of one's own responses and the ensuing consequences, perhaps by some formal means such as keeping a list or drawing a graph, may assist in the recognition and memory of behavioral consequences, and thus assist self-control.[35]

Sometimes the connection between the self-control response and its outcome may seem tenuous, uncertain, and this can hinder self-control. As discussed in Chapter 3, as the certainty of a future event decreases, the advantages accruing from waiting for that event also decrease. One way in which a larger, more delayed outcome may be uncertain in a self-control experiment, resulting in decreased self-control, is related to the trust that the subject has in the experimenter.[36] The experimenter may have told the subject that he or she will receive the larger, more delayed reinforcer, but the subject may not believe that the experimenter will actually deliver on that promise. In that case, there is no point to the subject demonstrating self-control. This sort of mechanism may explain the fact that children are more likely to show self-control when tested by other children rather than by adults, and blacks are more likely to show self-control when tested by blacks than by whites.[37]

Subjects' self-statements also appear to influence the subjects' perceptions of the response-outcome contingencies. Subjects who make statements during the waiting periods reminding themselves of what will happen if they wait, or reminding themselves of what they have to do in order to receive the larger reinforcer, are more likely to show self-control.[38] In one experiment, children aged 2.5 to 4 years had difficulty responding slowly in order to receive rewards. However, when they were taught to sing a song about responding slowly, they were able to respond slowly enough to obtain the rewards. (For older children, ordinary instructions were sufficient to obtain slow responding.)[39] Nevertheless, some research has shown that self-verbalization about the reinforcer contingencies is less effective at increasing self-control than is self-distraction[40] (described above).

Self-statements may increase self-control through providing stimuli that are associated with the response-outcome contingency, thus reminding the subject of that contingency. Analyzed in this way, similar stimuli can be provided to nonhuman subjects. In fact, when colored lights are present during delay periods, with the precise color used being identical to the color of the choice button that has been pecked, pigeons show more self-control than when such delay lights are not used.[41] Complex language behavior is not necessary in order for stimuli to function as reminders of the response-outcome contingencies and for self-control to be increased.

CONCLUSION

This chapter has discussed a large number of possible ways that self-control can be increased and possibly decreased. Some of these ways seem more directed at influencing the effect of outcome delay, some at influencing the effect of outcome size, and some at influencing the effect of the response-outcome contingencies. However, in many cases, it is not clear precisely why a particular technique is effective in increasing self-control, or even if there is any solid empirical evidence that the technique is effective. Much more could be done to identify successful mechanisms for increasing and decreasing self-control. Although people do seem to acquire many self-control techniques without explicit training as a part of normal development (see Chapter 4), there are still many situations in which specific training could increase the probability of adaptive responses within a self-control paradigm. Some of the particular situations that could benefit from such knowledge will be described in the following chapters in Part III: Applications.

REFERENCES

1. Ainslie, G., and Herrnstein, R. J. (1981). "Preference Reversal and Delayed Reinforcement." *Animal Learning and Behavior*, 9, 476–482.

    Fantino, E. (1966). "Immediate Reward Followed by Extinction vs. Later Reward without Extinction." *Psychonomic Science*, 6, 233–234.

    Green, L., Fisher, E. B., Perlow, S., and Sherman, L. (1981). "Preference Reversal and Self Control: Choice as a Function of Reward Amount and Delay." *Behaviour Analysis Letters*, 1, 43–51.

    Mischel, W., and Grusec, J. (1967). "Waiting for Rewards and Punishments: Effects of Time and Probability on Choice." *Journal of Personality and Social Psychology*, 5, 24–31.

2. Litrownik, A. J., Franzini, L. R., Geller, S., and Geller, M. (1977). "Delay of Gratification: Decisional Self-control and Experience with Delay Intervals." *American Journal of Mental Deficiency*, 82, 149–154.

    Walls, R. T., and Smith, T. S. (1970). "Development of Preference for Delayed Reinforcement in Disadvantaged Children." *Journal of Educational Psychology*, 61, 118–123.

3. Eisenberger, R., and Adornetto, M. (1986). "Generalized Self-control of Delay and Effort." *Journal of Personality and Social Psychology*, 51, 1020–1031.

4. Grosch, J., and Neuringer, A. (1981). "Self-control in Pigeons under the Mischel Paradigm." *Journal of the Experimental Analysis of Behavior*, 35, 3–21.

5. Eisenberger, R., and Masterson, F. A. (1987). "Effects of Prior Learning and Current Motivation on Self-control." In J. A. Nevin and H. Rachlin (Eds.), *Quantitative Analyses of Behavior: Vol. 5, The Effects of Delay and of Intervening Events on Reinforcement Value* (pp. 267–282). Hillsdale, NJ: Erlbaum.

    Grosch and Neuringer, "Self-control in Pigeons," 3–21.

6. Logue, A. W., and Peña-Correal, T. E. (1984). "Responding During Reinforcement Delay in a Self-control Paradigm." *Journal of the Experimental Analysis of Behavior*, 41, 267–277.

    Logue, A. W., Rodriguez, M. L., Peña-Correal, T. E., and Mauro, B. C. (1984). "Choice in a Self-control Paradigm: Quantification of Experience-based Differences." *Journal of the Experimental Analysis of Behavior*, 41, 53–67.

    Mazur, J. E., and Logue, A. W. (1978). "Choice in a `Self-control' Paradigm: Effects of a Fading Procedure." *Journal of the Experimental Analysis of Behavior*, 30, 11–17.

    Schweitzer, J. B., and Sulzer-Azaroff, B. (1988). "Self-control: Teaching Tolerance for Delay in Impulsive Children." *Journal of the Experimental Analysis of Behavior*, 50, 173–186.

7. Eisenberger, R., Mitchell, M., and Masterson, F. A. (1985). "Effort Training Increases Generalized Self-control." *Journal of Personality and Social Psychology*, 49, 1294–1301.

   Eisenberger, R., Weier, F., Masterson, F. A., and Theis, L. Y. (1989). "Fixed-ratio Schedules Increase Generalized Self-control: Preference for Large Rewards Despite High Effort or Punishment." *Journal of Experimental Psychology: Animal Behavior Processes*, 15, 383–392.

   Mahoney, M. J., and Bandura, A. (1972). "Self-reinforcement in Pigeons." *Learning and Motivation*, 3, 293–303.

8. Eisenberger, R. (1992). "Learned Industriousness." *Psychological Review*, 99, 248–267.

9. Grosch, and Neuringer, "Self-control in Pigeons," 3–21.

   Mischel, W., and Ebbesen, E. B. (1970). "Attention in Delay of Gratification." *Journal of Personality and Social Psychology*, 16, 329–337.

   Mischel, W., Ebbesen, E. B., and Zeiss, A. R. (1972). "Cognitive and Attentional Mechanisms in Delay of Gratification." *Journal of Personality and Social Psychology*, 21, 204–218.

10. Shakespeare, W. (1936). "The Tragedy of Othello, the Moor of Venice." In W. A. Wright (Ed.), *The Complete Works of William Shakespeare* (pp. 937–979). Garden City, NY: Garden City Books.

11. Mischel and Ebbesen, "Attention in Delay," 329–337.

12. Grosch and Neuringer, "Self-control in Pigeons," 3–21.

    Mischel and Ebbesen, "Attention in Delay," 329–337.

    Yates, J. F., and Revelle, G. L. (1979). "Processes Operative During Delay of Gratification." *Motivation and Emotion*, 3, 103–115.

13. Mischel, W., and Patterson, C. J. (1976). "Substantive and Structural Elements of Effective Plans for Self-control." *Journal of Personality and Social Psychology*, 34, 942–950.

    Patterson, C. J., and Mischel, W. (1976). "Effects of Temptation-inhibiting and Task-facilitating Plans on Self-control." *Journal of Personality and Social Psychology*, 33, 209–217.

14. Ainslie, G., and Haslam, N. (1992). "Self-control." In G. Loewenstein and J. Elster (Eds.), *Choice Over Time* (pp. 177–209). New York: Russell Sage Foundation.

15. Skinner, B. F. (1948). *Walden Two*. New York: Macmillan, pp. 107–108.

16. Larrick, R. P., Morgan, J. N., and Nisbett, R. E. (1990). "Teaching the Use of Cost-benefit Reasoning in Everyday Life." *Psychological Science*, 1, 362–370.

17. Bandura, A., and Mischel, W. (1965). "Modification of Self-imposed Delay of Reward through Exposure to Live and Symbolic Models." *Journal of Personality and Social Psychology*, 2, 698–705.

    LaVoie, J. C., Anderson, K., Fraze, B., and Johnson, K. (1981). "Modeling, Tuition, and Sanction Effects on Self-control at Different Ages." *Journal of Experimental Child Psychology*, 31, 446–455.

18. Cabanac, M. (1986). "Money Versus Pain: Experimental Study of a Conflict in Humans." *Journal of the Experimental Analysis of Behavior*, 46, 37–44.

    Fantino, "Immediate Reward," 233–234.

Grusec, J. E. (1968). "Waiting for Rewards and Punishments: Effects of Reinforcement Value on Choice." *Journal of Personality and Social Psychology*, 9, 85–89.

Herzberger, S. D., and Dweck, C. S. (1978). "Attraction and Delay of Gratification." *Journal of Personality*, 46, 214–227.

19. King, G. R., and Logue, A. W. (1990). "Choice in a Self-control Paradigm: Effects of Reinforcer Quality." *Behavioural Processes*, 22, 89–99.

20. Blakely, E., Starin, S., and Poling, A. (1988). "Human Performance Under Sequences of Fixed-ratio Schedules: Effects of Ratio Size and Magnitude of Reinforcement." *The Psychological Record*, 38, 111–119.

21. Ainslie and Haslam, "Self-control," pp. 177–209.

Baron, J. (1988). *Thinking and Deciding*. New York: Cambridge University Press.

22. Mischel, W., Shoda, Y., and Rodriguez, M. L. (1989). "Delay of Gratification in Children." *Science*, 244, 933–938.

23. Mischel, W., and Baker, N. (1975). "Cognitive Appraisals and Transformations in Delay Behavior." *Journal of Personality and Social Psychology*, 31, 254–261.

24. Grosch and Neuringer, "Self-control in Pigeons," 3–21.

25. Mischel, W., and Moore, B. (1973). "Effects of Attention to Symbolically Presented Rewards on Self-control." *Journal of Personality and Social Psychology*, 28, 172–179.

26. Karniol, R., and Miller, D. T. (1981). "The Development of Self-control in Children." In S. S. Brehm, S. M. Kassin, and F. X. Gibbons (Eds.), *Developmental Social Psychology: Theory and Research* (pp. 32–50). Oxford: Oxford University Press.

Little, V. L., and Kendall, P. C. (1979). "Cognitive-behavioral Interventions with Delinquents: Problem Solving, Role-taking, and Self-control." In P. C. Kendall, and S. D. Hollon (Eds.), *Cognitive-behavioral Interventions* (pp. 81–115). New York: Academic Press.

27. Kanfer, F. H. (1971). "The Maintenance of Behavior by Self-generated Stimuli and Reinforcement." In A. Jacobs, and L. Sachs (Eds.), *The Psychology of Private Events* (pp. 39–59). New York: Academic Press.

O'Leary, S. G., and Dubey, D. R. (1979). "Applications of Self-control Procedures by Children: A Review." *Journal of Applied Behavior Analysis*, 12, 449–465.

28. Ainslie, G. (1975). "Specious Reward: A Behavioral Theory of Impulsiveness and Impulse Control." *Psychological Bulletin*, 82, 463–496.

Ainslie and Haslam, "Self-control," pp. 177–209.

29. Elster, J. (1985). "Weakness of Will and the Free-rider Problem." *Economics and Philosophy*, 1, 231–265.

Logue and Peña-Correal, "Responding During Reinforcement Delay," 267–277.

30. Ainslie, "Specious Reward," 463–496.

Rachlin, H. (1974). "Self-control." *Behaviorism*, 2, 94–107.

31. Ainslie, "Specious Reward," 463–496 (p. 474).

32. Ainslie, G. W. (1974). "Impulse Control in Pigeons." *Journal of the Experimental Analysis of Behavior*, 21, 485–489.

Deluty, M. Z., Whitehouse, W. G., Mellitz, M., and Hineline, P. N. (1983). "Self-control and Commitment Involving Aversive Events." *Behaviour Analysis Letters*, 3, 213–219.

Rachlin, H., and Green, L. (1972). "Commitment, Choice and Self-control." *Journal of the Experimental Analysis of Behavior*, 17, 15–22.

Solnick, J. V., Kannenberg, C. H., Eckerman, D. A., and Waller, M. B. (1980). "An Experimental Analysis of Impulsivity and Impulse Control in Humans." *Learning and Motivation*, 11, 61–77.

33. Mazur and Logue "Choice in a `Self-control' Paradigm," 11–17.

34. Kendall, P. C. (1982). "Individual Versus Group Cognitive-behavioral Self-control training: 1-year Follow-up." *Behavior Therapy*, 13, 241–247.

    Kendall, P. C., and Zupan, B. A. (1981). "Individual Versus Group Application of Cognitive-behavioral Self-control Procedures with Children." *Behavior Therapy*, 12, 344–359.

35. Mischel, W. (1990). "Personality Dispositions Revisited and Revised: A View after Three Decades." In L. A. Pervin (Ed.), *Handbook of Personality: Theory and Research* (pp. 111–134). New York: Guilford.

    Rachlin, "Self-control," 94–107.

36. Shybut, J. (1968). "Delay of Gratification and Severity of Psychological Disturbance among Hospitalized Psychiatric Patients." *Journal of Consulting and Clinical Psychology*, 32, 462–468.

37. Lew, M. B. (1982). "Child and Adult Experimenters: Some Differential Effects." *Child Study Journal*, 12, 223–235.

    Strickland, B. R. (1972). "Delay of Gratification as a Function of Race of the Experimenter." *Journal of Personality and Social Psychology*, 22, 108–112.

38. Anderson, W. H., and Moreland, K. L. (1982). "Instrumental vs. Moralistic Self-verbalizations in Delaying Gratification." *Merrill-Palmer Quarterly*, 28, 291–296.

    Kendall, P. C. (1977). "On the Efficacious Use of Verbal Self-instructional Procedures with Children." *Cognitive Therapy and Research*, 1, 331–341.

    Meichenbaum, D. H., and Goodman, J. (1971). "Training Impulsive Children to Talk to Themselves." *Journal of Abnormal Psychology*, 77, 115–126.

39. Bentall, R. P., and Lowe, C. F. (1987). "The Role of Verbal Behavior in Human Learning: III. Instructional Effects in Children." *Journal of the Experimental Analysis of Behavior*, 47, 177–190.

40. Anderson, W. H. (1978). "A Comparison of Self-distraction with Self-verbalization under Moralistic Versus Instrumental Rationales in a Delay-of-gratification Paradigm." *Cognitive Therapy and Research*, 2, 299–303.

41. Logue, A. W., and Mazur, J. E. (1981). "Maintenance of Self-control Acquired Through a Fading Procedure: Follow-up on Mazur and Logue (1978)." *Behaviour Analysis Letters*, 1, 131–137.

Part III

Applications

6

Eating

Eating plays an enormous role in our daily lives. From when we (and other animals) wake, to when we go to sleep, we must repeatedly choose what we will eat, how much we will eat, and when we will eat. Often, in every animal's daily life, such choices are between a food of lesser value that can be obtained sooner and a food of more value that can only be obtained later (for example see Box 6.1). In those cases, the two choices can be described as im-

A principle of self-control: In looking at a menu, ask not what will taste good but what will feel good an hour or so from now.[1] [B. F. Skinner]

Box 6.1

pulsiveness and self-control. Further, eating disorders such as overeating, anorexia nervosa, and bulimia nervosa can be described as involving excessive self-control and impulsiveness. Finally, in our society, many people view self-control as a virtue, and a trim body as excellent evidence of self-control.[2] Thus, in many ways self-control and eating are inextricably intertwined.

This chapter will discuss self-control and impulsiveness in relation to food rewards. The first section of the chapter will be concerned with self-control and impulsiveness as part of animals' daily search for food, in other words, as part of foraging behavior. This section will also consider some possible evolutionary bases for this type of self-control and impulsiveness. The next section will describe overeating as a self-control problem as well as some physiological mechanisms that may be responsible for impulsive overeating. The final sections will discuss anorexia nervosa and bulimia nervosa.

FORAGING

In their daily lives, both humans and nonhumans must often make choices between foods that are of different values and that are available at different times in the future. This behavior is one aspect of what has been called *foraging*—to "wander or rove in search of food or other provisions."[3] Some choices that foragers must make are equivalent to choosing between self-control and impulsiveness. For example, a protein-deficient bear may have to choose between staying in a field to eat berries or going to the bank of a stream where fish occasionally swim by. Similarly, a hungry human in a supermarket may have to choose between buying a precooked, rubbery chicken or a fresh chicken that will take several hours to cook.

Delay-Reduction Hypothesis

Many researchers have tried to develop theories to explain the choices of foraging animals. One such approach has been Edmund Fantino's *delay-reduction hypothesis*.[4] This model is particularly relevant for the present discussion because the delay-reduction hypothesis has also been specifically used to explain self-control behavior. According to this model, when animals make choices they are choosing between different stimuli (in this case, between food-related stimuli). Further, these stimuli are rewarding to the degree that they are associated with a reduction in the amount of time that the animal has to wait until it receives food. In other words, a stimulus which, in the past, has been associated with the animal's food waiting time being drastically shortened is much more rewarding than a stimulus which, in the past, has been associated with the animal's waiting time being shortened only to a small degree. According to the delay-reduction hypothesis, animals should choose the alternative with the stimulus or stimuli that are associated with greatest reduction in delay time to food access. For example, according to the delay-reduction hypothesis, a hungry pigeon should be more likely to fly to a gray office building where, in the past, the pigeon has never had to wait very long before an office worker placed some food on a windowsill, than to a tan office building where, in the past, the pigeon has had to wait a very long time before an office worker placed some food on a windowsill.

Delay-reduction theory was not originally designed for situations in which the two choice alternatives differed in the amount of reward available as well as the degree to which each alternative was associated with a reduction in the delay to reward (i.e., self-control and impulsive choices). However, it is possible to modify this theory so that it can describe choices between rewards of different sizes. The delay-reduction hypothesis has successfully explained much data from both the self-control and the general foraging literatures.

Optimal Foraging Theory

The most commonly used approach for explaining the food choices of foraging animals is *optimal foraging theory*. This theory takes as a given that adequate eating is critical for survival and inclusive fitness. The theory therefore assumes that evolution must have shaped the behavior of animals so that they forage in ways that maximize energy input per unit of time spent foraging.[5] However, determining what is the animal's optimal choice is not always simple. In addition to how much energy will be obtained from each choice, there are a number of different factors that must be taken into account.

One factor that must be taken into account in determining the optimal choice for a foraging animal is the degree of risk or danger associated with each choice.[6] As indicated in Chapter 3, with delayed food outcomes there is some uncertainty as to whether or not the outcome will actually occur. While the deer waits for the berries to ripen, another animal could steal them, a rainstorm could spoil them, or the deer could be killed by a predator. Even in the case of the foraging human described above, while waiting for the chicken to cook, a burglar could demand the chicken, the thermostat in the oven could malfunction resulting in inedible burnt chicken, or the human could die of a heart attack. Researchers studying foraging often refer to such possible happenings as risk. Risk (uncertainty) decreases the value of delayed outcomes, including food outcomes, because risk means that those outcomes may never be received. Risk must be taken into account in assessing the value of any choice. The existence of risk means that sometimes it is most advantageous to choose the smaller, less delayed food item—sometimes it is most advantageous to take advantage of every feeding opportunity as it arises, rather than waiting for better, but riskier, feeding opportunities (see Box 6.2).

> *Potior est, qui prior est* (first come first served, or, the early bird catches the worm). [Terence]

Box 6.2

Another factor that must be taken into account in determining a foraging animal's optimal choice is the degree to which the animal is food-deprived. If an animal is hungry, then it may need a larger rather than a smaller amount of food, and might therefore be expected to show self-control rather than impulsiveness. However, if an animal is extremely food deprived, to the point at which it may not have enough energy to consume the larger, more delayed food reward when it is finally received—if the animal is so food-deprived that it may even die before receiving the larger, more delayed reward—then the optimal choice is the smaller, less delayed food reward.[7] In this case, only by choosing the smaller, less delayed reward will the animal have a chance of survival (see Box 6.3). A large number of experiments have

> WARBUCKS:
> The New Deal, in my opinion, is badly planned, badly organized and badly administered. You don't think your programs through, Franklin, you don't think of what they're going to do to the economy in the long run.
> FDR:
> People don't eat in the long run.[8] [*Annie*]

Box 6.3

been conducted to try to determine whether or not deprivation level affects self-control. Some experiments have found that increasing deprivation does increase impulsiveness for food rewards, but other experiments have found no effect or an increase in self-control.[9] Because the procedures used in these experiments differed in many respects, it is difficult to say what might be responsible for these differing results. Following are examples of several experiments that have and have not found that deprivation level affects self-control.

The first example comes from an experiment that used pigeons.[10] This experiment first determined what is called the pigeons' free-feeding weights—their weights when they could eat as much as they wanted every day. Then the pigeons were food deprived so that they weighed 70, 80, or 90 percent of their free-feeding weights. No matter what the pigeons' weights, they were consistently impulsive. The pigeons chose no more of the larger (but more delayed) food rewards when they were more food-deprived. In this experiment, the pigeons' impulsiveness was very unadaptive because the procedure of this experiment ensured that no matter what choice was made, one reward was received each minute. Thus, if large amounts of food were needed, the only way to obtain them was to choose the larger, more delayed rewards. However, it is important to remember that this laboratory procedure may not have been that similar to the choices that a pigeon must usually face in nature. In nature, delay of reward and frequency of reward are usually confounded. In other words, shorter delay of reward usually goes along with higher frequency of reward and vice versa, so that making an impulsive response will not necessarily result in the receipt of less total reward.

Pigeons in the wild may not need to be sensitive to overall reward frequency in order to maximize their total food intake, and therefore may not have evolved to have this sensitivity. Alternatively, perhaps due to birds' high, constant needs for energy, they are unlikely to survive if they wait for a larger food reward, and so they have evolved to be consistently impulsive, despite changes in deprivation level.[11]

A related foraging choice problem has been studied extensively in birds that must acquire enough energy before sundown in order to enable them to live through a possibly cold, long night.[12] When one of these birds is extremely food-deprived and is given a choice between a risky alternative that may result in either a small amount of food or in a large amount of food, and a nonrisky alternative that will always result in a medium amount of food, the bird is more likely to choose the risky alternative. For birds that are extremely food-deprived, only the large amount of food reward is sufficient for survival, and therefore only the risky alternative carries the possibility of survival. However, if the bird is not very food-deprived, so that it does not need the large food reward in order to survive, the bird is more likely to choose the nonrisky alternative. Rats, in contrast, consistently choose the nonrisky alternative despite their deprivation level.[13] This difference in findings between the experiments with birds and with rats may be due to procedural differences between the experiments with birds and rats, or to the fact that rats have larger internal energy stores than do birds, or to differences in the prefrontal cortex of birds and rats, or to some other factor.[14]

The final example comes from an experiment that used adult human females.[15] Each subject repeatedly chose between shorter, sooner access to her favorite juice and longer, later access to her favorite juice. Some of the subjects showed impulsiveness, some indifference, and some self-control. There was no relationship between the degree of self-control demonstrated by a subject and either the number of calories that she had consumed in the twelve hours prior to the experimental sessions or the degree to which she was underweight or overweight. Finally, even though during the sessions, as they consumed increasing amounts of juice, the subjects' desire for the juice decreased, self-control did not change. All of these findings appear to suggest that deprivation level does not affect self-control in humans. However, this experiment also found that subjects who reported that they were currently dieting were significantly more impulsive than subjects who reported that they were not currently dieting. There are at least two possible explanations for these seemingly contradictory findings. First, it is possible that subjects who said that they were currently dieting were in some as yet critical, unmeasured way actually more food-deprived than those who said that they were not dieting. If so, these subjects, by being impulsive, may have been evidencing their evolutionary heritage—they may have been demonstrating a tendency to obtain immediate food when deprivation threatened their future ability to obtain food. Another possible explanation for the finding of more impulsiveness in subjects who reported that they were dieting is that these subjects chose the impulsive alternative on purpose because in that way, consistent with their diets, they would have less access to the juice. In other words, perhaps the subjects chose the impulsive alternative as a sort of pre-commitment strategy (see Chapter 5); by choosing the impulsive alternative, the subjects ensured that they would not have an opportunity to consume large amounts of juice. If this were true, then for these subjects the impulsive alternative was really the self-control alternative. This explanation reinforces the point made in Chapter 2 that self-control and impulsiveness are so defined only in relation to other events occurring in a subject's life.

A final factor that must be taken into account in determining optimal foraging choices is how much energy expenditure each choice requires.[16] If the larger, more delayed alternative requires more energy expenditure than does the smaller, less delayed alternative, then it may be more advantageous for the animal to choose the smaller, less delayed alternative. In other words, in such cases it may be more advantageous for the animal to be impulsive. Sometimes situations may arise in which both deprivation level and energy expenditure play a role in identifying the optimal choice (see Box 6.4).

In all that time they came upon nothing they could eat, and the meager stores they had been able to bring with them were nearly depleted.

"Tomorrow," Varnak said, as they huddled in the bare lee of their sleds on the third night, "we shall eat none of our stores. Because I feel certain that on the next day we shall come to better land."

"If the land is to be better," one of the men asked, "why not trust that we will find food there?" and Varnak reasoned: "If the food is there, we shall have to be strong enough to run it down, and fight it when we overtake it, and dare much. And to do all that, we must have food in our bellies."[17]
[James Michener]

Box 6.4

Optimal foraging does not necessarily describe the behavior of all animals all of the time. Indeed, the preceding material indicates that there are many reasons why an animal may not forage optimally. For example, an animal may not have the cognitive ability to determine what response will maximize survival (see the discussion of the time horizon in Chapter 4). In addition, the animal may have evolved in an environment different from the one in which it is being studied, so that responses that would be adaptive in its original or natural environment are now unadaptive. Finally, animals must have both the physical capacity and the information necessary to make the optimal response.[18] It is important to remember that what appears to be a particular inability of an animal to forage optimally during laboratory experimentation may not be an inability in nature; the animal may be perfectly well suited to getting the food that it needs given the particular contingencies in its ecological niche.[19]

Hoarding

A special type of foraging behavior that is relevant to the study of self-control is *hoarding*: "the handling of food to conserve it for future use."[20] When animals hoard they take edible food and store it so that it will be available for consumption later. It is possible to conceive of hoarding as self-control in that the animal is giving up eating valuable food now in return for having even more valuable food later.[21] However, if the animal has plenty of food now, then hoarding may not involve giving up anything, and it may be inappropriate to describe such hoarding behavior as self-control. Research has indicated that at least one rodent species does appear to demonstrate hoarding that can clearly be defined as self-control. When hamsters are food deprived they tend to increase their hoarding; they give up current food that they need in order to have food later when they might need it even more. In contrast, when gerbils are food-deprived they tend to increase their current feeding.[22] In other words, deprivation tends to increase hoarding and self-control in hamsters but not in gerbils. It would be useful to find out whether, during times of food scarcity, the natural environments of hamsters and gerbils differ in ways that would tend to make hoarding more adaptive for hamsters than gerbils.

OVEREATING

The term *overeating* is used when too much is consumed—when more food is consumed than is healthy or desired. In other words, choosing to overeat means *not* choosing some more valued, but usually more delayed, alternative such as having a healthier or more attractive body, or *not* choosing to have an appetite for dinner later that day. Thus overeating can be conceived of as an impulsive response. Most people say that they at least occasionally overeat. If it is indeed only occasionally then this is not a serious problem. However, some people overeat repeatedly, and then serious health or social problems may arise.

An understanding of the reasons why people impulsively overeat could be very useful in decreasing overeating. One way in which to examine the causes of impulsive overeating involves an evolutionary approach. Chapter 3 pointed out that during much of humans' evolutionary past, food was scarce and periods of famine not infrequent. In such an environment, with great uncertainty about food sources, it is in a human's or any animal's best interest to take advantage of every food source that is encountered. In such an environment, times of food surplus are often followed by times of food scarcity. Therefore, in this type of environment, eating large amounts when food is present is unlikely to result in any permanent health damage— a period of food deprivation will usually follow. However, in our current environment, when most people in the United States have easy access to cheap food, eating large amounts of food can occur continuously, and the results can be extremely detrimental to physical and possibly mental well-being.

Thus, as discussed previously in the book, overeating may be just one aspect of the impulsiveness we inherited as a result of evolution. However, a belief that evolution has given us a tendency to overeat says nothing about what physiological mechanisms are responsible for that overeating, or about what environmental factors can affect those physiological mechanisms. An understanding of the physical and environmental causes of overeating can help decrease overeating. Therefore the remainder of this section will describe some of the possible physiological mechanisms responsible for impulsive overeating, as well as the environmental stimuli that affect overeating, ending with some speculations concerning how this knowledge might be applied to decreasing overeating.

Overeating Involving All Kinds of Food

There are many different physiological mechanisms involved in overeating, some of which are primarily involved in the long-term regulation of body weight, and some of which are primarily involved in the short-term regulation of food consumption. For each physiological mechanism there are a variety of different environmental events that can affect the operation of that mechanism. There are also environmental events that affect overeating through some as yet unknown physiological mechanism.

One example of a physiological mechanism involved in long-term regulation of body weight and that we know affects overeating is the number of adipose cells that someone has. *Adipose cells* are the cells in the body that store fat. When these cells are full of fat, there is less hunger; when they are not full of fat, there is more hunger. Therefore two people could have the same amount of fat but if one of the people stored that fat in fewer fat cells, that person would be less hungry than the other person who stored it in more fat cells.[23] The number of fat cells that someone has is affected by that person's genes. In addition, being overweight can increase the number of fat cells at any time in a person's life (particularly in childhood). The number of fat cells can never decrease.[24] Therefore someone who weighs less than his or her maximum lifetime weight may be continually hungry. This hunger can result in overeating so that the lost weight is regained.

There are other factors affecting overeating that are involved in short-term regulation of feeding. For example, some people impulsively overeat whenever there is food present, apparently independently of a physiological need for food. Such people are said to be externally responsive to food stimuli. Externally responsive people tend to demonstrate particular physiological responses to food stimuli. When such people simply see or smell food, their insulin level increases which, in turn, increases their hunger level and the tendency for any food consumed to be stored as fat. In other words, externally responsive people are literally turned on by the sight of food.[25] Women who obtain high scores on a questionnaire that measures their tendency to become hungry in the presence of food stimuli also tend to be impulsive for food rewards in the laboratory.[26]

Food stimuli are not the only stimuli that will induce overeating. Other environmental stimuli that in the past occurred at the same time as food also have this effect. For example, Harvey P. Weingarten showed that if rats were given a light/tone combination that had previously predicted the presence of a meal, the rats would eat even if they were not food-deprived.[27] An example of a similar effect in humans could be the following. Suppose you have just had an early dinner and you take a stroll down Columbus Avenue in New York City. It is a beautiful summer evening and many people are eating in outdoor cafes. You run into an old friend of yours who is eating in one of the cafes. Your friend, who is just about to order, invites you to sit down. A few minutes ago you felt full, but now you decide you will order just a little something. When the evening is over, you realize that despite trying to watch your weight, you have consumed the equivalent of two dinners. It is possible that stimuli associated with food, for both rats and humans, induce an insulin response, increase hunger, and increase impulsive overeating.

The above example may illustrate another possible cause of impulsive overeating. People eat more in social situations than they do alone. Experiments have shown that both male and female undergraduates eat more ice cream when they eat in groups than when they eat alone.[28] Similarly, men eat more lasagna when they eat in groups than when they eat alone.[29] Janet Polivy and her colleagues have shown that women tend to eat a lot when they eat with another woman who also eats a lot. In contrast, women tend to eat less if they eat with another woman who says that she is dieting.[30] There is as yet no evidence with regard to what physiological mechanism or mechanisms may be responsible for these social effects on overeating.

Another way that environmental stimuli can affect overeating of all types of food involves stimuli that signal an upcoming period of food deprivation. Marcie Greenberg Lowe hypothesized that people eat (often, overeat) when confronted with such stimuli. Such stimuli could occur, for example, when someone has broken a reducing diet by eating a small amount of something forbidden by the diet. Now the person has to think about going back on the diet, and that means thinking about all kinds of stimuli that are associated

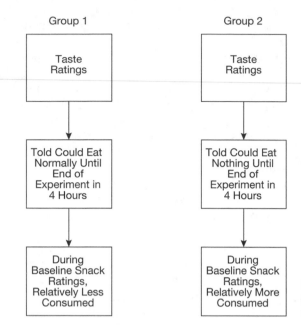

Group 1

Taste
Ratings

Told Could Eat
Normally Until
End of
Experiment in
4 Hours

During
Baseline Snack
Ratings,
Relatively Less
Consumed

Group 2

Taste
Ratings

Told Could Eat
Nothing Until
End of
Experiment in
4 Hours

During
Baseline Snack
Ratings,
Relatively More
Consumed

Figure 6.1. Diagram of the procedure used in Lowe's experiment.[31]

with future food deprivation. For example, the person who has just broken his diet might start thinking about going back on the diet in terms of such events as having to forgo cookies that someone brings to the office. According to Lowe's hypothesis, presentation of stimuli associated with future food deprivation and anticipation of the diet should result in even more overeating. Lowe did an experiment to test her hypothesis (see Figure 6.1). She told her subjects that they were participating in an experiment concerned with the effects of hunger on taste perception. Then she asked the subjects to practice making taste ratings on some snacks. Next, just before asking the subjects to make baseline snack ratings, she told half of the subjects that until the final part of the experiment, four hours later (timed so that either lunch or dinner should have occurred during the four hours), they could eat normally. She told the other half of the subjects that they could eat nothing during that time. Finally, before the four-hour break occurred, she asked each subject to make baseline snack ratings. While tasting and rating the snacks, subjects who thought they were about to skip lunch or dinner before making the last ratings ate significantly more of the snacks than did the subjects who thought that they were not about to skip a meal. Lowe's hypothesis was confirmed.[32]

Food variety can also result in overeating. When people eat the same food over and over again their preference for that food decreases. This is called the *sensory-specific satiety effect*. Eating a variety of foods prevents or decreases the sensory-specific satiety effect, making overeating more likely.[33] In our industrialized society, it is fairly common to have a variety of foods available at each meal, and this variety contributes to overeating.

As a final example regarding how some aspects of the environment can influence overeating, being led to believe that you have consumed alcohol can also result in overeating. This effect is particularly likely to occur if someone is a *restrained eater*. Restrained eaters have been defined as people who eat less than they wish. Then, by definition, people on weight-loss diets are restrained eaters. Janet Polivy and C. Peter Herman studied a sample of female college student subjects who had been identified as restrained eaters. Half of the subjects were given a drink containing alcohol, and half were given a drink containing vitamin C. For each of these two groups of subjects, half of the subjects thought that they had drunk alcohol and half thought that they had not, resulting in four groups of subjects (this is known as a *balanced placebo* design).[34] Whether or not these subjects had actually consumed alcohol, when they were told that they had consumed alcohol (as opposed to a vitamin C drink) they ate more ice cream.[35] This experiment shows that alcohol by itself is not necessary to cause overeating by restrained eaters; a restrained eater has only to think that she has consumed alcohol for her to overeat. When a restrained person's belief that she has consumed alcohol is correct, the overeating may be more problematic than if that belief is incorrect, because the alcohol, as well as the additional food eaten, contain calories.

Overeating Involving Specific Kinds of Food

Overeating is also affected by the type of food that is available for consumption. Humans are genetically predisposed to prefer sweet and salty foods. These preferences can be affected by experiences with sweet and salty foods, but the majority of people prefer sweet and salty foods from the time that they are able to taste them (at birth for sweet tastes; at about four months of age for salty tastes). In addition, we appear to be genetically predisposed to prefer foods that contain a high concentration of calories. This genetic predisposition often results in a preference for fatty foods, because the number of calories in a gram of fat is twice that in a gram of protein or carbohydrate. All of these genetically predisposed preferences were very helpful when humans were evolving and identifiable food sources were scarce. People needed to find and consume as much of high-calorie foods as possible, such as fatty and very sweet foods. Sugar is an excellent source of energy. Further, in nature, sugar is most often found in ripe fruits, which contain not only energy but also much-needed vitamins. Salt is also necessary for human bodies to function, and in nature, salt is not easy to find. Therefore the genetic predispositions for sweet, salty, and high-calorie foods helped early humans to eat what they needed to survive. Now, however, when so much fatty, sweet, and/or salty foods are so easily and cheaply available, humans' tendency to eat these foods whenever they are available can result in overeating, along with diabetes, cancer, high blood pressure, and other health problems.[36] Experiments with both rats and humans have shown that when large amounts of very tasty foods are available, subjects will overeat and become obese.[37]

Many researchers have paid special attention to the role of sweet tastes in inducing overeating. Many, but not all, of these experiments appear to indicate that sweet tastes can increase general appetite and overeating, and that this is true for artificial, noncaloric as well as natural, caloric sweeteners.[38] This effect may be due in part to the increase in insulin level that occurs following tasting something sweet. The increased insulin level decreases blood sugar level and thus increases hunger and overeating. Alternatively, eating sweet foods may increase hunger by means of causing the liver to lower blood sugar and to increase storage of consumed food as fat.[39]

Some people overeat due to carbohydrate craving. One example of such overeating involves the small proportion of obese people who suffer from *seasonal affective disorder* (*SAD*). SAD tends to occur among susceptible people during the winter months, when these people are exposed to less light. SAD is characterized by depression, a craving for carbohydrates, overeating, and weight gain.[40] This type of carbohydrate craving may be due to a dysfunction in serotonergic transmission in the brain. More specifically, carbohydrate craving due to SAD is thought to be due to insufficient amounts of serotonin stimulating the brain.[41] *Serotonin*, a chemical substance that transmits signals between some nerve cells, is believed by some, but not by others, to be involved in the appetite for carbohydrates.[42] Consumption of a predominately carbohydrate meal increases the amount of *tryptophan* (an amino acid) that enters the brain. Tryptophan is the chemical precursor for serotonin. Therefore when predominately carbohydrates are consumed, serotonin in the brain can increase.[43]

Another example of overeating due to carbohydrate craving is seen in some women in the luteal (postovulatory) phase of the menstrual cycle, in other words, in the second half of the menstrual cycle. Some researchers believe that, similar to SAD, serotonin may be involved in these cases of carbohydrate craving.[44] Another possible explanation is based on the fact that during the second half of the menstrual cycle, a woman's basal metabolic rate is higher than during the first half.[45] The resulting increased energy expenditure could therefore explain the premenstrual craving for high-calorie foods such as sweet carbohydrates (particularly chocolate). However, although energy expenditure has been found to be from 8 percent to 20 percent higher in the second than in the first half of the menstrual cycle, the total number of calories consumed in the second as compared to the first half has been found to be from 20 percent to 30 percent higher.[46] Therefore removal of an energy deficit cannot be the sole explanation of the food cravings present during the second half of the menstrual cycle; there is a tendency to eat more than is necessary to maintain weight during the second half of the menstrual cycle. A possible explanation of this overeating is based on evolution. Given that pregnancy and lactation require so many additional calories for both a woman and her child to be healthy (50,000 to 80,000 additional calories for pregnancy, and 765 to 980 calories per day for lactation[47]), and given that we evolved in an environment whose food supplies were often uncertain, it would not be surprising if women's bodies had evolved so that they would store some additional energy as fat during the second half of the menstrual cycle, the time at which pregnancy begins.[48] Thus, for women who actually become pregnant, the food cravings during the second half of the menstrual cycle may not really involve overeating. However, in our society, most women experience many more menstrual cycles than they experience pregnancies, and even if they do become pregnant, sufficient food supplies are usually present throughout pregnancy. Therefore, in our society, the cravings during the second half of the menstrual cycle do indeed constitute overeating.

Finally, stress can also be responsible for overeating of certain foods. Many experiments, using both human and nonhuman subjects, have shown that under conditions of physical or emotional stress, eating of preferred, familiar foods increases. One way of studying the effect of stress in the laboratory rat has been to give these rats repeated, mild tail pinches. In one such experiment, conducted by Neil E. Rowland and Seymour M. Antelman, rats whose tails were pinched for ten to fifteen minutes, six times per day, for up to five days, gained an average of 63 grams (18 percent of their average initial weight). Control rats whose tails were not pinched gained an average of only 17 grams.[49] As another example, Michael B. Cantor and his colleagues showed that information-processing tasks will induce eating in humans. They found that when humans work on a tracking task involving aiming a stylus at a rotating dot, they tend to consume snacks. When the task is made more difficult, the tendency to consume snacks increases.[50] There have been many attempts to explain stress-induced overeating. For example, John E. Morley and Allen S. Levine have postulated that opiates manufactured by subjects' own bodies (that is, endorphins) are involved in stress-induced eating, because, in rats, injections of naloxone, an opiate antagonist, eliminate stress-induced eating.[51]

Methods for Decreasing Overeating

The previous sections have presented many different ways in which impulsive overeating can occur, including some of what we know about the factors that tend to exacerbate impulsive overeating. For some of these types of impulsive overeating, we know something about the physiological mechanism involved, but for others we do not. However, even though our knowledge is incomplete, what is known about the causes of impulsive overeating can provide useful suggestions about how to prevent it, particularly when combined with the general suggestions for increasing self-control found in Chapter 5.

For example, one general method for increasing self-control, precommitment, can be modified specifically to prevent impulsive overeating. Precommitment procedures can be used to ensure that someone avoids: food stimuli, nonfood stimuli that have been associated with food, stimuli that have been associated with food deprivation, social eating occasions, meals containing a lot of different foods, alcohol consumption when food is present, sweet foods, salty foods, high-fat foods, situations in which stress is likely to occur with food present, or simply too many opportunities to eat. For all of these situations, some preplanning can ensure that the person who wishes to prevent overeating is not faced with tempting situations. For instance, when a person goes grocery shopping, that person can take only a limited amount of money. Then, unless the person is able to persuade someone at the store to provide a loan (see Box 6.5), it will be impossible for that person to buy large

WIMPY:
I will gladly pay you Tuesday for a hamburger today. [Popeye cartoon]

Box 6.5

amounts of food. Practically speaking, of course, using precommitment procedures to avoid all of these different types of tempting situations is extremely difficult.

When someone wishes to avoid a specific kind of food, such as processed sugar, that person can sign a contract (which is a form of precommitment) making engaging in pleasurable activities contingent on consuming decreased levels of processed sugar. Such contracts have been used successfully to decrease the consumption of nonhealthy foods while increasing the consumption of healthy foods, as well as to decrease food consumption in general.[52]

Use of precommitment procedures to prevent impulsive overeating involves manipulation of events in the external environment, which in turn, somehow affect the internal environment (that is, physiology) to increase self-control. A similar process is probably involved when exposure to bright light is used to decrease SAD and its associated carbohydrate craving.[53] Events in the internal environment can also be modified by means of specific drugs. For example, there are drugs that raise serotonin level and that also appear to be helpful in alleviating some types of carbohydrate craving. In the case of stress-induced overeating, a drug such as naloxone that removes the effect of endorphins may be effective in removing the overeating. Finally, drugs that can prevent the blood sugar level from decreasing, particularly in response to food-related stimuli, could be useful in preventing impulsive overeating. However, development of all of these types of drugs is still in its infancy.

This section has presented a number of possible suggestions for decreasing impulsive overeating (see also the section at the end of the book, Further Information and Self-Help Organizations). Nevertheless, it is important to remember that decreasing impulsive overeating, even when this means increasing dieting behavior, is not necessarily equal to successful weight loss. Weight loss is a function of not only how much food is consumed, but also of metabolic rate. Metabolic rate is genetically lower in some people than others, and may be permanently decreased by dieting. Thus, just because someone is eating less does not necessarily mean that the person will lose weight. The influence of metabolic rate is probably the reason for the fact that despite a great deal of research, behavior modification programs have been able to induce only moderate weight losses in the average person engaging in those programs. However, recent research shows that if someone will engage in lengthy aerobic exercise, weight reduction may be possible, perhaps through increasing metabolic rate[54] (see Chapter 8 for a discussion of exercise avoidance as impulsiveness—choosing to avoid the immediate small pain of exercise instead of choosing to avoid the large delayed pain of poor health).

ANOREXIA NERVOSA

According to the American Psychiatric Association's *Diagnostic and Statistical Manual of Mental Disorders*, the eating disorder called *anorexia nervosa* is defined as "refusal to maintain body weight over a minimal normal weight for age and height; intense fear of gaining weight or becoming fat, even though underweight; a distorted body image; and amenorrhea (in females)."[55] This disorder usually occurs in middle- or upper-class females ranging in age from their teens to their thirties. Estimates of the prevalence of anorexia nervosa range from 1 in 100 to 1 in 1,000 girls, depending on the group studied. It is a very serious disorder, with mortality estimates ranging up to approximately 18 percent.[56]

It is possible to classify anorexia nervosa as either self-control or impulsiveness. From the anorexic's point of view, her failure to eat constitutes self-control. Her larger, more delayed reward is to be as thin as possible, and not eating helps her to attain that goal. As far as an anorexic herself is concerned, any food consumption that will not allow her to remain or become extremely thin is impulsive.

On the other hand, from just about everyone else's point of view, an anorexic's failure to eat is impulsive. From this perspective, the larger, more delayed reward is a long, healthy life, and the smaller, less delayed reward is being thin. Even if an anorexic does not die, her extremely restrained eating and lowered body weight can severely inhibit her ability to reproduce. Thus, from this perspective, not eating is the more shortsighted, impulsive choice. Anorexia nervosa provides a good example of how context can determine whether a behavior is classified as self-control or impulsiveness.

A study by Staffan Sohlberg and his colleagues supports the classification of anorexia nervosa as impulsiveness.[57] These researchers interviewed thirty-five adults with anorexia nervosa or bulimia nervosa (described in the next section). Each subject was given an impulsiveness rating based on the subject's tendency to engage in four impulsive behaviors: binge eating, stealing, drug and alcohol abuse, and recent suicide attempts. Four to six years later, those subjects who had been rated as more impulsive were more likely to show anorectic symptoms. The impulsiveness ratings tended to predict only anorectic symptoms; in the years following when the impulsiveness ratings were made, although subjects who were rated as more impulsive were more likely to demonstrate anorectic symptoms, these subjects were not more likely to be depressed or to show overall worse mental health.

Putting anorexia nervosa in a self-control framework suggests that men and women do differ regarding some aspects of self-control and impulsiveness (see the section on gender differences in Chapter 4). Putting anorexia nervosa in a self-control framework also suggests that one part of treating anorexia nervosa might consist of doing whatever possible to make the delay to the long-term aversive consequences of the disorder seem shorter. For example, it is possible that speaking with women who have encountered some of the health problems caused by anorexia nervosa might be a useful part of the treatment. At the same time, it might be useful to try to decrease the value of being thin for the anorexic by taking steps to convince her that despite the media's depiction of attractive women as being extremely thin, people do not find her standard of thinness to be attractive. However, these treatment suggestions will certainly be insufficient by themselves. Anorexia nervosa is notoriously difficult to treat, and it is probably best to employ a combination of treatments including individual and group psychotherapy, family therapy, medication, and nutritional assistance and counseling[58] (see also the section at the end of the book, Further Information and Self-Help Organizations).

BULIMIA NERVOSA

The American Psychiatric Association's definition of bulimia nervosa is similar in some respects to its definition of anorexia nervosa. The definition of *bulimia nervosa* is: "recurrent episodes of binge eating (rapid consumption of a large amount of food in a discrete period of time); a feeling of lack of control over eating behavior during the eating binges; self-induced vomiting, use of laxatives or diuretics, strict dieting or fasting, or vigorous exercise in order to prevent weight gain; and persistent overconcern with body shape and weight."[59] In other words, bulimics, similar to anorexics, are extremely concerned about their body weight and take steps to prevent themselves from gaining weight. Also similar to anorexia nervosa, bulimics tend to be young adult females; estimates of prevalence among college-age populations range from 1 to 19 percent. In addition, bulimics, similar to anorexics, are subject to severe physiological problems as a result of their eating disorder. Repeated vomiting, for example, can result in sore throats, severe tooth decay, dehydration, cardiac arrhythmias, and death. The critical difference between anorexics and bulimics is that the latter, instead of avoiding eating entirely, eat large amounts of food (usually between 1,000 and 55,000 calories in a single binge) and then use various means to remove the caloric effects of those foods.[60] Thus, from a bulimic's perspective, she is alternating between impulsiveness (binging) and self-control (purging). However, from just about everyone else's point of view, a bulimic is alternating between one type of impulsiveness (eating too much, binging) and another (using nonhealthy ways to remove the caloric consequences of the food). Neither binging nor purging are behaviors that will result in long-term health.

Audrey J. Ruderman has also seen bulimics' binges as an example of impulsiveness.[61] According to Ruderman, when a bulimic overeats, she perceives this behavior as a disruption in self-control. This perception, in turn, precipitates more overeating, ultimately resulting in a binge. Ruderman's description of the causes of a bulimic's binging is similar to descriptions of the *abstinence violation effect* (*AVE*), originally studied to help explain relapse in abstinent former drug abusers. According to the AVE, once relapse has occurred, in other words, once self-control has not been maintained, the person sees himself or herself as a weak nonabstainer, thereby making future self-control more difficult. The AVE has been postulated as a mechanism involved in many types of overeating and other cases of impulsiveness.[62] Consistent with the classification of bulimics' binges as instances of the AVE, these binges have been shown to consist of a higher proportion of high-fat foods (considered forbidden, i.e., impulsive, by the bulimics) than is found with bulimics' nonbinge eating.[63]

As with anorexia nervosa, treatment of bulimia nervosa may be assisted by techniques designed to increase the self-control choice of long-term health. In addition, many researchers believe that antidepressants can be effectively used to ameliorate binging and purging.[64] This treatment strategy would appear consistent with other findings indicating that stress and aversive moods in general tend to increase impulsive overeating.[65] There may be some common physiological mechanism responsible for all of these cases of impulsive overeating involving anxiety and depression. In any case, also similar to anorexia nervosa, bulimia nervosa is a serious eating disorder that requires professional treatment (see the section at the end of the book, Further Information and Self-Help Organizations).

CONCLUSION

As with many other aspects of our behavior, feeding behavior appears frequently impulsive—many of us frequently overeat, and some of us are anorectic or bulimic. In the most common case of impulsive feeding, overeating, this behavior would probably have been adaptive in the environment in which we evolved. Overeating, when there was food available to overeat, would have helped to protect us against subsequent periods of starvation. Now, however, due to the more consistent food supply, overeating can occur continuously, and this continuous overeating is not conducive to good health over the long term—it is impulsive. With respect to feeding, as with respect to other aspects of behavior, it appears that evolution has best prepared humans for a world unlike the one in which humans currently reside. Therefore, in order to eat in a healthy way, many people need to take special steps to prevent some of the effects of their evolutionary heritage. Further, due to the critical role of feeding in survival, it would not be surprising if humans', and other species', bodies have evolved with specialized physiological mechanisms to encourage overeating whenever possible. To at least some degree, this does indeed appear to be the case. Therefore, although much of human behavior appears to be impulsive, in the case of impulsive feeding, unique physiological mechanisms may be responsible.

REFERENCES

1. Skinner, B. F. (1980). *Notebooks*. Englewood Cliffs, NJ: Prentice Hall, p. 59.
2. Brownell, K. D. (1991). "Dieting and the Search for the Perfect Body: Where Physiology and Culture Collide." *Behavior Therapy*, 22, 1–12.
3. Menzel, E. W., and Wyers, E. J. (1981). "Cognitive Aspects of Foraging Behavior." In A. C. Kamil and T. D. Sargent (Eds.), *Foraging Behavior: Ecological, Ethological, and Psychological Approaches* (pp. 355–377). New York: Garland (p. 355).
4. Fantino, E. (1981). "Contiguity, Response Strength, and the Delay-reduction Hypothesis." In P. Harzem and M. D. Zeiler (Ed.), *Predictability, Correlation, and Contiguity* (pp. 169–201). New York: Wiley.
    Fantino, E., and Abarca, N. (1985). "Choice, Optimal Foraging, and the Delay-reduction Hypothesis." *The Behavioral and Brain Sciences*, 8, 315–330.
5. Kamil, A. C., and Sargent, T. D. (1981). "Introduction." In A. C. Kamil and T. D. Sargent, *Foraging Behavior: Ecological, Ethological, and Psychological Approaches* (pp. xiii–xvii). New York: Garland.
6. Stephens, D. W., and Krebs, J. R. (1986). *Foraging Theory*. Princeton, NJ: Princeton University Press.
7. Logue, A. W. (1988). "Research on Self-Control: An Integrating Framework." *Behavioral and Brain Sciences*, 11, 665–709.
8. *Annie*. (1981, October 20). Manuscript in the Theatre Collection in the New York Public Library for the Performing Arts, New York, NY.
9. Bradshaw, C. M., and Szabadi, E. (1992). "Choice between Delayed Reinforcers in a Discrete-trials Procedure: The Effect of Deprivation Level." *The Quarterly Journal of Experimental Psychology*, 44B, 1–16.
    Christensen-Szalanski, J. J. J., Goldberg, A. D., Anderson, M. E., and Mitchell, T. R. (1980). "Deprivation, Delay of Reinforcement, and the Selection of Behavioural Strategies." *Animal Behaviour*, 28, 341–346.
    Collier, G. H. (1982). "Determinants of Choice." In D. J. Bernstein (Ed.), *Nebraska Symposium on Motivation 1981* (pp. 69–127). Lincoln, NE: University of Nebraska Press.
    Eisenberger, R., and Masterson, F. A. (1987). "Effects of Prior Learning and Current Motivation on Self-Control." In J. A. Nevin and H. Rachlin (Ed.), *Quantitative Analyses of Behavior: Vol. 5, The Effects of Delay and of Intervening Events on Reinforcement Value* (pp. 267–282). Hillsdale, NJ: Erlbaum.

Logue, A. W., and Peña-Correal, T. E. (1985). "The Effect of Food Deprivation on Self-control." *Behavioural Processes*, 10, 355–368.

Snyderman, M. (1983). "Optimal Prey Selection: The Effects of Food Deprivation." *Behaviour Analysis Letters*, 3, 359–369.

10. Logue, A. W., Chavarro, A., Rachlin, H., and Reeder, R. W. (1988). "Impulsiveness in Pigeons Living in the Experimental Chamber." *Animal Learning and Behavior*, 16, 31–39.

11. Logue, "Research on Self-control," 665–709.

12. Caraco, T. (1983). "White-crowned Sparrows (*Zonotrichia leucophrys*): Foraging Preferences in a Risky Environment." *Behavioral Ecology and Sociobiology*, 12, 63–69.

Caraco, T., Martindale, S., and Whittam, T. S. (1980). "An Empirical Demonstration of Risk-sensitive Foraging Preferences." *Animal Behaviour*, 28, 820–830.

Stephens and Krebs, *Foraging Theory*.

13. Kagel, J. H., MacDonald, D. N., Battalio, R. C., White, S., and Green, L. (1986). "Risk Aversion in Rats (*Rattus norvegicus*) Under Varying Levels of Resource Availability." *Journal of Comparative Psychology*, 100, 95–100.

14. Tobin, H., and Logue, A. W. (in press). "Self-control Across Species (*Columba livia, Homo sapiens, and Rattus norvegicus*)." *Journal of Comparative Psychology*.

15. Logue, A. W., and King, G. R. (1991). "Self-control and Impulsiveness in Adult Humans when Food Is the Reinforcer." *Appetite*, 17, 105–120.

16. Stephens and Krebs, *Foraging Theory*.

17. Michener, J. A. (1988). *Alaska*. New York: Fawcett Crest, p. 47.

18. Collier, "Determinants of Choice," pp. 69–127.

Houston, A. I., and McNamara, J. M. (1985). "The Variability of Behaviour and Constrained Optimization." *Journal of Theoretical Biology,* 112, 265–273.

McNamara, J. M., and Houston, A. I. (1985). "Optimal Foraging and Learning." *Journal of Theoretical Biology*, 117, 231–249.

19. Real, L. A. (1991). "Animal Choice Behavior and the Evolution of Cognitive Architecture." *Science*, 253, 980–986.

20. Vander Wall, S. B. (1990). *Food Hoarding in Animals*. Chicago: University of Chicago Press, p. 1.

21. Cole, M. R. (1990). "Operant Hoarding: A New Paradigm for the Study of Self-control." *Journal of the Experimental Analysis of Behavior*, 53, 247–261.

22. Wong, R. (1984). "Hoarding Versus the Immediate Consumption of Food Among Hamsters and Gerbils." *Behavioural Processes*, 9, 3–11.

23. Le Magnen, J. (1985). *Hunger*. New York: Cambridge University Press.

Sjöström, L. (1978). "The Contribution of Fat Cells to the Determination of Body Weight." In A. J. Stunkard (Ed.), *Symposium on Obesity: Basic Mechanisms and Treatment* (pp. 493–521). Philadelphia: W. B. Saunders.

24. Björntorp, P. (1987). "Fat Cell Distribution and Metabolism." In R. J. Wurtman and J. J. Wurtman (Eds.), *Human obesity* (pp. 66–72). New York: New York Academy of Sciences.

Sjöström, "The Contribution of Fat Cells," pp. 493–521.

25. Rodin, J. (1985). "Insulin Levels, Hunger, and Food Intake: An Example of Feedback Loops in Body Weight Regulation." *Health Psychology*, 4, 1–24.

26. Forzano, L. B., and Logue, A. W. (1992). "Predictors of Adult Humans' Self-control and Impulsiveness for Food Reinforcers." *Appetite*, 19, 33–47.

27. Weingarten, H. P. (1983). "Conditioned Cues Elicit Feeding in Sated Rats: A Role for Learning in Meal Initiation." *Science*, 220, 431–433.

28. Berry, S. L., Beatty, W. W., and Klesges, R. C. (1985). "Sensory and Social Influences on Ice Cream Consumption by Males and Females in a Laboratory Setting." *Appetite*, 6, 41–45.

29. Edelman, B., Engell, D., Bronstein, P., and Hirsh, E. (1986). "Environmental Effects on the Intake of Overweight and Normal-weight Men." *Appetite*, 7, 71–83.

30. Polivy, J., Herman, C. P., Younger, J. C., and Erskine, B. (1979). "Effects of a Model on Eating Behavior: The Induction of a Restrained Eating Style." *Journal of Personality*, 47, 100–117.

31. Lowe, M. G. (1982). "The Role of Anticipated Deprivation in Overeating." *Addictive Behaviors*, 7, 103–112.

32. Ibid.

33. Clifton, P. G., Burton, M. J., and Sharp, C. (1987). "Rapid Loss of Stimulus-specific Satiety after Consumption of a Second Food." *Appetite*, 9, 149–156.

    Rolls, B. J., Rowe, E. A., Rolls, E. T., Kingston, B., Megson, A., and Gunary, R. (1981). "Variety in a Meal Enhances Food Intake in Man." *Physiology and Behavior*, 26, 215–221.

34. George, W. H., and Marlatt, G. A. (1983). "Alcoholism: The Evolution of a Behavioral Perspective." In M. Galanter (Ed). *Recent Developments in Alcoholism* (Vol. 1, pp. 105–138). New York: Plenum.

    Marlatt, G. A., Demming, B., and Reid, J. B. (1973). "Loss of Control Drinking in Alcoholics: An Experimental Analogue." *Journal of Abnormal Psychology*, 81, 233–241.

35. Polivy, J., and Herman, C. P. (1976). "Effects of Alcohol on Eating Behavior: Influence of Mood and Perceived Intoxication." *Journal of Abnormal Psychology*, 85, 601–606.

36. Logue, A. W. (1991). *The Psychology of Eating and Drinking: An Introduction* (2nd ed.). New York: Freeman.

    Simopoulos, A. P. (1987). "Characteristics of Obesity: An Overview." In R. J. Wurtman and J. J. Wurtman (Eds.), *Human Obesity* (pp. 4–13). New York: New York Academy of Sciences.

37. Bobroff, E. M., and Kissileff, H. R. (1986). "Effects of Changes in Palatability on Food Intake and the Cumulative Food Intake Curve in Man." *Appetite*, 7, 85–96.

    Jordan, H. A., and Spiegel, T. A. (1977). "Palatability and Oral Factors and Their Role in Obesity." In M. R. Kare and O. Maller (Eds.), *The Chemical Senses and Nutrition* (pp. 393–410). New York: Academic Press.

    Sclafani, A., and Springer, D. (1976). "Dietary Obesity in Adult Rats: Similarities to Hypothalamic and Human Obesity Syndromes." *Physiology and Behavior*, 17, 461–471.

38. Blundell, J. E., and Hill, A. J. (1986, May 10). "Paradoxical Effects of an Intense Sweetener (Aspartame) on Appetite." *The Lancet*, pp. 1092–1093.

    Brala, P. M., and Hagen, R. L. (1983). "Effects of Sweetness Perception and Caloric Value of a Preload on Short-Term Intake." *Physiology and Behavior*, 30, 1–9.

Porikos, K. P., and Koopmans, H. S. (1988). "The Effect of Non-nutritive Sweet-eners on Body Weight in Rats." *Appetite*, 11 (Supplement), 12–15.

Tordoff, M. G., and Friedman, M. E. (1989). "Drinking Saccharin Increases Food Intake and Preference, I. Comparison with Other Drinks." *Appetite*, 12, 1–10.

39.   Geiselman, P. J. (1988). "Sugar-induced Hyperphagia: Is Hyperinsulinemia, Hy-poglycemia, or Any Other Factor a Necessary' Condition?" *Appetite*, 11 (Sup-plement), 26–34.

Rodin, "Insulin Levels, Hunger, and Food Intake," 1–24.

Simon, C., Schlienger, J. L., Sapin, R., and Imler, M. (1986). "Cephalic Phase In-sulin Secretion in Relation to Food Presentation in Normal and Overweight Sub-jects." *Physiology and Behavior*, 36, 465–469.

Tordoff, M. G., and Friedman, M. I. (1989). "Drinking Saccharin Increases Food Intake and Preference, IV. Cephalic Phase and Metabolic Factors." *Appetite*, 12, 37–56.

Vasselli, J. R. (1985). "Carbohydrate Ingestion, Hypoglycemia, and Obesity." *Appetite*, 6, 53–59.

40.   Wurtman, R. J., and Wurtman, J. J. (1989). "Carbohydrates and Depression." *Scientific American*, 360, 68–75.

41.   Silverstone, T. (1987). "Mood and Food: A Psychopharmacological Enquiry." In R. J. Wurtman and J. J. Wurtman (Eds.), *Human Obesity* (pp. 264–268). New York: New York Academy of Sciences.

Wurtman, J. J. (1987). "Disorders of Food Intake: Excessive Carbohydrate Snack Intake Among a Class of Obese People." In R. J. Wurtman and J. J. Wurtman (Eds.), *Human Obesity* (pp. 197–202). New York: New York Academy of Sci-ences.

Wurtman, and Wurtman, "Carbohydrates and Depression," 68–75.

42.   Wurtman, J. J. (1981). "Neurotransmitter Regulation of Protein and Carbohy-drate Consumption." In S. A. Miller (Ed.), *Nutrition and Behavior* (pp. 69–75). Philadelphia: Franklin Institute.

Wurtman, R. J., and Wurtman, J. J. (1984). "Nutrients, Neurotransmitter Syn-thesis, and the Control of Food Intake." In A. J. Stunkard and E. Stellar (Eds.), *Eating and Its Disorders* (pp. 77–86). New York: Raven Press.

Wurtman, R. J., and Wurtman, J. J. (1988). "Do Carbohydrates Affect Food In-take Via Neurotransmitter Activity?" *Appetite*, 11 (Supplement), 42–47.

43.   Logue, *The Psychology of Eating and Drinking*.

44.   Wurtman, and Wurtman, "Carbohydrates and Depression," 68–75.

45.   "Energy Expenditure During the Menstrual Cycle," (1987). *Nutrition Reviews*, 45, 102–103.

Leiter, L. A., Hrboticky, N., and Anderson, G. H. (1987). "Effects of *l*-Trypto-phan on Food Intake and Selection in Lean Men and Women." In R. J. Wurtman and J. J. Wurtman (Eds.), *Human Obesity* (pp. 327–328). New York: New York Academy of Sciences.

St. Jeor, S. T., Sutnick, M. R., and Scott, B. J. (1988). "Nutrition." In E. A. Blech-man and K. D. Brownell (Eds.), *Handbook of Behavioral Medicine for Women* (pp. 269–290). New York: Pergamon.

46.   "Energy Expenditure," 102–103.

Leiter, Hrboticky, and Anderson, "Effects of *l*-Tryptophan," pp. 327–328.

St. Jeor, Sutnick, and Scott, "Nutrition," pp. 269–290.

47. Frisch, R. E. (1988). "Fatness and Fertility." *Scientific American*, 258, 88–95.

~~St. Jeor, Sutnick, and Scott, "Nutrition," pp. 269–290.~~

48. Logue, *The Psychology of Eating and Drinking*.

49. Rowland, N. E. and Antelman, S. M. (1976). "Stress-induced Hyperphagia and Obesity in Rats: A Possible Model for Understanding Human Obesity." *Science*, 191, 310–312.

50. Cantor, M. B., Smith, S. E., and Bryan, B. R. (1982). "Induced Bad Habits: Adjunctive Ingestion and Grooming in Human Subjects." *Appetite*, 3, 1–12.

51. Morley, J. E., and Levine, A. S. (1980). "Stress-induced Eating Is Mediated Through Endogenous Opiates." *Science*, 209, 1259–1261.

    Morley, J. E., and Levine, A. S. (1981). "Endogenous Opiates and Stress-induced Eating." *Science*, 214, 1150–1151.

52. McReynolds, W. T., Green, L., and Fisher, E. B. (1983). "Self-control as Choice Management with Reference to the Behavioral Treatment of Obesity." *Health Psychology*, 2, 261–276.

    Nelson, L. J., and Hekmat, H. (1991). "Promoting Healthy Nutritional Habits by Paradigmatic Behavior Therapy." *Journal of Behavior Therapy and Experimental Psychiatry*, 22, 291–298.

53. Wurtman, and Wurtman, "Carbohydrates and Depression," 68–75.

54. Logue, *The Psychology of Eating and Drinking*.

55. American Psychiatric Association, (1987). *Diagnostic and Statistical Manual of Mental Disorders* (3rd ed. rev.). Washington, DC: Author, p. 65.

56. Logue, *The Psychology of Eating and Drinking*.

57. Sohlberg, S., Norring, C., Holmgren, S., Rosmark, B. (1989). "Impulsivity and Long-term Prognosis of Psychiatric Patients with Anorexia Nervosa." *The Journal of Nervous and Mental Disease*, 177, 249–258.

58. Bemis, K. M. (1978). "Current Approaches to the Etiology and Treatment of Anorexia Nervosa." *Psychological Bulletin*, 85, 593–617.

    Garfinkel, P. E., and Garner, D. M. (1982). *Anorexia Nervosa*. New York: Brunner/Mazel.

59. American Psychiatric Association, (1987). *Diagnostic and Statistical Manual of Mental Disorders* (3rd ed. rev.). Washington, DC: Author, p. 67.

60. Logue, *The Psychology of Eating and Drinking*.

61. Ruderman, A. J. (1986). "Dietary Restraint: A Theoretical and Empirical Review." *Psychological Bulletin*, 99, 247–262.

62. Marlatt, G. A., and Gordon, J. R. (1980). "Determinates of Relapse: Implications for the Maintenance of Behavior Change." In P. O. Davidson and S. M. Davidson (Eds.), *Behavioral Medicine: Changing Health Lifestyles* (pp. 410–452). New York: Brunner/Mazel.

63. Kales, E. F. (1990). "Macronutrient Analysis of Binge Eating in Bulimia." *Physiology and Behavior*, 48, 837–840.

64. Agras, W. S. (1987). *Eating Disorders: Management of Obesity, Bulimia, and Anorexia Nervosa*. New York: Pergamon.

Hudson, J. I., Pope, H. G., and Jonas, J. M. (1984). "Treatment of Bulimia with Antidepressants: Theoretical Considerations and Clinical Findings." In A. J. Stunkard and E. Stellar (Eds.), *Eating and Its Disorders* (pp. 259–273). New York: Raven Press.

Walsh, B. T., Stewart, J. W., Wright, L., Harrison, W., Roose, S. P., and Glassman, A. H. (1982). "Treatment of Bulimia with Monoamine Oxidase Inhibitors." *The American Journal of Psychiatry*, 139, 1629–1630.

65. Logue, *The Psychology of Eating and Drinking*.

7

Drug Abuse

From any perspective, drug abuse is a major problem in the United States. For the purposes of this chapter, drug abuse will be defined as "the use of a substance in a manner, in amounts, or in situations such that the drug use causes problems or greatly increases the chances of problems occurring. The problems may be social (including legal), occupational, psychological, or physical."[1] In this country, approximately 5.5 million people are addicted to illegal drugs.[2] Among these 5.5 million people, there are, for instance, about one to three million cocaine abusers who are estimated to be in need of treatment.[3] There is also a great deal of use of legal drugs which, despite their legality, are still potentially quite harmful. For example, there are about 54 million smokers in the United States.[4] Further, approximately 13 percent of the American adult population have at some point in their lives satisfied the American Psychiatric Association's criteria for alcohol abuse or alcohol dependence, and many more have had less serious problems with alcohol.[5] In addition, from coffee and tea alone, per capita consumption in the United States of caffeine is approximately 200 milligrams per day,[6] the equivalent of two cups of brewed coffee. Adding caffeine consumption from soft drinks (one soft drink contains about as much caffeine as a half cup of coffee)[7] would boost these statistics on caffeine consumption significantly. The list of drugs frequently abused in the United States goes on and on.

There are two ways in which drug abuse can involve impulsiveness. First, taking the drugs can itself be described as impulsiveness. Taking each one of these drugs, while resulting in some immediate pleasure, also carries with it the possibility of some future, long-lasting, serious harm. More specifically, drug abuse can be described as a choice between the immediate benefits of the pleasures of taking the drug along with the immediate benefits of

avoiding the suffering that may be present due to withdrawal; versus the delayed benefits of avoiding an unhealthy body, a disastrous family life, an un-
successful career, etc. Too often people choose the former, impulsive choice.

Nevertheless, taking these drugs does not always constitute impulsiveness. Defining drug usage as impulsiveness is dependent on there being some
long-term negative consequences for doing so. However, drug usage is not
always followed by negative consequences, particularly if that drug usage is
very limited. For example, someone who occasionally consumes a single
drink of alcohol, and who has no medical conditions that would be aggravated by alcohol, cannot be considered as engaging in impulsive behavior.
With many drugs, problems only occur when the drug is taken repeatedly.

The second way in which drug abuse can involve impulsiveness is that
taking of some, although certainly not all, drugs can increase someone's tendency to be impulsive. In other words, the effects of the drug may be such
that they increase future impulsiveness. Such drug-induced impulsiveness
may be exhibited in the taking of still more drugs, or in general impulsiveness in many aspects of the drug taker's life.

This chapter will consider both drug taking as a form of impulsiveness,
and impulsiveness resulting from drug taking. The focus will be on five drugs
of specific concern in many areas of the world including the United States: alcohol, cocaine, marijuana, nicotine, and caffeine. The last part of the chapter
will present a partial list of possible suggestions for decreasing drug abuse—
suggestions specifically based on a consideration of drug abuse within a self-
control/impulsiveness framework. Some of these suggestions will involve
manipulations of the environment in ways that might help to decrease drug
abuse; drugs of abuse are rewards, and behavior directed at obtaining them
is subject to many of the same environmental effects as is behavior directed
at obtaining other types of rewards.[8] In addition, this part of the chapter will
present some methods for decreasing drug abuse that involve pharmacological manipulation of the physiological state of the drug abuser.

ABUSE OF SPECIFIC DRUGS
AND IMPULSIVENESS

Alcohol

Repeated heavy consumption of alcohol fits well within the definition
of impulsiveness. First, repeatedly consuming alcohol often gives the consumer some immediate pleasure. For example, some people drink alcohol for
the reduction in tension that they feel (although tension reduction is not
widely applicable as an explanation of alcoholism).[9] In addition, for many alcoholics, alcohol consumption results in the fairly immediate removal of the
very unpleasant feelings of withdrawal. However, many other supposed
pleasurable effects of alcohol consumption may be more due to consumers'

expectations concerning alcohol's effects than to the actual physiological effects of the alcohol. Experimenters can determine that drinkers are experiencing something due to expectations concerning the alcohol, not the physiological effects of the alcohol, if subjects (1) show the effect when they think that they have consumed alcohol but they have not, and (2) do not show the effect when they think that they have not consumed alcohol but they have.[10] For example, alcohol's supposed ability to improve mood and to increase sexual behavior are actually both due to consumers' expectations concerning the effects of alcohol, and are not due to the physiological effects of the alcohol.[11] Mood improves and sexual behavior increases if subjects believe that they have consumed alcohol but they have not; mood does not improve and sexual behavior does not increase if subjects believe that they have not consumed alcohol but they have. Some drinkers may take advantage of the general public's ignorance of the limited nature of alcohol's physiological effects by using alcohol consumption as an excuse to perform some behavior that is generally considered unacceptable.[12] Using such an excuse can prevent others from negatively characterizing a drinker's sexual or other inappropriate behavior as impulsive ("he could not help himself, he was drunk"). In sum, whether due to expectations or to the physiological effects of alcohol, many people find immediate pleasure in consuming alcohol.

Alcohol can also give the consumer some delayed negative consequences. Although consumption of a single drink will not harm most people, repeated heavy consumption of alcohol can eventually have devastating effects. Excessive alcohol consumption is associated with: an increased probability of all types of accidents, aggravation of diseases such as bleeding peptic ulcers, a decreased probability of someone's detecting when he or she needs medical attention, an increased probability of suicide and of being a victim of a homicide, a possibility of dying due to acute alcohol poisoning (alcohol depresses the central nervous system, particularly in interaction with other drugs), a possibility of dying due to diseases caused by chronic alcoholism, an increased probability of committing a crime (see Chapters 9 and 10 for additional discussion of impulsiveness and criminal behavior), an increased probability of inadequate work performance, an increased probability of inadequate social relationships,[13] etc.

With so few definitive positive consequences following the consumption of alcohol, and so many possible negative consequences following its repeated consumption, it may seem surprising that anyone ever drinks excessively. However, the effective negative impact of all of the negative consequences outlined above may be decreased, or discounted, due to the fact that these are usually delayed consequences, and thus uncertain (see Chapter 5). This uncertainty is greater than that resulting simply from delay, because the negative consequences of alcohol abuse described above would not necessarily occur even if there were no delay—they will only occur given that the alcohol abuser's body is in a certain physiological state and/or a certain environment is present. In other words, the negative consequences of alcohol abuse are very uncertain events, and it is difficult for such events to have much impact on someone's behavior. There is still another reason why it may be very difficult to affect alcoholics' behavior by the negative consequences of alcohol abuse: Alcoholics' behavior in general appears to be less affected by negative consequences than is the behavior of nonalcoholics. For example, giving shocks to alcoholics for pressing buttons to obtain pennies suppresses their button pressing less than it suppresses button pressing in nonalcoholics.[14] As another example, nausea and vomiting following consumption of a food are apparently less likely to result in a subsequent aversion to eating that food in hospitalized alcoholics than in nonalcoholics.[15]

In addition to alcohol consumption itself being definable as impulsiveness, alcohol consumption can also increase impulsiveness in two ways: It can increase subsequent alcohol consumption and it can increase general impulsiveness. *Gamma alcoholism*, as currently defined by the American Psychiatric Association, is an example of alcohol consumption increasing subsequent alcohol consumption: "Gamma alcoholism involves problems with `control': once the person with gamma alcoholism begins to drink, he or she is unable to stop until poor health or depleted financial resources prevent further drinking."[16]

The use of alcohol may also increase impulsiveness more generally. There is no question that one of the physiological effects of some doses of alcohol is to increase aggression,[17] and therefore also impulsive criminal acts of aggression (see Chapters 9 and 10 for additional discussion of criminal behavior). Further, although there is not a great deal of relevant empirical evidence, researchers have argued that someone who has consumed alcohol may discount delayed events to a greater degree than someone who has not consumed alcohol.[18] One way in which this might occur is by alcohol disrupting humans' verbal statements that they use to remind themselves of delayed events[19] and to maintain the value of those events despite the delay (see Chapter 5). For example, alcohol consumption might disrupt drivers' statements to themselves about what could happen if they speed. Some people may take advantage of the increased discounting caused by alcohol by consuming alcohol in order to engage in a behavior that the person should do but does not have the courage to do.[20] Consider, for example, a case in which, during a war, in order to escape a country where death is guaranteed, someone has no choice but to travel on a tanker ship that is a likely candidate for bombing. Alcohol consumption during the trip could make the trip more bearable.

It has been proposed that alcohol causes humans to do things they would not otherwise do, including behaviors that in the long term are not the best strategy, by means of its effects on various parts of the brain including the *hippocampus* and the septum[21] (see Figure 7.1). There is some evidence for this hypothesis in rats. When these parts of the brain are destroyed, rats are less likely to choose a delayed alternative.[22] Researchers believe that destruction of these parts of the brain causes the rats to focus on immediate rewards.[23]

Finally, alcohol consumption can apparently increase impulsiveness

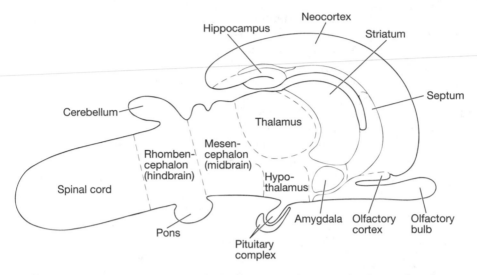

Figure 7.1. Location of the septum and the hippocampus in the mammalian brain, adapted from Nauta, J. H., and Feirtag, M. (1986). *Fundamental Neuroanatomy*. New York: Freeman.

across generations. A woman who engages in alcohol binges while she is pregnant is more likely to give birth to a child who makes impulsive errors on tests involving vigilance than is a woman who does not engage in alcohol binges while she is pregnant.[24] Such effects may be related to *fetal alcohol syndrome (FAS)*. This syndrome occurs when pregnant women consume alcohol, resulting in a child who is mentally retarded as well as facially deformed.[25] The amount of alcohol that a pregnant woman must consume in order for her baby to suffer from FAS is controversial.[26] It is possible that amounts too small to cause obvious mental retardation or facial deformities may nonetheless by some means affect the child's discounting of delayed rewards. Additional research is clearly needed in this area.

Cocaine

Cocaine is well-known for its ability to provide pleasurable feelings. More specifically, cocaine use tends to result in feelings of well-being, confidence, and even euphoria.[27] Inhaling cocaine powder ensures quick occurrence of these pleasurable feelings, injecting cocaine makes the pleasurable feelings occur even more quickly, and smoking the crack form of cocaine makes the pleasurable feelings occur still more quickly. Because the pleasurable feelings caused by cocaine are usually followed by negative feelings (anxiety, depression, fatigue, etc.),[28] repeatedly taking cocaine not only causes pleasurable feelings to occur but can remove some unpleasant ones caused by previous cocaine use.

Yet taking cocaine regularly eventually brings with it some extremely negative, possibly permanent, consequences. For example, due to the fact that cocaine abusers have little interest in rewards other than the rewards associated with the drug, cocaine abusers' social and work relationships usually deteriorate severely.[29] Further, use of cocaine may permanently damage the effectiveness of the substance dopamine (a *neurotransmitter*) in transmitting messages in the brain, thus resulting in depression lasting long after cocaine use has stopped. This depression can result in suicide.[30] Cocaine abuse can kill in many other ways also, including death from cardiac arrhythmia or respiratory paralysis.[31]

Due to cocaine abuse resulting in relatively immediate pleasure, and relatively delayed negative consequences, there is no question that cocaine abuse fits well within the definition of impulsiveness. In fact, it is possible that people who tend to be generally impulsive are more likely to abuse cocaine than are other people. Nathan Smithberg and Joseph Westermeyer demonstrated that a group of female cocaine abusers tended to receive high scores on a personality test measuring their impulsiveness, nonconformity, and poor judgment.[32] Nevertheless, it is not clear from such a questionnaire study whether the impulsiveness or some other factor resulted in the cocaine abuse.

In addition to research suggesting that impulsive people may be more likely to become cocaine abusers, perhaps cocaine also causes impulsiveness. First consider the possibility that cocaine use results in increased impulsive cocaine use. One way to investigate whether cocaine use can increase future impulsive cocaine use is to look at patterns of cocaine abuse among people who inhale versus inject cocaine. Recall that the pleasurable effects of cocaine are more immediate for people who inject cocaine than for people who inhale cocaine powder. Therefore, according to the definition of impulsiveness in use here, one would expect intravenous users of cocaine to be even more likely than powder inhalers to develop an apparently compulsive pattern of cocaine usage—a pattern in which the abuser appears unable to stop searching for and using the drug despite the long-term negative consequences. Research indicates that there is, indeed, a greater tendency towards compulsive cocaine use among people who inject versus inhale cocaine.[33] In at least some cases, cocaine abuse does appear to cause impulsive drug taking.

Regular use of cocaine may also increase impulsiveness for other types of rewards. Alexandra W. Logue and her colleagues recently developed a laboratory method for examining the effects of cocaine on self-control in rats.[34] The rats were first made hungry and were then given repeated choices between two levers, one of which delivered longer, more delayed access to a reward (milk) than did the other lever. The rats were exposed to this procedure for many days. Immediately before each session they were injected. In the first and third parts of the experiment, the rats were injected with saline. However, in the second, middle, part they were injected with cocaine. Figure 7.2 shows the results. The chronic injections of cocaine significantly decreased the rats' self-control for the milk. There is a general perception in our society that drug abuse, including use of cocaine, somehow contributes to impulsiveness (e.g., stealing, job absenteeism, and dropping out of school), and cor-

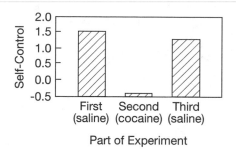

Figure 7.2. Self-control in rats in the three different parts of the experiment (in the first and third parts the rats received injections of saline, and in the second part they received injections of cocaine). A self-control measure of 0.0 represents no control over choice behavior by reward size as compared with reward delay, and a self-control measure of 2.0 represents twice as much control over choice behavior by reward size as compared with reward delay (in other words, higher bars represent greater self-control).

relations have been obtained between, for example, cocaine use and criminal behavior.[35] However, this is the first laboratory evidence suggesting that there may indeed be some effect of cocaine on general impulsiveness.

We do not know why it is that use of cocaine may, under some circumstances, increase general impulsiveness. One possibility is based on the fact that cocaine increases the effective action of the neurotransmitter dopamine. Previous research has shown that drugs that enhance dopaminergic function result in rats responding as if time periods are longer than the time periods seem when there is no drug exposure. Similarly, exposure to drugs that inhibit dopaminergic function result in rats responding as if time periods are shorter than the time periods seem when there is no drug exposure.[36] Further, if rats have been exposed to cocaine they wait longer to respond for rewards that are available after a fixed interval of time than if they have not been exposed to cocaine.[37] If drug-exposed rats are responding as if time periods are longer than when the rats are not drug exposed, then the drug-exposed rats' behavior will be more affected by those time periods and impulsiveness will be more likely. Thus, cocaine may increase general impulsiveness by making time seem to pass more slowly (see also Chapter 5).

Marijuana

Smoking marijuana usually quickly generates a sense of well-being. However, marijuana smoking can also impair driving ability (thus causing accidents) and can cause panic attacks. Repeated marijuana smoking can harm the lungs, can decrease testosterone levels in men, can interfere with the functioning of the immune system, and may cause brain damage.[38] Therefore, the smoking of marijuana, particularly the repeated smoking of marijuana, can be classified as impulsiveness.

Similar to cocaine, it is possible that the use of marijuana can not only be classified as impulsiveness, but can itself increase future impulsiveness.

People who regularly smoke marijuana sometimes seem to lack motivation;[39] they do not engage in behaviors that will result in long-term rewards. In other words, people who regularly smoke marijuana may not exhibit much self-control behavior. A possible explanation of this finding is that frequent users of marijuana tend to judge the passage of time as being significantly longer than do people who do not use marijuana.[40] Thus frequent marijuana users may see little point in waiting for what to them are *very* delayed rewards, resulting in an apparent lack of motivation and self-control.

Nicotine

Nicotine is another drug whose usual method of administration, inhalation, ensures rapid absorption of the drug into the body. Thus, smoking cigarettes quickly removes any unpleasant feelings resulting from withdrawal from nicotine, an addictive drug.[41] There may be other relatively immediate rewards for smoking (and, in fact, there must be for a smoker who is not yet addicted). For example, smoking can attract attention that the smoker finds rewarding. In addition, among at least some people, smoking provides the reward of a weight loss or a lack of a weight gain. A small proportion of people who start smoking actually do so in order to lose weight,[42] and on average, people who begin smoking do lose weight.[43] In addition, a fairly large proportion of people (about 47 percent of males and 59 percent of females in one survey) are afraid to stop smoking due to a possible weight gain.[44] There is also some factual basis for this belief; many people who stop smoking do tend to gain weight.[45]

At the same time, however, chronic smokers have an increased risk of heart disease, emphysema, cancer, and many other serious illnesses. In addition, today many businesses and social settings prohibit smoking, and therefore an addiction to nicotine can interfere with someone's work performance and social relationships.[46] Although prevention of excessive weight gain can sometimes be a healthy goal, on balance it would appear that smoking yields more short-term, rather than long-term, benefits, and should therefore be classified as impulsiveness.

Smoking does not appear to increase general impulsiveness. However, it certainly may contribute to increased impulsive smoking. Once someone starts smoking, the combination of the fact that nicotine withdrawal can cause very unpleasant symptoms, and the fact that the inhalation of nicotine causes rapid effects, makes chain smoking a not unlikely result. Further, the rapid effects of smoking make stopping smoking cigarettes more difficult than, for example, stopping chewing of tobacco.[47]

Caffeine

The final drug to be discussed in this chapter is caffeine. Caffeine is contained in coffee, tea, soda, chocolate, and many other foods and drinks, as well as in some over-the-counter medications. Similar to the other drugs discussed previously, consumption of caffeine brings with it some immediate, but relatively small, rewards, as well as the possibility of some delayed, but relatively large, negative consequences.

In terms of immediate, but relatively small, rewards, consumption of caffeine results in, for example, increased subjective reports of wakefulness and energy.[48] In addition, caffeine consumption can improve some, although not all, types of memory among people who have been identified as generally high in impulsiveness.[49] Because long-term consumption of caffeine can result in physiological dependence, the immediate rewards of consuming caffeine can also include the removal of withdrawal symptoms such as a withdrawal headache.[50] Possibly due to the removal of such symptoms, one experiment showed that subjects with a history of consuming a great deal of caffeine found taking capsules of caffeine more pleasant than taking placebo capsules. In other words, these subjects felt better taking caffeine capsules than placebo capsules even when the only way to tell whether or not the capsules contained caffeine was due to their post-ingestive physiological effects.[51]

Heavy and/or repeated consumption of caffeine can result in some more delayed, possibly very serious, negative consequences, however. Caffeine consumption can increase the probability or severity of gastrointestinal disease and heart disease. Further, in some people, consumption of as little as two cups of coffee can result in a disorder called *caffeinism* or *caffeine intoxication*, a syndrome whose symptoms include hyperactivity, an inability to sleep, water loss, and gastrointestinal distress. Large doses of caffeine can cause grand mal seizures, respiratory problems, and death.[52] In addition, studies using both female nonhuman animals and female humans have shown that caffeine consumption can result in various reproductive disorders, such as miscarriages and stillbirths. There is also some evidence that caffeine consumption may sometimes be linked to birth defects.[53]

Due to its relatively immediate positive consequences, and its more delayed negative consequences, caffeine consumption can be defined as impulsiveness. Similar to nicotine, there is currently no evidence indicating that caffeine consumption increases general impulsiveness. However, due to its addictive nature, consumption of caffeine certainly contributes to increased future impulsive consumption of caffeine.

METHODS FOR DECREASING DRUG ABUSE IMPULSIVENESS

This section will focus on suggested methods for decreasing drug abuse that derive from considering drug abuse within a self-control framework. There are many other successful methods for decreasing drug abuse that derive from other perspectives, but that are not within the scope of this book (see the section at the end of the book, Further Information and Self-Help Organizations).

Decrease Immediate Rewards

One obvious way to decrease drug abuse is to decrease the relatively immediate rewards that result from taking a drug. There are many ways in which this can be done. For example, if the drug is an addictive one, it may be possible to eliminate the drug-taking reward of removing withdrawal symptoms by the use of some medication that eliminates withdrawal symptoms. A related strategy is to remove what may be the permanent tendency towards depression caused by cocaine abuse by the use of antidepressants.[54] This strategy can help to prevent a cocaine abuser from taking cocaine to remove this depression.

Using medication, it may be possible to eliminate other positive feelings resulting from drug use as well. Michael A. Sherer and his colleagues accomplished this when they gave the medication carbamazepine to a cocaine abuser.[55] The carbamazepine prevented the cocaine abuser from experiencing the rush of positive feelings that he usually felt right after taking cocaine. There is also a medication that blocks the physical sensations accompanying the intoxication caused by alcohol consumption. However, so far, this medication has been tested only in rats. This medication apparently inhibits the effects of alcohol on the brain, although blood alcohol levels remain unaffected.[56] Nevertheless, even after this medication has been taken, high doses of alcohol will still result in intoxication.[57] Therefore use of this medication might induce alcoholics to consume even more alcohol in order to attain an intoxicated state. Further, although this medication might be useful in preventing drunk driving, it would not remove or even meliorate any of the potentially lethal damage done to body tissues by a high blood-alcohol level. Therefore use of this medication could possibly encourage drinking (such as by someone at a party who ordinarily would have abstained in order to drive home safely), and it could therefore cause great harm. For all of these reasons this medication may never be developed for commercial use.[58]

The immediate positive value of taking an abused drug can also be decreased by following its use with some immediate negative consequences. This is the principle behind the use of the medication Antabuse, which, if someone has taken it, and if that person has consumed alcohol, causes a profound physical reaction in that person including "nausea, vomiting, tachycardia, marked drop in blood pressure, and other symptoms of massive autonomic arousal."[59] Not all types of immediate negative consequences are successful in decreasing alcohol consumption, however. For example, immediately following drinking with shock will decrease alcohol consumption in the training, but not other, situations. Unlike following drinking with gastrointestinal illness, following drinking with shock does not affect the hedonic value of the alcohol. The brains of many animals, including humans, are apparently constructed so as to associate easily the tastes and smells of foods and drinks with gastrointestinal illness, but not with shock.[60]

Another, more indirect, method for decreasing the relatively immediate positive consequences that may follow use of an abused drug is to increase the value of other rewards present at the same time[61] (see also the section on relapse below). Chapter 2 indicated that the value of a reward is dependent on the value of other available rewards. A reward will seem to be of high value when other available rewards are relatively small and vice versa. There has been some laboratory testing of this type of strategy. For example, using monkeys responding to obtain the drug phencyclidine, Marilyn E. Carroll and her colleagues showed that responding to obtain the drug was significantly decreased when the monkeys could also respond to obtain saccharin.[62] As another example, Rudy E. Vuchinich and Jalie A. Tucker, using humans responding to obtain access to alcohol, showed that responding to obtain the drug was significantly decreased when the humans could make another response that resulted in relatively large amounts of money.[63] Unfortunately, this strategy for decreasing drug abuse is not easily applied to every type of drug abuse situation. To begin with, outside of the laboratory it may be much more difficult to control the sizes of all of the reinforcers available to the drug abuser than it is to control them in the laboratory. An even more fundamental problem is that this strategy of decreasing drug abuse through providing rewards for alternative behaviors will work best if the drug abuser is willing to substitute some amount of the rewards that follow these alternative behaviors for the rewards that follow drug abuse.[64] This strategy will not work, for example, if the primary reward the drug abuser is abusing the drugs for is alleviation of withdrawal symptoms, and alternative behaviors result in no reward that can help to alleviate such symptoms.

A final way to decrease the value of the relatively immediate rewards that can follow drug abuse is to delay these rewards, thus discounting their value. When drug abuse rewards are delayed, then the larger, more delayed rewards of lack of drug-related problems may have more value than taking the drug. Figure 7.3a (which is the same as Figure 3.2) shows the usual self-control choice between a larger, more delayed reward (e.g., lack of drug abuse) and a smaller, less delayed reward (e.g., drug abuse). Figure 7.3b is the same as Figure 7.3a with the exception that the delay to the smaller, less delayed reward has been increased. Note that in Figure 7.3a, self-control (e.g., lack of drug abuse) will be shown at point x, and impulsiveness (e.g., drug abuse) will be shown at point y. However, in Figure 7.3b, self-control will be shown at both points x and y. Sandra Rutter has advocated increasing the delay to the smaller reward to decrease cigarette smoking. If smokers are only given opportunities to choose whether or not to smoke another cigarette at times at which the next possible occasion for smoking is somewhat distant, they should be much more likely to choose not to smoke.[65]

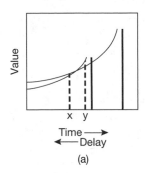 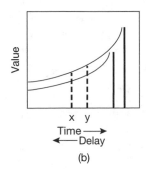

Figure 7.3. Hypothetical gradients of the value of two outcomes as a function of time—a larger, more delayed outcome and a smaller, less delayed outcome. The letters *x* and *y* indicate two points at which choices between the two outcomes might be made. (a) Large difference between the delays to the smaller and larger outcomes. (b) Small difference between the delays to the smaller and larger outcomes.

Precommitment

Figure 7.3 can illustrate what is involved in using a precommitment strategy to decrease drug abuse. In this case, the drug abuser should make the choice between taking the abused drug or not taking the abused drug at some time before the abused drug will actually be available (see point x on Figures 3.2 and 7.3a), thus increasing the delay to both the smaller, more immediate reward and the larger, more delayed reward. One way in which precommitment techniques have been used in the treatment of drug abuse is in the employment of contingency contracts.[66] In signing such a contract, a drug abuser might agree that if he or she abuses drugs then he or she agrees to accept certain negative consequences. However, if he or she does not abuse drugs then he or she might agree to accept certain positive consequences. The consequences are delivered by a therapist, family member, or friend. These contracts are signed when the drug abuser is not in a situation in which drugs are available. In other words, these contracts are signed when there is a delay to the choice to take or not to abuse drugs. Therefore, signing of the contingency contract constitutes the use of a precommitment device.

For example, the majority of methadone maintenance clinics use contingency contracting to some degree. In a typical contract, detection of drugs in the urine will be followed by a decrease in methadone dose, and no detection of drugs in the urine will be followed by an increase in methadone dose (up to some set limit).[67] The success of contingency contracts in decreasing drug abuse may be related to characteristics of the abusers such as their gender and recent drug history.[68]

Increase Delayed Rewards

Another set of strategies designed to decrease drug abuse involves increasing the value of the larger, more delayed rewards that result from not taking drugs. One way to do this is to decrease the delay to such rewards by giving some immediate rewards whenever a drug abuser chooses not to take an abused drug. This strategy has been used successfully, for example, with inpatient alcoholics by allowing them access to future alcohol only if they do not drink excessively.[69]

Another way of increasing the value of the more delayed, larger rewards that result from not taking abused drugs is to make the delays to those rewards seem shorter or, equivalently, to make the delays to the serious negative consequences that result from taking abused drugs seem shorter. An example of how this could be done would be to show pregnant women movies clearly demonstrating how the blood supply in an umbilical cord is severely decreased if the mother consumes even a single drink of 100-proof whiskey.[70] Box 7.1 shows another example of this type of strategy, a strategy intended to

[From a public service announcement televised frequently around 1990.]
A frying pan appears.
VOICE: This is drugs.
A pat of butter flies into the pan and starts to sizzle loudly as soon as it makes contact with the pan.
VOICE: This is your brain on drugs.
A raw egg is dropped into the pan, on top of the butter, where it immediately starts to hiss and pop loudly.
VOICE: Any questions?

Box 7.1

decrease all types of drug abuse. However, such strategies are unlikely to succeed unless the drug abuser has available sources of reward other than drugs[71] (see following section on relapse).

Relapse

One aspect of preventing drug abuse impulsiveness that has received a great deal of research attention concerns situations in which a former, abstinent, drug abuser loses self-control, in other words, relapses.[72] This research has focused on two aspects of relapse: relapse prevention and the effects of a relapse on subsequent abstinence. The majority of former drug abusers relapse.[73] Therefore, any comprehensive drug-abuse treatment program must include methods for decreasing and coping with relapse.

With regard to relapse prevention, researchers have shown that prevention of relapse can be assisted by, for example, making sure that engaging in drug abuse is not the only rewarding behavior available to the abstainer[74] (similar to one of the techniques discussed above for decreasing the size of the immediate rewards of drug abuse). This recommendation follows from a frequently studied theory of choice behavior, the *matching law*.[75] According to the matching law, the value of a reward is relative; the value of a reward depends on what other rewards are available. If reward A is being compared with reward B which is very large, then reward A will seem small. However, if reward A is being compared with reward C which is very small, then reward A will seem large. Thus if an abstinent former drug abuser has available one or more large rewards other than drug abuse, the value of drug abuse will seem relatively small and the abstainer will be less likely to relapse.

When a relapse (impulsiveness) does occur, the effect of that relapse can be to decrease future abstinence (self-control), due to the occurrence of the abstinence violation effect (AVE). As was described in Chapter 6, once relapse has occurred, the person who has relapsed can see himself or herself as a weak, nonabstainer, thereby making future self-control more difficult. The AVE may be a particular problem in cases of drug abuse because certain drugs give those people who take them a relatively immediate feeling of power. This relatively immediate feeling of power makes the reward of drug abuse seem even larger to a relapsed drug abuser who perceives himself or herself as a weak nonabstainer. In order to prevent the deleterious effects of the AVE when a relapse does occur, therapists work with their clients to help them understand that a relapse is a function of the client not yet having the skills necessary to avoid a relapse, rather than the client being a weak-willed failure. In addition, therapists help their clients to understand that a relapse does not mean that the client will never again be able to abstain. Therapists explain to clients that abstainers and nonabstainers are not two permanent categories of people. Most abstainers eventually relapse. Following a relapse, future abstention will be more likely if the relapse is seen as a cue for the client to engage in additional self-control techniques, rather than the client perceiving himself or herself as someone who will never again be an abstainer.[76]

CONCLUSION

This chapter has illustrated the serious nature and extent of the drug abuse problem, particularly in the United States. In addition, the chapter has demonstrated how drug abuse fits well within a self-control/impulsiveness framework. Drug abuse can be described as choosing smaller, but less delayed rewards over larger, but more delayed rewards. In other words, drug abuse can be described as impulsiveness. Examining drug abuse from this perspective may make it possible to generate some specific ideas concerning how to prevent and stop drug abuse. Finally, through consideration of drug abuse as impulsiveness, this chapter has shown some of the similarities between drug abuse and other types of impulsiveness. However, the chapter has also shown some of the differences. For example, the physiological systems involved in drug addiction withdrawal play a role in drug abuse, but not in other types of impulsiveness.

REFERENCES

1. Ray, O., and Ksir, C. (1993). *Drugs, Society, and Human Behavior*. St. Louis: Mosby, p. 4.
2. Holloway, M. (1991, March). "Rx for Addiction." *Scientific American*, pp. 94–103.
3. Gawin, F. H. (1991). "Cocaine Addiction: Psychology and Neurophysiology." *Science*, 251, 1580–1586.
4. Russell, P. O., and Epstein, L. H. (1988). "Smoking." In E. A. Blechman and K. D. Brownell (Eds.), *Handbook of Behavioral Medicine for Women* (pp. 369–383). New York: Pergamon.
5. American Psychiatric Association. (1987). *Diagnostic and Statistical Manual of Mental Disorders* (3rd ed. rev.). Washington, DC: Author.
6. Gilbert, R. M. (1981). "Caffeine: Overview and Anthology." In S. A. Miller (Ed.), *Nutrition and Behavior* (pp. 145–166). Philadelphia: Franklin Institute.
7. Brody, J. (1981). *Jane Brody's Nutrition Book*. New York: W. W. Norton.
8. Thompson, T. (1981). "Behavioral Mechanisms and Loci of Drug Dependence: An Overview." In T. Thompson and C. E. Johanson (Eds.), *Behavior Pharmacology of Human Drug Dependence* (pp. 1–10). Rockville, MD: U.S. Department of Health and Human Services.
9. Cappell, H. (1975). "An Evaluation of Tension Models of Alcohol Consumption." In R. J. Gibbins, Y. Israel, H. Kalant, R. E. Popham, W. Schmidt, and R. G. Smart (Eds.), *Research Advances in Alcohol and Drug Problems* (Vol. 2, pp. 177–209). New York: Wiley.
10. George, W. H., and Marlatt, G. A. (1983). "Alcoholism: The Evolution of a Behavioral Perspective." In M. Galanter (Ed.), *Recent Developments in Alcoholism* (Vol. 1, pp. 105–138). New York: Plenum.

    Marlatt, G. A., Demming, B. and Reid, J. B. (1973). "Loss of Control Drinking in Alcoholics: An Experimental Analogue." *Journal of Abnormal Psychology*, 81, 233–241.
11. Hull, J. G., and Bond, C. F. (1986). "Social and Behavioral Consequences of Alcohol Consumption and Expectancy: A Meta-analysis." *Psychological Bulletin*, 99, 347–360.

    Polivy, J. and Herman, C. P. (1976). "Effects of Alcohol on Eating Behavior: Influence of Mood and Perceived Intoxication." *Journal of Abnormal Psychology*, 85, 601–606.
12. Critchlow, B. (1986). "The Powers of John Barleycorn: Beliefs about the Effects of Alcohol on Social Behavior." *American Psychologist*, 41, 751–764.
13. Logue, A. W. (1991). *The Psychology of Eating and Drinking: An Introduction* (2nd ed.). New York: Freeman.

14. Vogel-Sprott, M. D., and Banks, R. K. (1965). "The Effect of Delayed Punishment on an Immediately Rewarded Response in Alcoholics and Nonalcoholics." *Behaviour Research and Therapy*, 3, 69–73.

15. Logue, A. W., Logue, K. R., and Strauss, K. E. (1983). "The Acquisition of Taste Aversions in Humans with Eating and Drinking Disorders." *Behaviour Research and Therapy*, 21, 275–289.

16. American Psychiatric Association, *Diagnostic and Statistical Manual of Mental Disorders*, p. 173.

17. Hull and Bond, "Social and Behavioral Consequences," 347–360.

18. Steele, C. M., and Josephs, R. A. (1990). "Alcohol Myopia: Its Prized and Dangerous Effects." *American Psychologist*, 45, 921–933.

19. Wilson, J. Q., and Herrnstein, R. J. (1985). *Crime and Human Nature*. New York: Simon & Schuster.

20. Ainslie, G. (1975). "Specious Reward: A Behavioral Theory of Impulsiveness and Impulse Control." *Psychological Bulletin*, 82, 463–496.

21. Newman, J. P., Gorenstein, E. E., and Kelsey, J. E. (1983). "Failure to Delay Gratification Following Septal Lesions in Rats: Implications for an Animal Model of Disinhibitory Psychopathology." *Personality and Individual Differences*, 4, 147–156.

22. Ibid.

    Rawlins, J. N. P., Feldon, J., and Butt, S. (1985). "The Effects of Delaying Reward on Choice Preference in Rats with Hippocampal or Selective Septal Lesions." *Behavioural Brain Research*, 15, 191–203.

23. Newman, Gorenstein, and Kelsey, "Failure to Delay Gratification," 147–156.

24. Sampson, P. D., Streissguth, A. P., Barr, H. M., and Bookstein, F. L. (1989). "Neurobehavioral Effects of Prenatal Alcohol: Part II. Partial Least Squares Analysis." *Neurotoxicology*, 11, 477–491.

    Streissguth, A. P., Barr, H. M., Sampson, P. D., Bookstein, F. L., and Darby, B. L. (1989). "Neurobehavioral Effects of Prenatal Alcohol: Part I. Research Strategy." *Neurotoxicology and Teratology*, 11, 461–476.

25. Abel, E. L. (1980). "Fetal Alcohol Syndrome: Behavioral Teratology." *Psychological Bulletin*, 87, 29–50.

    Streissguth, A. P., Landesman-Dwyer, S., Martin, J. C., and Smith, D. W. (1980). "Teratogenic Effects of Alcohol in Humans and Laboratory Animals." *Science*, 209, 353–361.

26. Logue, *The Psychology of Eating and Drinking*.

27. American Psychiatric Association, *Diagnostic and Statistical Manual of Mental Disorders*.

    Holloway, "Rx for Addiction," pp. 94–103.

28. American Psychiatric Association, *Diagnostic and Statistical Manual of Mental Disorders*.

    Ray, and Ksir, *Drugs, Society, and Human Behavior*.

    Resnick, R. B., and Resnick, E. B. (1984). "Cocaine Abuse and Its Treatment." *Psychiatric Clinics of North America*, 7, 713–728.

29. Ibid.

30. American Psychiatric Association, *Diagnostic and Statistical Manual of Mental Disorders*.

    Holloway, "Rx for Addiction," pp. 94–103.

31. American Psychiatric Association, *Diagnostic and Statistical Manual of Mental Disorders*.

32. Smithberg, N., and Westermeyer, J. (1985). "White Dragon Pearl Syndrome: A Female Pattern of Drug Dependence." *American Journal of Drug and Alcohol Abuse*, 11, 199–207.

33. Resnick, and Resnick, "Cocaine Abuse," 713–728.

34. Logue, A. W., Tobin, H., Chelonis, J., Wang, R., Geary, N., and Schachter, S. (1992). "Cocaine Decreases Self-control in Rats: A Preliminary Report." *Psychopharmacology*, 109, 245–247.

35. Kosten, T. R., Gawin, F. H., Rounsaville, B. J., and Kleber, H. D. (1986). "Abuse of Cocaine with Opioids: Psychological Aspects of Treatment." *National Institute on Drug Abuse Research Monograph Series*, 67, 278–282.

    Kosten, T. R., Gawin, F. H., Rounsaville, B. J., and Kleber, H. D. (1986). "Cocaine Abuse Among Opioid Addicts: Demographic and Diagnostic Factors in Treatment." *American Journal of Drug and Alcohol Abuse*, 12, 1–16.

    Nurco, D. N., Hanlon, T. E., and Kinlock, T. W. (1991). "Recent Research on the Relationship Between Illicit Drug Use and Crime." *Behavioral Sciences and the Law*, 9, 221–242.

36. Church, R. M., Broadbent, H. A., and Gibbon, J. (1992). "Biological and Psychological Description of an Internal Clock." In I. Gormezano and E. A. Wasserman (Eds.), *Learning and Memory: The Behavioral and Biological Substrates* (pp. 105–127). Hillsdale, NJ: Erlbaum.

    Meck, W. H. (1983). "Selective Adjustment of the Speed of Internal Clock and Memory Processes." *Journal of Experimental Psychology: Animal Behavior Processes*, 9, 171–201.

    Meck, W. H. (1986). "Affinity for the Dopamine D_2 Receptor Predicts Neuroleptic Potency in Decreasing the Speed of an Internal Clock." *Pharmacology, Biochemistry and Behavior*, 25, 1185–1189.

37. Logan, L., Carney, J. M., Holloway, F. A., and Seale, T. W. (1989). "Effects of Caffeine, Cocaine and Their Combination on Fixed-interval Behavior in Rats." *Pharmacology Biochemistry and Behavior*, 33, 99–104.

38. Ray and Ksir, *Drugs, Society, and Human Behavior*.

39. Ibid.

40. Varma, V. K., Malhotra, A. K., Dang, R., Das, K., and Nehra, R. (1988). "Cannabis and Cognitive Functions: A Prospective Study." *Drug and Alcohol Dependence*, 21, 147–152.

41. American Psychiatric Association, *Diagnostic and Statistical Manual of Mental Disorders*.

42. Klesges, R. C., and Klesges, L. M. (1988). "Cigarette Smoking as a Dieting Strategy in a University Population." *International Journal of Eating Disorders*, 7, 413–419.

43. Klesges, R. C., and Meyers, A. W. (1989). "Smoking, Body Weight, and Their Effects on Smoking Behavior: A Comprehensive Review of the Literature." *Psychological Bulletin*, 106, 204–230.

44. Klesges and Klesges, "Cigarette Smoking as a Dieting Strategy," 413–419.

45. Hall, S. M., McGee, R., Tunstall, C., Duffy, J., and Benowitz, N. (1989). "Changes in Food Intake and Activity After Quitting Smoking." *Journal of Consulting and Clinical Psychology*, 57, 81–86.

    Klesges and Meyers, "Smoking, Body Weight, and Their Effects on Smoking Behavior," 204–230.

46. American Psychiatric Association, *Diagnostic and Statistical Manual of Mental Disorders.*

    Russell and Epstein, "Smoking," pp. 369–383.

47. American Psychiatric Association, *Diagnostic and Statistical Manual of Mental Disorders.*

48. Elkins, R., Rapoport, J. L., Zahn, T., Buchsbaum, M. S., Weingartner, H., Kopin, I. J., Langer, D., and Johnson, C. (1981). "Acute Effects of Caffeine in Normal Prepubertal Boys." In S. A. Miller (Ed.), *Nutrition and Behavior* (pp. 167–176). Philadelphia: Franklin Institute.

    Gilbert, "Caffeine."

    Leathwood, P.D., and Pollet, P. (1982/1983). "Diet-induced Mood Changes in Normal Populations." *Journal of Psychiatric Research*, 17, 147–154.

    Rozin, P., and Cines, B. M. (1982). "Ethnic Differences in Coffee Use and Attitudes to Coffee." *Ecology of Food and Nutrition*, 12, 79–88.

49. Gupta, U. (1991). "Differential Effects of Caffeine on Free Recall After Semantic and Rhyming Tasks in High and Low Impulsives." *Psychopharmacology*, 105, 137–140.

50. American Psychiatric Association, *Diagnostic and Statistical Manual of Mental Disorders.*

51. Griffiths, R. R., Bigelow, G. E., and Liebson, I. A. (1989). "Reinforcing Effects of Caffeine in Coffee and Capsules." *Journal of the Experimental Analysis of Behavior*, 52, 127–140.

52. American Psychiatric Association, *Diagnostic and Statistical Manual of Mental Disorders.*

53. Gilbert, "Caffeine," pp. 145–166.

54. Resnick and Resnick, "Cocaine Abuse," 713–728.

55. Sherer, M. A., Kumor, K. M., and Mapour, R. L. (1990). "A Case in Which Carbamazepine Attenuated Cocaine `Rush.'" *American Journal of Psychiatry*, 147, 950.

56. Kolata, G. (1986). "New Drug Counters Alcohol Intoxication." *Science*, 234, 1198–1199.

    Suzdak, P. D., Glowa, J. R., Crawley, J. N., Schwartz, R. D., Skolnick, P., and Paul, S. M. (1986). "A Selective Imidazobenzodiazepine Antagonist of Ethanol in the Rat." *Science*, 234, 1243–1247.

57. Suzdak, P. D., Glowa, J. R., Crawley, J. N., Skolnick, P., and Paul, S. M. (1988). "Is Ethanol Antagonist Ro15-4513 Selective for Ethanol?" *Science*, 239, 649–650.

58. Kolata, "New Drug," 1198–1199.

59. Litman, G. K., and Topham, A. (1983). "Outcome Studies on Techniques in Alcoholism Treatment." In M. Galanter (Ed.), *Recent Developments in Alcoholism* (Vol. 1, pp. 167–194). New York: Plenum, p. 172.

60. Logue, *The Psychology of Eating and Drinking.*

61. Vuchinich, R. E., and Tucker, J. A. (1988). "Contributions from Behavioral Theories of Choice to an Analysis of Alcohol Abuse." *Journal of Abnormal Psychology*, 97, 181–195.

62. Carroll, M. E., Carmona, G. G., and May, S. A. (1991). "Modifying Drug-reinforced Behavior by Altering the Economic Conditions of the Drug and a Nondrug Reinforcer." *Journal of the Experimental Analysis of Behavior*, 56, 361–376.

63. Vuchinich, R. E., and Tucker, J. A. (1983). "Behavioral Theories of Choice as a Framework for Studying Drinking Behavior." *Journal of Abnormal Psychology*, 92, 408–416.

64. Hursh, S. R. (1991). "Behavioral Economics of Drug Self-administration and Drug Abuse Policy." *Journal of the Experimental Analysis of Behavior*, 56, 377–393.

65. Rutter, S. (1990). "Cigarette-smoking Reduction in University Students." *Psychological Reports*, 66, 186.

66. Resnick, and Resnick, "Cocaine Abuse," 713–728.

Schelling, T. C. (1992). "Self-command: A New Discipline." In G.Loewenstein and J. Elster (Eds.), *Choice Over Time* (pp. 167–176). New York: Russell Sage Foundation.

67. Calsyn, D. A., Saxon, A. J., and Barndt, D. C. (1991). "Urine Screening Practices in Methadone Maintenance Clinics: A Survey of How the Results Are Used." *The Journal of Nervous and Mental Diseases*, 179, 222–227.

Nolimal, D., and Crowley, T. J. (1990). "Difficulties in a Clinical Application of Methadone-dose Contingency Contracting." *Journal of Substance Abuse Treatment*, 7, 219–224.

68. Curry, S. J., Marlatt, G. A., Gordon, J., and Baer, J. S. (1988). "A Comparison of Alternative Theoretical Approaches to Smoking Cessation and Relapse." *Health Psychology*, 7, 545–556.

Dolan, M. P., Black, J. L., Penk, W. K., Robinowitz, R., and DeFord, H. A. (1986). "Predicting the Outcome of Contingency Contracting for Drug Abuse." *Behavior Therapy*, 17, 470–474.

69. Caddy, G. R., and Block, T. (1983). "Behavioral Treatment Methods for Alcoholism." In M. Galanter (Ed.), *Recent Developments in Alcoholism* (Vol. 1, pp. 139–165). New York: Plenum.

70. Altura, B. M., Altura, B. T., Carella, A., Chatterjee, M., Halevy, S., and Tejani, N. (1983). "Alcohol Produces Spasms of Human Umbilical Blood Vessels: Relationship to Fetal Alcohol Syndrome (FAS)." *European Journal of Pharmacology*, 86, 311–312.

71. Miller, W. R. (1985). "Motivation for Treatment: A Review with Special Emphasis on Alcoholism." *Psychological Bulletin*, 98, 84–107.

72. Marlatt, G. A., and Gordon, J. R. (1980). "Determinants of Relapse: Implications for the Maintenance of Behavior Change." In P. O. Davidson and S. M. Davidson (Eds.), *Behavioral Medicine: Changing Health Lifestyles* (pp. 410–452). New York: Brunner/Mazel.

Tucker, J. A., and Vuchinich, R. E. (1992). "Substance Abuse Relapse." In R. R. Watson (Ed.), *Drug Abuse Treatment* (pp. 71–98). Totowa, NJ: Humana Press.

73. Ibid.

74. Ibid.

Vuchinich, R. E., and Tucker, J. A. (1988). "Contributions from Behavioral Theories of Choice to an Analysis of Alcohol Abuse." *Journal of Abnormal Psychology*, 97, 181–195.

75. Herrnstein, R. J. (1970). "On the Law of Effect." *Journal of the Experimental Analysis of Behavior*, 13, 243–266.

76. Marlatt, and Gordon, "Determinants of Relapse," pp. 410–452.

    Tucker, and Vuchinich, "Substance Abuse Relapse," pp. 71–98.

8

Other Health-Related Behaviors

Many of the diseases from which we suffer can be prevented by engaging in healthy behaviors.[1] In other words, there are behaviors in which we can engage now that will prevent severe illness later. We can choose to behave in a way that will result in the large reward of good health later; alternatively, we can choose to behave in a way that may bring with it some small immediate pleasure, but is not likely to result in a healthy body later (see Boxes 8.1 and 8.2). Choices of this sort are choices involving self-control and impulsiveness.

> An ounce of prevention is worth a pound of cure.

Box 8.1

> However long I live, I want to be healthful and zestful, free of disease and disability. I am convinced that my future health largely depends on how I care for myself in the present.[2]

Box 8.2

Self-control is extremely important with regard to maintaining a healthy body.[3] It is important, first, because individuals can help to remain healthy by using self-control. In addition, people who make decisions regarding health and safety policies often need to think about the long-term, and not just the short-term, health consequences of their decisions. Further, health and safety policy decision makers need to have a good understanding of how people in general think about and respond to various kinds of short- and long-term health risks.[4]

This book has already discussed many health-related self-control behaviors in the previous two chapters on eating and drug abuse. This chapter will cover some additional health-related self-control behaviors including those involving sexual behavior, accident prevention, exercise, coping with environmental stress, and coping with illness. Throughout the chapter, there will be suggestions regarding ways to increase health-related self-control behaviors for particular types of situations.

As was described earlier in the book, one of the reasons that it may be difficult for people to engage in health-related self-control behaviors is that even if there were no delay, many of the unhealthy outcomes of unhealthy behaviors might not occur. For example, independent of the inevitable delay in determining that someone has contracted the HIV virus, people do not contract HIV every time they have unprotected sexual intercourse (that is, sexual intercourse without a condom). This is so even when they have unprotected sexual intercourse with a person who is known to be infected with HIV. Contracting HIV is more likely in the event of unprotected intercourse with an infected person than in the event of protected intercourse with an infected person, but for unprotected intercourse with an infected person the probability of contracting HIV is not equal to 1.0. Thus, for many health-related behaviors, the outcome of poor health is very uncertain, as well as delayed.

SEXUAL BEHAVIOR

No in-depth analysis is needed to realize that much of sexual behavior is impulsive. People often engage in sex for the resulting immediate pleasure, taking no precautions against the possible unwanted long-term consequences: pregnancy, syphilis, gonorrhea, herpes, AIDS, etc. Some of these consequences may be very delayed. A pregnancy may not be discovered for several months, and still more months will pass before the woman will experience a possibly painful and dangerous childbirth and an expensive, time-consuming baby will appear. AIDS can take many years to develop following someone's initial infection with the HIV virus. Thus it is not surprising that many people find it difficult to take such consequences into account when deciding whether or not to engage in sexual behavior; the sometimes very long delays until the occurrence of these consequences can result in their impact being severely discounted.

There has been extensive analysis of the adaptiveness of different aspects of human sexual behavior.[5] Impulsive sexual behavior may have been adaptive in our evolutionary past. During that time, sexually transmitted diseases were less frequent than they are now (AIDS, for example, was nonexistent). In addition, pregnancies were much less likely to result in a live birth, children were much less likely to survive to adulthood, and adults often did not live to the end of their reproductive years. In this type of situation, in order to ensure that their genes were present in future generations, it was clearly adaptive for humans to reproduce as much as possible; frequent sexual behavior would have maximized inclusive fitness. The immediate pleasure provided by sexual intercourse may thus have had an evolutionary basis; this pleasure may have ensured that humans reproduced whenever they could. In the evolutionary past, there may have been more positive than negative long-term consequences to individual humans engaging in frequent sexual behavior, so that frequent sexual behavior was not impulsive.[6]

However, our present environment is not similar to this previous one. Extensive sexual behavior now results in a great many surviving children, so that feeding and caring for them can be very difficult. In addition, sexually transmitted diseases are causing much pain and even death among large segments of the world's population. Thus, in our current environment, frequent sexual behavior can indeed be impulsive.

It is difficult to decrease frequent sexual behavior because of the built-in pleasure it provides. The tendency of the media to remind people of sexual behavior, and to model it for them, may make it even more difficult to decrease frequent sexual behavior. However, there are many ways in which to decrease impulsive sexual behavior, that is, sexual behavior that results in immediate pleasure but long-term negative consequences such as disease and unwanted pregnancy. Some of these ways are suggested specifically by the use of a self-control theoretical framework. For example, precommitment devices can be used to ensure that sexual behavior is not likely to result in disease or unwanted pregnancy. Such precommitment devices could include men having a vasectomy, thus ensuring that their sexual behavior will result in no pregnancies no matter what sort of sexual temptations are encountered. They could also include women having hormonal implants that will ensure contraception for many years. By guaranteeing that a man or woman is never in a situation in which sexual intercourse is possible, precommitment strategies can also be used to ensure abstinence. Such a strategy is being used when someone refuses to date someone else except in public settings, and refuses offers of car rides and homemade meals by the date. As a very extreme example, castration will definitely precommit that person to a decrease in the immediate pleasure provided by sexual activity and will reduce sexual activity.[7] However, due to the loss of rewards related to self-image and self-esteem, plus the pain involved, no one in our society is likely to use castration as a self-control technique for decreasing sexual activity.

ACCIDENT PREVENTION

Accident prevention is another way in which behavior can result in a large, delayed positive outcome (in this case, a lack of accidents; the self-control alternative). Not engaging in accident prevention results in a smaller, less delayed positive outcome (not having to take the precautions necessary to prevent accidents; the impulsive alternative). The use of seat belts is one example of such self-control.[8] Most people find wearing seat belts somewhat unpleasant; most people would not choose to wear seat belts if wearing seat belts had no consequences. However, by wearing a seat belt someone helps to ensure the large, delayed consequence of minimal bodily harm if there is an accident. Another example of self-control in the form of accident prevention, an example well known to young parents, is baby proofing—making an apartment or house safe for a baby or young child. Baby proofing is quite time-consuming and requires the purchase of many baby-proofing devices (for example, outlet plugs and toilet and cabinet locks). No one would engage in such behavior just for the fun of it. However, many parents gladly spend many hours and dollars on baby proofing in order to prevent their children from having many types of home accidents. Decreasing the relatively immediate negative consequences of baby proofing by having someone do much of the work and/or provide the materials free of charge could encourage more parents to baby proof their homes. Still other examples of self-control in the form of accident prevention include: taking your car for regular inspection and maintenance; using a rubber mat in the bathtub; using a spotter in a gymnastics class; wearing ear plugs, gloves, and a face shield when using a chain saw; standing in an open field rather than under a tree during a lightning storm; carpeting slippery wood stairs; etc.

EXERCISE

Exercise has many positive long-term health benefits. These include weight control (see Chapter 6), cardiovascular fitness, increased muscle tone, bone strength, and, in men, an increase in the high density lipoprotein cholesterol content of the blood (which is associated with decreased cardiovascular risk).[9] On the other hand, actually doing the exercise is not necessarily that much fun. Doing exercise at the very least requires time and some uncomfortable physical sensations. In fact, some people feel that it is impossible to obtain the positive benefits from exercise without experiencing a great deal of uncomfortable sensations (see Box 8.3). Doing exercise can also require buying and putting on special clothing (for example, a bathing suit), buying special accessories (for example, a squash racket), and joining a health club (which, in New York City, can easily cost around $1,000 for one year). Thus, exercising can be described as self-control, and not exercising can be described as impulsiveness.[10]

No pain, no gain.

Box 8.3

Many people use a variety of precommitment devices to ensure that they exercise. For example, they exercise as part of an exercise class, making it more difficult to quit exercising after ten minutes. Or they exercise with a friend, making it more difficult to skip a scheduled exercise session.

Maryann Leslie and Pamela A. Schuster used the precommitment strategy of contingency contracting to try to increase both exercise and the knowledge of the benefits of exercise among patients who needed cardiac rehabilitation. Half of the patients signed weekly contracts that specified that they would receive rewards if they attained that week's exercise goals. The results indicated that using the contingency contracts did not increase exercise more than simply giving the patients a weekly one-hour group education session (which all of the patients received). However, those patients who made weekly contracts seemed to acquire more knowledge about the benefits of exercise than the patients who did not make contracts.[11]

Engaging in healthful behaviors such as exercise can also be increased by increasing the immediate positive consequences and decreasing the immediate negative consequences provided by those behaviors. For example, a corporation could build a free fitness center in the building in which most of its employees work, thus decreasing the employees' time and monetary costs of exercising. Further, the corporation could provide paycheck bonuses to those employees who use the fitness center regularly.

In our evolutionary past, when food was much more scarce, lack of desire to exercise may have been adaptive. During that time, when there were no cars, elevators, or electric vacuum cleaners, people got enough exercise for health purposes during their daily lives, and any more exercise would have simply used up more calories, possibly increasing the probability of starvation. However, today, with all of our work-saving devices, we need to exercise in order to maintain our health. Using a self-control framework may be helpful in getting us to improve our long-term health through the use of exercise.

Coping with Environmental Stress

There are many experiments demonstrating that certain kinds of environmental stress can have detrimental physical effects. For example, in certain susceptible people, the psychological stress resulting from competitive mental tasks can result in salt and fluid being retained in the body, thus increasing the possibility of high blood pressure.[12] In addition, we know that certain kinds of work environments, notably those in which people have few possibilities for controlling which events will occur, are likely to result in burnout, including a decreased motivation to engage in any sort of work effort.[13] Further, people of the personality that has been labeled Type A respond more quickly than do other people when rewards are delivered after variable numbers of responses.[14] Thus Type A people may be more likely to overexert themselves in stressful situations of unlikely positive outcome than other people. Stress can also increase people's susceptibility to infectious ill-nesses, presumably through its effects on immune function.[15] These are just some of the ways in which stress can have detrimental effects (see also Chapter 6 for a discussion of stress-induced eating). In general, much research has shown that stressful environments are associated with a variety of diseases.[16]

Clearly, methods are needed to help people cope with stressful situations in ways that will minimize the physical and emotional damage that can be caused by such situations. One approach is to avoid the stressful situations, and this is the type of approach in which self-control can play a role. People can use precommitment devices to ensure that they are not placed in a stressful situation. An office worker can quit a particularly stressful job and look for a less stressful one. An employee of an organization can change positions within that organization (for example, a faculty member can return to laboratory research after serving as an administrator). A student can decide to take only easy courses, or even to major in something that does not require difficult courses. In accordance with the definitions of self-control discussed in Chapter 2, such strategies can be seen as ways in which to avoid the harm that can be caused by stress, or alternatively, as ways in which to make a long, healthy life more likely.

Coping with Illness

Self-control can also play a useful role in our coping with illnesses once they actually occur, both in terms of getting initial treatment for an illness, and in terms of carrying through on a prescribed treatment regimen. Consider first the situation of someone discovering a symptom that may indicate that he or she is seriously ill. That person has a choice. He or she can choose either to visit or not to visit the appropriate health care professional in order to find out what is wrong and to engage in appropriate treatment. Many factors can influence whether this visit does or does not occur.[17] An examination of the advantages and disadvantages of making the visit makes apparent that the choice to visit the doctor is a self-control choice. For example, the advantages to not visiting a health care professional are avoidance of a relatively immediate possibly painful or time-consuming treatment, avoidance of a relatively immediate possibly large expenditure of money, and avoidance of being given relatively immediately a possibly unpleasant prognosis. On the other hand, the advantages of visiting a health care professional when someone thinks that he or she is ill consist of the possibly relatively immediate alleviation of whatever unpleasant symptoms the ill person is experiencing, and the often delayed possible prevention of the worsening of the disease. Therefore, from a self-control perspective, given that many very serious diseases can initially have very mild symptoms (such as a small, nonpainful, lump in the breast that can signal breast cancer), and given the relatively immediate unpleasant possible consequences of visiting a health care professional (such as spending money to receive a diagnosis of breast cancer and a recommendation for a mastectomy), it is not at all surprising that many people do not engage in such visits when ill. In other words, it is not at all surprising that many people behave impulsively with regard to seeking medical attention when they are ill.

Further, based on this analysis, it is not at all surprising that many people avoid regular checkups—visits to the doctor or dentist that are supposed to occur even when someone is experiencing no symptoms of illness whatsoever. The main purpose of regular checkups is to find any symptoms of illness that may be at present unobservable to the patient (for example, a suboptimal level of iron in the blood). Thus the potential patient would appear to have even less to gain and more to lose by going to a regular checkup than in going to the doctor or dentist when the patient is experiencing some unpleasant symptoms of illness.

Many organizations value the health of their employees, but also recognize the tendency among many people to avoid regular checkups and to stay away from physicians and dentists when illness may be a possibility. Therefore these organizations provide group health care to their employees (which may also serve as an incentive for an employee to work for a particular organization), thus removing the possibility of someone incurring financial risk by visiting a health care professional. In some cases, organizations even require their employees to have an annual physical examination, paid for, of course, by the organization.

Sometimes someone is ill and there is little or nothing that a health care professional can do to alleviate the resulting debilitating symptoms. In such cases, self-control can play a role in how the ill person copes with these symptoms in trying to maintain a normal life. For example, Michael Rosenbaum and Arnon Rolnick studied sailors in the Israeli Navy.[18] They divided the sailors into those who did and did not get seasick as the result of a stormy sea. The researchers also gave each sailor a questionnaire measuring his degree of self-control. This questionnaire asked the sailors to report the degree to which they were likely to use self-control behaviors in a wide variety of situations in everyday life. More specifically, this questionnaire measured: "(a) use of cognitive and 'self-statements' to control emotional and physiological responses; (b) application of problem-solving strategies (e.g., planning, problem definition, evaluating alternatives, anticipation of consequences); (c) ability to delay immediate gratification; and (d) general perceived self-efficacy."[19] Rosenbaum and Rolnick found that there were no differences in self-control between sailors who did and did not get seasick; some factor other than a general tendency to show self-control determined whether a sailor would become seasick. However, among the seasick sailors, those who obtained high self-control scores were able to perform their jobs better when seasick than were those who obtained low self-control scores. Unfortunately, Rosenbaum and Rolnick did not report which specific aspects of the self-control behaviors measured by their questionnaire were related to the high self-control seasick sailors performing better than the low self-control seasick sailors. One possibility is that the sailors used precommitment strategies (such as telling colleagues that they were not sick, and relieving another sailor on duty) to ensure that they had to perform their assigned tasks.

Finally, many people (e.g., diabetics) are faced with situations in which they are told by a medical care professional to engage in a specific treatment program. The treatment may be unpleasant with only long-term beneficial effects (e.g., blood monitoring accompanied by changes in diet, plus insulin shots or pills), and the underlying illness may have few, if any, currently debilitating symptoms. Given such circumstances, it is not surprising that many people have great difficulty adhering to the treatment program; they behave impulsively and do not maintain the treatment. Contingency contracting, a precommitment strategy discussed previously, may prove helpful in getting patients to adhere to their treatment programs, if the patients are sufficiently motivated and sufficiently intelligent to use this self-control technique.[20]

Patients are not the only ones who have to face self-control issues when an illness has occurred. Health care professionals are also faced with self-control decisions. Health care professionals must sometimes decide whether to give the patient a treatment that only quickly alleviates the patient's symptoms, or a treatment that will take some time to have an effect but will result in better long-term health. For example, in treating anorexia nervosa (see Chapter 6 for a discussion of anorexia nervosa), doctors can choose between force feeding (which will certainly result in a weight gain, but cannot be continued for long periods of time, and certainly not outside of the hospital) or psychotherapy (which may take a long period of time to have any effect but may result in some long-lasting benefit). Given that many anorexics will die if they do not gain weight immediately, many physicians choose to begin with temporary force feeding, and then to start psychotherapy as soon as the patient is able.[21] Luckily, the two treatments are not mutually exclusive. Note, however, that if force feeding is needed to prevent immediate starvation, it is inaccurate to describe this treatment as an impulsive one (see Chapter 6). A similar example would be giving a patient an artificial heart (an immediate but temporary solution) rather than a heart transplant (which has the possibility of keeping the patient alive for a much longer period of time). If the patient is about to die, and a suitable heart is not available for transplanting, then an artificial heart is not an impulsive solution.

An example in which doctors and their patients might sometimes be tempted to choose an impulsive alternative concerns the prescription of antibiotics. Many patients visit doctors when the patient is suffering from a virus against which antibiotics have little effect, as opposed to a bacterial infection, against which antibiotics are often very effective. Doctors would like their patients to feel that they have been helped, and patients often feel helped when they have been given a prescription. Therefore, even though a doctor might be aware that antibiotics can do little for a viral illness, the doctor might be tempted to prescribe them when a patient is suffering from a virus; and a patient might be tempted to ask a doctor to prescribe antibiotics for a viral illness. The patient's virus illness would then clear up on its own; the patient would be happy, ascribing the cure to the antibiotic and a wonderful doctor;

and the doctor would be happy, due to having a cured illness and a grateful patient. Thus, prescribing and taking antibiotics in this situation would bring some immediate benefits in terms of patient and doctor satisfaction. However, there could also be some long-term negative consequences. Frequent prescription of antibiotics can encourage the growth of antibiotic-resistant strains of bacteria. Therefore doctors and their patients need to think carefully about the long-term, and not just the short-term, consequences of prescribing antibiotics.

CONCLUSION

This chapter, as well as the previous two chapters, have shown how a self-control analysis can be useful in identifying choices involving healthy behaviors—behaviors that are likely to result in long-term good health. Once healthy behaviors are conceived of as self-control—choice of larger, more delayed rewards—it is easy to see why it is so difficult for many people to engage in these behaviors. The consequence of a long, healthy life may be very delayed and therefore its (discounted) value may play a small role when choices are being made between healthy and nonhealthy behaviors. We can use the self-control techniques described in Chapter 5 to increase choices of healthy behaviors, and these techniques can be adapted so as to be most effective in particular health-related situations. The concept of self-control can help guide us to longer and healthier lives.

REFERENCES

1.   Brody, J. (1983). *Jane Brody's The New York Times Guide to Personal Health*. New York: Avon.
     Jeffrey, R. W. (1989). "Risk Behaviors and Health: Contrasting Individual and Population Perspectives." *American Psychologist*, 44, 1194–1202.
2.   Brody, *Jane Brody's The New York Times Guide*, p. xiii.
3.   Fisher, E. B., Levenkron, J. C., Lowe, M. R., Loro, A. D., and Green, L. (1982). "Self-initiated Self-control in Risk Reduction." In R. B. Stuart (Ed.), *Adherence, Compliance and Generalization in Behavioral Medicine* (pp. 169–191). New York: Brunner/Mazel.
     Jeffrey, R. W. (1989). "Risk Behaviors and Health: Contrasting Individual and Population Perspectives." *American Psychologist*, 44, 1194–1202.
4.   Slovic, P. (1987). "Perception of Risk." *Science*, 236, 280–285.
5.   Buss, D. M., and Schmitt, D. P. (1993). "Sexual Strategies Theory: An Evolutionary Perspective on Human Mating." *Psychological Review*, 100, 204–232.
6.   Konner, M. (1987, May/June). "Why the Reckless Survive." *The Sciences*, pp. 2–4.
7.   Beck, R. C. (1990). *Motivation: Theories and Principles*. Englewood Cliffs, NJ: Prentice Hall.

8. Jeffrey, "Risk Behaviors and Health," 1194–1202.

9. Logue, A. W. (1991). *The Psychology of Eating and Drinking: An Introduction* (2nd ed.). New York: Freeman.

10. McReynolds, W. T., Green, L., and Fisher, E. B. (1983). "Self-control as Choice Management with Reference to the Behavioral Treatment of Obesity." *Health Psychology*, 2, 261–276.

11. Leslie, M., and Schuster, P. A. (1991). "The Effect of Contingency Contracting on Adherence and Knowledge of Exercise Regimens." *Patient Education and Counseling*, 18, 231–241.

12. Light, K. C., Koepke, J. P., Obrist, P. A., and Willis, P. W. (1983). "Psychological Stress Induces Sodium and Fluid Retention in Men at High Risk for Hypertension." *Science*, 220, 429–431.

13. Glass, D. C., McKnight, J. D., and Valdimarsdottir, H. (1993). "Depression, Burnout, and Perceptions of Control." *Journal of Consulting Psychology*, 61, 147–155.

14. Krantz, D. S., Grunberg, N. E., and Baum, A. (1985). "Health Psychology." *Annual Review of Psychology*, 36, 349–383.

15. Ader, R., and Cohen, N. (1993). "Psychoneuroimmunology: Conditioning and Stress." *Annual Review of Psychology*, 44, 53–85.

16. Glass, D. G. (1977). *Behavior Patterns, Stress, and Coronary Disease*. Hillsdale, NJ: Erlbaum.

    Rodin, J., and Salovey, P. (1989). "Health Psychology." *Annual Review of Psychology*, 40, 533–579.

17. Taylor, S. E. (1986). *Health Psychology*. New York: Random House.

18. Rosenbaum, M., and Rolnick, A. (1983). "Self-control Behaviors and Coping with Seasickness." *Cognitive Therapy and Research*, 7, 93–97.

19. Ibid. pp. 93–94.

20. Morgan, B. S., and Littell, D. H. (1988). "A Closer Look at Teaching and Contingency Contracting with Type II Diabetes." *Patient and Education Counseling*, 12, 145–158.

21. Logue, *The Psychology of Eating and Drinking*.

9

Education, Management, and Money

Self-control plays an important role in education. Whether or not teachers and students show self-control can affect how successful education is—how much students learn and how well they are prepared for their future careers. In addition, decisions concerning educational policy sometimes involve issues of self-control (weighing more immediate consequences against more delayed consequences). When school careers are over and work careers have begun, workers need to manage their earnings and self-control is again involved. Further, managers in organizations and businesses may need to take into account both short- and long-term consequences when making managerial decisions, decisions that can affect the employees, clients, and/or neighbors of the organization or business. Sometimes, rather than earning money, people choose to obtain it through gambling or theft, strategies likely to result in positive consequences only in the short term, at best. This chapter is about all of these particular aspects of self-control and impulsiveness, and how self-control can be increased in these types of situations.

EDUCATION

Grades and Studying

One of the primary reasons that students attend school is to obtain a degree. In order to obtain a degree, certain grades are necessary. Grades are supposed to provide some measure of how much students have learned. In addition, they are supposed to provide some indication regarding which students are least and best qualified for more advanced work, or for certain kinds of jobs. Many teachers consider grades to be the main motivator available to them for encouraging students to study.[1]

However, can grades be much of a motivator given that they are often very delayed from the time when the graded work is performed? This is so not just for final course grades, but even grades for individual tests and papers. Some teachers rarely return weekly graded homework assignments with less than a month's delay, being either unable to return them more quickly or seeing no purpose to doing so. In addition, many teachers, particularly college and university faculty, design their courses such that there are only occasional graded examinations of performance. For all of these reasons, much studying can be unrewarded by any immediate graded feedback.

The result of all of these delays is that the motivational value of grades is severely discounted for students. This allows other smaller, but more immediate, rewards to have more value for the students. For example, it is hard for a student in a class whose only grade comes from a final examination to choose, at the beginning of the course, to study, rather than to go to a party, to go to a movie, to talk on the telephone, or simply to daydream. Near the end of the course, when the consequence of a grade is much less delayed, the student is more likely to choose to study. However, by then, it is often too late to learn all of the course material, particularly when the student may be experiencing the same sequence of events simultaneously for several courses. Then the student's grades are harmed.

Another temptation with which students are frequently faced is the temptation to work at a paying, but time-consuming, job. Many students work many hours each week at jobs in order to obtain sufficient money to attend school, or even to purchase luxury items such as a fancier car. These jobs deposit money in the students' pockets at fairly short intervals, usually at much shorter intervals than grades are delivered. Too many students are thus tempted to work many hours for nonessential money, leaving little time for studying for good grades.

Both teachers and students can take actions to help students study more and obtain better grades. First, teachers can increase the number of times that they grade students on their performance during a course and can ensure that the grades are returned quickly. Second, students can use precommitment devices to ensure that they study throughout the course and are not tempted to engage in nonstudy behaviors. For example, students can join study groups. Members of study groups use social rewards and punishers to ensure that all members of the group meet and go over course material at regular intervals throughout the school year, regardless of the temptations that arise. Students may also learn to give themselves rewards for studying, thus adding to the rewarding value of studying provided by (discounted, delayed) grades.[2] Using self-control skills that make time seem to go faster while studying may encourage longer study times (see Box 9.1). Developing general self-control skills may help to prevent later failure in school.[4]

> PATIENCE
> The clock will go slow
> If you watch it, you know;
> You must work right along
> and forget it.
> To study your best
> Till it's time for a rest,
> The clock will go fast, if you
> let it![3]

Box 9.1

Cheating

Cheating, including cheating on tests as well as plagiarism and fabrication of research data, seems to be extremely common in our academic institutions. In fact, some researchers believe that cheating is becoming increasingly prevalent in the American culture.[5] This is a very serious problem because without faith in academic honesty, the value of the products of these institutions (in other words, the value of awarded degrees and of research) is worthless. The entire academic system is founded on the integrity of its constituents.

Understanding and decreasing cheating can be assisted by viewing cheating as impulsiveness. Students and researchers who cheat have a choice between cheating now to obtain some immediate good grade or publication, versus not cheating and working to obtain good grades or publications later along with avoiding the aversive consequences of being caught. Conceptualized in this way, cheating can be seen to be a function of the relative strengths of immediate and delayed rewards, and of someone's ability to use self-control techniques to increase choices of larger, more delayed rewards.[6] For example, K. Daniel O'Leary demonstrated that in the experimenter's absence, first-grade boys are more likely to follow instructions about when not to press a telegraph key if they have been told to verbally remind themselves about what is and is not permitted.[7]

Robert Eisenberger, using a self-control conceptual framework, has done extensive research on possible causes of cheating and on ways to train students not to cheat. He has repeatedly shown that in both preadolescent and college-age students, experience with rewards that are obtained only after long delays or after much effort increases the students' subsequent tendency to show self-control or not to cheat. This research suggests that one possible cause of cheating is that the cheaters have never had much experience with delayed, effortful, rewards, and that cheating can be prevented by giving students experience with such rewards. In other words, the experience of delayed or effortful rewards may generalize to situations other than the one in which the original experience occurred, and can result in someone having a generalized tendency to show self-control and not to cheat.[8]

Impulsive Children

In general, children are more impulsive than adults (see Chapter 4). However, some children are unusually impulsive. For example, approximately 3 percent of children evidence *attention-deficit hyperactivity disorder* (*ADHD*; most of the children with this disorder are boys). This disorder involves impulsiveness, and can seriously interfere with school performance.[9] Children suffering from ADHD show "developmentally inappropriate degrees of inattention, impulsiveness, and hyperactivity." Examples of how the impulsiveness associated with this disorder can interfere with education are: "not sticking with tasks sufficiently to finish them and . . . having difficulty organizing and completing work correctly. . . . work is often messy, and performed carelessly and impulsively. . . . blurting out answers to questions before they are completed, making comments out of turn, failing to await one's turn in group tasks, failing to heed directions fully before beginning to respond to assignments, interrupting the teacher during a lesson, and interrupting or talking to other children during quiet work periods. . . . initiating a diverting activity on the spur of the moment instead of attending to a previous commitment."[10] The behavior of children with ADHD appears to be strongly controlled by immediate rewards and very weakly controlled by delayed rewards.

Central nervous system abnormalities are thought to be predisposing factors for ADHD.[11] In one theory concerning ADHD, deficits in the parts of the brain called the septum and the hippocampus (see Figure 7.1) have been proposed as a physiological analogy for the steep discounting of delayed events and thus the impulsiveness of children with ADHD. Rats with lesions in the septum display the increased attention to immediate, as opposed to delayed, rewards that is consistent with a diagnosis of ADHD in humans (see Chapter 7). However, there are no data specifically linking ADHD with a deficit in the septum.[12]

Consistent with a brain deficit explanation of ADHD, certain medications, such as the central nervous system stimulant *methylphenidate* (structurally related to amphetamine),[13] have been found effective in treating ADHD.[14] It is thought that these medications help to increase the attention of hyperactive children to cognitive tasks. Because sustaining attention on a cognitive task is incompatible with activity, ADHD children who are administered amphetamines are less active. This effect of amphetamines on ADHD children is in contrast to the effect of amphetamines on adults who, when administered amphetamines, appear to become more active.[15] Children with ADHD who are administered amphetamines, and whose attention span thus increases, will show less discounting of delayed rewards and will be more likely to demonstrate self-control.

However, amphetamines are powerful drugs with many side effects. For example, children given amphetamines for long periods of time may not grow as tall as children not given amphetamines.[16] In addition, administering amphetamines results in only short-term improvements in behavior.[17] Therefore, many researchers have taken advantage of the conception of ADHD as impulsiveness in order to develop behavioral methods of treatment for ADHD, treatments that focus on using manipulations of the environment in order to ensure that a child with ADHD chooses the larger, more delayed reward. Such treatments attempt to make long-lasting changes in the behavior patterns of children with ADHD.

For example, Julie B. Schweitzer and Beth Sulzer-Azaroff adapted the fading procedure originally developed for increasing self-control in pigeons (see Chapter 5) for increasing self-control in children who had been identified as impulsive by their teachers.[18] Children sat in front of a panel and repeatedly made choices between two boxes that partially extended from the panel. Touching the top of one or the other box resulted in, sometimes after a delay, the box being fully extended. After a box was fully extended, it could be opened to obtain food items or stickers (the rewards). At first, the children chose between immediate small and immediate large rewards. Then, over many days and 49 to 81 choices, the delay to the larger reward was gradually increased until the children were choosing between an immediate smaller reward and a larger reward delayed between 20 and 65 seconds, depending on the child. After the children had been exposed to this fading procedure, they were much more likely to choose the larger, more delayed reward box than before they had been exposed to this fading procedure.

Other researchers, such as Philip C. Kendall, have taken a cognitive-behavioral approach, one that attempts to change impulsive behavior in children through changing the environment as well as through changing cognitions (thoughts and emotions). These researchers have worked with children in improving their self-control in specific educational settings, as well as in play settings. In educational settings, the treatments specifically involved, for example, training the children to plan how to solve various types of test problems, to focus their attention on the test problems, and to reward themselves when they performed correctly. In addition, the researchers removed rewards when the children made errors on the test problems. Kendall and his associates have stated that the cognitive capacity of an impulsive child is important with regard to the type of treatment that will be successful with that child.[19]

There are many different techniques that can be used with some success to treat children with ADHD and other impulsive disorders. A combination of treatments may provide the best treatment. For example, ADHD children's classroom behavior can benefit from combinations of pharmacotherapy, parent training, and self-control training.[20] Early treatment may be very important, because there is some evidence indicating that when they have reached adulthood, extremely impulsive children may be more likely than other children to engage in impulsive behaviors such as drug abuse.[21]

Teaching and Research Productivity

There are also many situations in which self-control demonstrated by teachers can improve the education of their students, as well as enhance the teachers' own careers. The previous section on studying has already indicated that teachers can help students learn in a particular course by providing frequent, immediate feedback, in the form of frequent assignments and tests whose grades are returned promptly.[22] Such behaviors may require that teachers give up their own immediate rewards, such as going to a movie or concert, in order to have time to grade and return assignments and tests. However, by giving up these immediate rewards, teachers can ultimately receive the delayed reward of having students who have learned a great deal of course material by the end of the term.

Another way in which teachers can find it useful to exert self-control concerns their attempts to control classroom behavior. Every teacher, regardless of the age of the teacher's students, at least occasionally has disruptive students in the classroom. In such situations, the teacher can find it very tempting to try to decrease the disruptions by rebuking or punishing the student or students who are being disruptive. Nevertheless, if this is the only method used to decrease the disruptions, this technique can backfire. Particularly in large classrooms, students may find it very difficult to obtain teacher attention except by being disruptive; rebuking or punishing a student necessarily involves giving some attention to that student. Students quickly learn that in some classrooms, the way to get the attention of the teacher is to behave in inappropriate ways. The teacher continues to follow this strategy of classroom control because the act of rebuking or punishing the responsible student(s) does temporarily eliminate the disruption. However, research has shown that due to the rewarding nature of teacher attention, this classroom control technique does not result in a decrease in disruptions over the long term. A classroom control technique that focuses on rewarding those students who are behaving appropriately is much more likely to result in a well-behaved class in which students focus on their work.[23] Teachers need to consider the long-term, as well as the short-term, consequences of the classroom control techniques that they employ, and not be tempted by what seems to be an immediate (but ultimately less effective) strategy.

In addition to ensuring that their students learn course material effectively, today many college and university faculty need to do research and to publish that research in order to be promoted or even to keep their jobs. Many faculty find this part of their jobs extraordinarily difficult.[24] Using a self-control framework to analyze this situation can be helpful in understanding one of the reasons why so many faculty have trouble conducting sufficient research. Many colleges and universities provide little in the way of rewards for research productivity until it is time for a contract renewal, for promotion, or for tenure consideration, events of potentially very large reward value that can be spaced many years apart. On the other hand, most college and university faculty are required to teach from one to four courses per semester. For each of these courses, the faculty member must meet with the students several hours per week, and the faculty member usually functions in the position of the primary presenter of course material. Thus, several times per week or even per day, a faculty member must publicly display his or her knowledge and must face the possibility of appearing to have inadequate knowledge, a possibility that most people find extremely aversive. Further, during these same sessions with students, it will be apparent to the faculty member if the students strongly like or dislike the course as well as the faculty member, outcomes that can have great positive or negative value for faculty. Finally, many faculty, particularly nontenured faculty, are extremely concerned about the consequences if even a single disgruntled student goes to the chair of the department to complain about the faculty member. Nontenured faculty worry that such an incident will ensure that the faculty member does not receive tenure.[25] Thus, faculty have a choice: spend time preparing for classes so as to obtain immediate, but smaller, rewards; or spend time on research to obtain a larger, but very delayed reward. Just as many students put off studying to the end of the term, many faculty put off research until the end of their contract when it is too late, and instead spend most of their contract years devoting countless hours to their courses. In fact, faculty have been described as following the "Law of Delay" (see Box 9.2).[26]

> *The Law of Delay:* That which can be delayed will be.[27]

Box 9.2

Early in their careers, many faculty need assistance in devoting more time to research and less time to teaching while still maintaining the quality of their teaching. They can be shown time-saving techniques for effective teaching, as well as techniques for finding time for research during busy days. They can also be disabused of the notion that there would be any large negative impact if there were a single student complaint about something such as unclear lectures. In addition, committees can be set up to monitor the progress of these faculty, with the monitored faculty annually or biannually detailing for that committee what research they expect to accomplish in the near future. At the same time, faculty can arrange to conduct research with other faculty. In other words, social pressure can be used to enforce a faculty member's precommitment to conduct research and not to devote all of his or her time to teaching.[28]

Educational administrators also need to take principles of self-control into account in order to improve teaching and education. One example is in the return of teaching evaluations. Many college and university students dutifully and carefully fill out these evaluations at the end of a term, but then, all too frequently, the results may not be returned to the professor until many months later. As a result, much time passes in which corrections or refinements of the professor's teaching style, corrections that could have been made had the evaluations been returned promptly, go unmade. In addition, when the student evaluations finally do arrive, they may end up having little impact on the professor's future teaching behavior due to the large temporal gap between the past teaching behavior and its consequences (in other words, the impact of the teaching evaluations is discounted due to the large delay between the teaching behavior and its evaluations). It is essential that educational administrators ensure that teaching evaluations are returned quickly. Even better, just as grades are more effective if they are given more often, so that grades can follow continuous studying at relatively short intervals, so teaching evaluations are more effective as modifiers of teaching behavior if they occur more often, and not just at the end of the term. Teaching evaluations should ideally be conducted and returned to the faculty at least once during the term, thus allowing faculty to modify their teaching behavior before the end of a course.[29]

Finally, even educational administrators' careers can be adversely affected by their choosing short-term over long-term consequences. Just as faculty tend to devote their time to obtaining the immediate rewards provided by adequate teaching, rather than devoting their time to obtaining the delayed rewards provided by research, so educational administrators, even those who wish to remain involved with research, tend to devote their time to obtaining the immediate rewards provided by adequate administration, rather than to obtaining the delayed rewards provided by research. If continued, such impulsiveness may eventually make it impossible for an educational administrator to return to a full-time research career; the administrator will be too out-of-date and too out-of-touch with respect to current research. The administrator may not realize what has happened until it is too late (see Box 9.3). All faculty who wish to be active in research, including faculty who serve as administrators and faculty who teach, should use precommitment and other self-control techniques to ensure that blocks of time are regularly set aside for research.

Earning and Managing Money

In controlled laboratory experiments, most adult human subjects show a great deal of self-control for points exchangeable for money. (In contrast, when working for food, these subjects are often impulsive; see Chapter 6.) Self-control in the laboratory for points exchangeable for money probably results from the fact that the money cannot be spent until the subjects leave the experiment. Therefore, within the experimental sessions, there is no point in the subjects obtaining smaller, but less delayed rewards.[31] Outside of the laboratory, the contingencies are often quite different for choices involving money. Money available in these situations is usually money that can be immediately spent. Therefore it is not surprising that in the world outside of the laboratory, choices between larger, more delayed and smaller, less delayed amounts of money so often result in impulsiveness.

This section describes some of the self-control and impulsiveness issues that confront those who must make choices outside of the laboratory concerning earning and managing money. Such choices may involve decisions about personal money or decisions about money belonging to other people

Since administrators are usually recruited from the ranks of successful researchers as they reach mid-life, Walcott's story of intensely conflicting demands, and consequent internal stress, echoes a pervasive and honest refrain heard from the helm of scientific institutions. Administrators are chosen because they understand research—meaning that they both love the work and do it well. The story is as old as Walcott's beloved Cambrian mountains. You begin with a promise to yourself: I won't have as much time for research, but I will be more efficient. Others have fallen by the wayside, but I will be different; I will never abandon my research; I will keep working and publishing at close to full volume. Slowly, the perverseness of creeping inevitability takes over. Research fades. You never abandon the ideal, or the original love. You will get back to it, after this term as director, after retirement, after. . . . Sometimes, you really do enjoy an old age of renewed scholarship; more often as in Walcott's case, death intervenes.[30]

Box 9.3

(such as the fiscal choices made by organizational managers and administrators). Impulsiveness with regard to money causes many problems in our society. Perhaps examining this type of impulsiveness using a self-control framework can help suggest ways for decreasing such impulsiveness.

An example of self-control involving money is saving (see also Chapter 4). When someone has earned money, that person has a choice between spending the money on something that will give the person some immediate pleasure, or saving the money for a future use. For example, someone could save money for something that is not needed now but will be needed in the future (in other words, will have a very high value in the future; see Box 9.4), such as replacing property that might be stolen at some time in the future. Al-

Save money for a rainy day.

Box 9.4

ternatively, someone could save money in order to purchase something that cannot be purchased except with an accumulation of money, such as a new home. These are examples of self-control.[32] Saving money can be encouraged by the payment of interest on saving accounts. Paying interest increases the value of the delayed large reward (that reward being the money when it is finally removed from the savings account for spending). Another method for encouraging saving, one that is more under the control of the potential saver than is interest rate, is joining a savings plan. In many such plans, each week the potential saver's employer automatically deposits into savings some of the potential saver's earnings, so that the saver essentially precommits to saving money.[33] With a savings plan, the portion of earnings automatically deposited into savings is not available for impulsive spending. Nevertheless, with any saving method, saving money may be particularly difficult for children due to their having a higher discount rate than do adults.[34] Finally, it should be noted that saving money does not always constitute self-control. If someone saves more money than he or she needs to save, and if this saving is at the expense of his or her current enjoyment of life (e.g., if saving more money than will be needed results in a gregarious person having too little money this year to go to his or her high school reunion, to take a group tour, or to throw a party), then the value of spending money now may be greater than if the money is saved for later.

When individual savers or financial managers have money that they do not have to spend and want to save (at least for a while), they must decide how to invest the money. Some investments, such as three-month treasury bills, pay money to the investor after relatively short periods of time, with all earnings occurring within a few months of purchase of the treasury bills. Other investments, such as zero-coupon bonds, pay money to the investor after relatively long periods of time (earnings are not realized until after many years). Even when investors feel fairly confident that they will have no need for the money within a short period of time, they may be more likely to choose a short-term investment that earns them relatively little due to not valuing as much an amount of money that is larger but is earned after much more time. Investors tend to underestimate long-term investment earnings.[35]

A related savings issue is that of saving for retirement. Assuming that someone's expenditures do not change on retirement, a retiree needs to have more money in savings during retirement than when he or she is working because a retiree's earnings are substantially less after retirement. Therefore, assuming that someone expects to live beyond retirement, saving for retirement results in a large, delayed reward. Nevertheless, discounting the value of delayed events makes it difficult for many people to save during their working years.[36] During those years, other expenses, such as a larger house, children's educational expenses, a nice vacation, or a new car, often seem more important than saving for retirement. Recognizing the difficulty that many people have in saving for retirement, many employers make available retirement plans (these plans also attract potential employees to employers who offer those plans). Retirement plans put some of an employee's weekly earnings into a retirement investment account. To ensure that the employee is not tempted to spend this money on more immediate needs, the money in the retirement account is usable only if the employee retires. Sometimes organizations give their employees the option of saving additional funds for retirement, and a number of different investment options for those funds. Some options may permit borrowing of the money thus saved for retirement in order for the employee to meet more immediate needs. However, employees may sometimes (for example, at the State University of New York at Stony Brook) elect an optional retirement savings plan that does not allow any borrowing, the primary advantage of such a plan being that it prevents the employee from being tempted to spend the money on needs more immediate than retirement. In other words, participation in a retirement plan that does not allow removal or borrowing of the money saved constitutes the use of a precommitment device. The United States government also helps people to precommit to saving for retirement by requiring workers to pay social security tax.

Spending money can also involve issues of self-control and impulsiveness.[37] Some spending is for necessary items or uses money that is not needed for anything else. Such spending does not qualify as impulsiveness. However, some spending is for items that are of little use to the buyer, or uses money that would be better spent on something else. This type of spending does indeed qualify as impulsiveness. Approximately 6 percent of people of all income levels continually spend despite having insufficient funds for their expenditures.[38]

The frequency of impulsive spending can be increased by the use of credit cards and other types of borrowing. For example, people who make purchases with credit cards do not have to pay any money for a month. Thus, with credit card purchases, the actual cost of what is purchased is delayed and discounted; the actual cost of the item does not seem as large as it really is. Further, if they agree to pay a finance charge, purchasers who use a credit card can wait even longer than one month to pay. Due to the fact that the payment of the finance charge is also delayed, the negative impact of the finance charge, as well as that of the original cost of the item, is discounted, and thus an agreement to pay the finance charge may be made too readily. It is hard to turn down buying a striking new jacket when the jacket can be bought and worn right away, and the cost of the jacket as well as the finance charge need not be paid until many months later.

Many people have several credit cards, each with its own line of credit, and the resulting temptation to buy as much as the cards will allow can be overwhelming and ultimately financially devastating. One consumer avoided such temptation by literally freezing her credit cards in a six-inch block of ice (although she used springwater so that the ice would be clear and she could still see her credit cards).[39] For consumers who do not use such clever precommitment devices, however, the bills can mount up. In some cases, when the bills finally come due, it is simply impossible to pay them all. Commercials for lending institutions offer to extract you from such situations by giving you another, very large loan that you can use to pay off all of your other creditors. The lending institution points out, accurately, that you can end up paying less per month this way, and might even have some money left over to buy something else (one commercial suggests using that leftover money to purchase a small item—a new deck for your house). What they do not tell you is that the reason you will be paying less per month is that you will now be paying for many more months. Even knowing this, many people may take advantage of this type of very long-term, large loan. It may be the only way that they can pay back their creditors. In this case, taking out the loan does not constitute impulsiveness. Alternatively, someone may take out such an extended, large loan because, even though the loan is not absolutely necessary, paying money later does not have as much negative value as paying money sooner. Then taking out the new loan does constitute impulsiveness. People who borrow beyond their means to pay back previous loans will eventually experience the negative consequences of their actions, but perhaps by then there will be another lending institution ready to give them another loan to spread out the payments still further. . . .

Impulsive spenders clearly need to avoid repayment problems by spending and therefore borrowing less. To do this, they can limit the cash and checks that they carry, as well as the number of credit cards that they own. They can also keep a budget (thus precommitting themselves to spend pre-set maximum amounts in various expense categories) and they can reward themselves for not spending.[40] Joining a self-help organization such as Debtors Anonymous (see the section at the end of the book entitled Further Information and Self-Help Organizations) may be of additional help in curbing spending as well as in speeding repayment of borrowed funds.

In general, administrators, government officials, and managers need to think about the long-term, and not just the short-term, consequences of their policies concerning allocation of financial resources (see Box 9.5). For example, secondary school educational administrators should not devote resources to improving students' standardized test scores at the expense of

If we trivialize our approach to public affairs . . . we will spoonfeed [sic] the present at the expense of the future. Instant gratification is not a sound policy objective for responsible government, for responsible education, or for responsible journalism.[41]

Box 9.5

teaching the students behaviors that will help promote life-long learning. University deans need to monitor carefully their commitments to future funds; there may be a tendency to discount the value of these funds and/or the probability of these funds actually having to be expended. Personnel officers need to engage in the relatively small, immediate, aversive behavior of either firing or trying to change the behavior of an unsatisfactory employee, rather than engaging in the relatively large, delayed aversive behavior of repairing for many years the problems caused by that employee. Countries containing rain forests may be tempted to cut down some of the forest and replace it with farmland in order to better feed their citizens. However, in the long run, such destruction of the environment could lead to disaster for everyone. Factory owners may find it very difficult to spend money on modernization of their facilities, particularly if it will be several years before that modernization will result in increased profits. However, without that modernization, old-fashioned factories will soon be run out of business by factories that have been modernized or by new factories. When modernization is needed primarily to decrease pollution rather than to increase profits, laws will probably be needed to ensure that modernization occurs; without enforcement by law, factory owners are unlikely to devote funds to an enterprise that will affect the owners' health only many years hence.

In general, it may be easier for those supervising a particular group of workers in an organization to put into effect long-term, as opposed to short-term, strategies for those workers than for those workers to put such strategies into effect themselves. This is particularly true if the workers could directly benefit from the short-term strategies (e.g., if the decision to be made was between increasing the workers' salaries versus investing more funds in the organization's infrastructure).[42]

Henry Rosovsky, who was for many years dean of arts and sciences at Harvard University, has offered a compelling analogy between universities and baseball teams that aptly illustrates some of the advantages and disadvantages of short- and long-term managerial strategies. According to Rosovsky, similar to a university, a baseball team has a choice between purchasing expensive star players (i.e., faculty) who will give instant recognition to the team (but who may be past their prime), or devoting its energies to a farm system in which young players' talents are fostered for many years so that some (unfortunately, usually not all) of them may become star players.[43]

Particularly when a financial or a publicity crisis looms (e.g., if a university or other organization is said to be going downhill), it may seem as if every managerial decision must be made based on immediate survival. Managers also may not be motivated to take long-term consequences into account if they are working in a field in which managers tend to switch frequently (so that managers are unlikely to ever personally experience any of the long-term consequences of their decisions). But if there are any choices available at all, and if there is any stability in their organizations' environments, managers should be encouraged, in making their decisions, to factor in the long-term consequences of their choices.[44] Managers' choices may significantly influence a future that will eventually arrive, whether the managers choose to take that future into account or not.

OBTAINING MONEY OR GOODS WITHOUT WORKING

There are many ways of obtaining money or valuable goods without working. This section will discuss two of the more common ways: gambling and theft.

Gambling

In its most general sense, gambling is any activity that involves a risk of loss of something valuable.[45] This section will be particularly concerned with types of gambling in which people pay some money in order to have a possibility of winning a larger amount of money. This category of gambling includes lotteries, bingo, football pools, slot machines, race track betting, etc. In the United States, much of this gambling is legal. Most states now run lotteries, many religious groups sponsor bingo games, and Las Vegas and Atlantic City are famous for their legalized casino gambling which includes huge rooms lined with slot machines.

Many people engage in legal, as well as illegal, gambling. In 1990, New York State collected approximately $95 million from track and off-track betting alone. That year in New York State, approximately 475,000 people participated in this type of gambling, betting an average of $200 each.[46] Clearly, gambling is an exceedingly popular activity.

The primary purpose of legalized gambling in the United States is to earn a profit for the sponsoring group. The only way that a profit can be earned is to have people pay more to play than they are paid, on average, when they win. In other words, in the long run, the games are designed so that people engaging in these sorts of gambling will lose money. If someone gambles only occasionally, and can easily spare the money, then gambling can be seen as a form of entertainment or as a form of charity and is not a problem. However, some people lose more in gambling than they can afford. About 2 to 3 percent of adults can be classified as pathological gamblers.[47] The American Psychiatric Association defines pathological gambling as "a chronic and progressive failure to resist impulses to gamble, and gambling behavior that compromises, disrupts, or damages personal, family, or vocational pursuits."[48] Pathological gamblers are engaging in behavior that results in long-term harm to themselves and their families.

There has been a great deal of research concerning the causes of non-pathological and pathological gambling. Much of this research has been devoted to determining how people evaluate risks, to determining how they make decisions, and to identifying what personality types are likely to become pathological gamblers. Research with both human and nonhuman subjects has demonstrated that the particular response-reward contingencies involved in gambling are very likely to generate high rates of responding that persist despite many unrewarded responses.[49] These are all useful approaches in understanding the causes of gambling. The remainder of this section will focus on the approach of particular concern here—a description of gambling as a type of impulsiveness.

In order to understand why gambling qualifies as impulsiveness, it is necessary to understand the costs and rewards associated with multiple, as well as single, opportunities to gamble. When people have an opportunity to gamble they have a choice between paying money and possibly winning a great deal of money, or not paying money and having the money to spend on something later. However, most people do not gamble just once. They repeatedly put a coin in the slot machine, bet on a horse, or buy a lottery ticket. Many of these times they lose but sometimes they win. Therefore, when people have the opportunity to gamble, they may treat the probability of winning as a (somewhat variable) delay to winning. A low probability means that on the average, they will have to wait a long time before playing will result in a win, and a high probability means that on the average, they will have to wait a short time before playing will result in a win.[50] Chapter 3 of this book described how a delayed reward is also an uncertain reward. Analysis of gambling demonstrates that uncertainty of reward can function as a delay to reward. Thus, when people gamble repeatedly, they are repeatedly choosing between spending some small amount of money in return for possibly quickly receiving a large sum of money (but, in reality, over time a net loss of money), versus not spending that money and having it to spend later (impulsiveness versus self-control).

Additional analysis based on the assumption that delay decreases reward value can help to explain why people gamble. When people repeatedly gamble, they may perceive their gambling as a series of losses with each series terminated by a win. Some series are long and some are short. The value of a series depends on its length. Long series involve many gambles with many payments to play, and so the amount won is likely to be less than the amount spent (in other words, long series have a net negative value). On the other hand, short series involve few gambles with few payments to play, and so the amount won is likely to be more than the amount spent (in other words, short series have a net positive value). If, due to delay discounting, the consequence of a long series (a net loss of money) has less impact on choice than does the consequence of a short series (a net gain of money), then people will perceive gambling, on the average, as resulting in receipt of more money than actually occurs.[51]

Seen in this way, the tendency to gamble should be a function of, at least in part, the cost of playing, the probability of winning, and the amount that can be won. Consistent with this view of gambling, people of lower socioeconomic status, in other words, those for whom receipt of even a small amount of money has high value, are more likely to gamble than are people of higher socioeconomic status, for whom receipt of a small amount of money has little value. In fact, people of lower socioeconomic status may perceive gambling as the only way in which they can obtain large amounts of money.[52] For such people, if they are in severe financial need, it is questionable whether gambling should still be classified as impulsiveness (similar to not classifying as impulsiveness the choice by starving animals of receiving sooner, smaller amounts of food; see Chapter 6).

Given that gambling is a function of the cost of playing, the probability of winning, and the amount that can be won, manipulating all of these factors can change the frequency of gambling. However, when someone who gambles too much is trying to gamble less, these are not the factors that are likely to be under the person's control; they are under the control of the organization sponsoring the gambling. Therefore, someone who gambles too often must use self-control techniques in order not to give in to the temptation and to gamble. Such people can avoid trips to Las Vegas or can only enter a casino with a limited amount of funds. These are examples of precommitment strategies—one important component of treating pathological gambling (for further information about treating pathological gambling, see the final section of the book).

Theft

Another, all too popular, way of obtaining money without a job is by means of theft, taking money or goods from someone who has not given them to you. Theft is an example of impulsiveness because, although a thief may obtain some money in the short term, in the long run a thief risks going to jail.[53] The larger the value of what can be stolen, the more someone will be tempted to steal.[54] The value of what can be stolen may be large because, for example, it is a large amount of money. Or it may be large because the potential thief greatly needs money (as could occur with a drug abuser). Thus it is not surprising that drug abusers tend to engage in criminal behavior.[55] People also steal because the aversive consequences of stealing (imprisonment, fines, community service, loss of esteem), if they occur at all, are often very delayed from when the choice to steal occurs, and therefore the impact of these aversive consequences is significantly discounted.

Identifying criminality as impulsiveness does not, of course, mean that a generally impulsive person is doomed to a life of crime. Lack of opportunity, use of precommitment devices, lack of criminal role models, etc., can all result in a law-abiding person, even though that person is generally impulsive.[56] In an extreme case, even someone who is extremely inclined to engage in criminal behavior will not do so if that person is in jail.

It has been hypothesized that people who tend to engage in criminal behavior tend to have shorter time horizons than people who do not tend to engage in criminal behavior. For example, it has been postulated that the reason that theft among adults decreases with age is due to an increased time horizon (see Chapter 4) among older adults; in other words, among older adults delayed events are discounted less than among younger adults. It has also been postulated that people are more likely to steal if they are of less intelligence because lower intelligence is associated with a shorter time horizon.[57] However, there has been a great deal of controversy concerning how low intelligence might or might not be related to criminal behavior, and whether any such relationship is primarily genetically or environmentally mediated.[58]

According to this view of theft, in addition to imprisoning someone so that theft is impossible, methods for increasing the time horizon should be useful for decreasing theft. Such methods might include exposing potential thieves to proven thieves who have been caught and who have suffered for their crimes. Alternatively, decreasing the delay between crime and punishment or increasing the severity of punishment should help to decrease theft. All of these actions impose additional costs on society, however, costs that society may be unwilling to pay.

CONCLUSION

Principles of self-control and impulsiveness can be very useful in guiding education and management, and in understanding why people gamble and steal. Overall, in our current environment, a productive life depends a great deal on the ability to demonstrate self-control. Research on self-control can provide many suggestions with regard to how a productive life can be achieved by using self-control.

REFERENCES

1. McKeachie, W. J. (1978). *Teaching Tips* (7th ed.). Lexington, MA: D. C. Heath.
2. Beneke, W. M., and Harris, M. B. (1972). "Teaching Self-control of Study Behavior." *Behaviour Research and Therapy*, 10, 35–41.
3. Burgess, G. (1928). *Goops and How to Be Them: A Manual of Manners for Polite Infants Inculcating Many Juvenile Virtues Both by Precept and Example with Ninety Drawings*. Philadelphia: J. B. Lippincott Company, p. 39.
4. Mischel, W., Shoda, Y., and Rodriguez, M. L. (1989). "Delay of Gratification in Children." *Science*, 244, 933–938.
5. Putka, G. (1992, June 29). "Blackboard Jungle: A Cheating Epidemic at a Top High School Teaches Sad Lessons." *Wall Street Journal*, pp. A1, A4, A5.
6. Mischel, W., and Gilligan, C. (1964). "Delay of Gratification, Motivation for the Prohibited Gratification, and Responses to Temptation." *Journal of Abnormal and Social Psychology*, 69, 411–417.

7. O'Leary, K. D. (1968). "The Effects of Self-instruction on Immoral Behavior." *Journal of Experimental Child Psychology*, 6, 297–301.

8. Eisenberger, R., and Adornetto, M. (1986). "Generalized Self-control of Delay and Effort." *Journal of Personality and Social Psychology*, 51, 1020–1031.

Eisenberger, R., and Masterson, F. A. (1983). "Required High Effort Increases Subsequent Persistence and Reduces Cheating." *Journal of Personality and Social Psychology*, 44, 593–599.

Eisenberger, R., Mitchell, M., and Masterson, F. A. (1985). "Effort Training Increases Generalized Self-control." *Journal of Personality and Social Psychology*, 49, 1294–1301.

Eisenberger, R., and Shank, D. M. (1985). "Personal Work Ethic and Effort Training Affect Cheating." *Journal of Personality and Social Psychology*, 49, 520–528.

9. American Psychiatric Association. (1987). *Diagnostic and Statistical Manual of Mental Disorders* (3rd ed. rev.). Washington, DC: Author.

10. Ibid. pp. 50–51.

11. American Psychiatric Association, *Diagnostic and Statistical Manual of Mental Disorders*.

12. Gorenstein, E. E., and Newman, J. P. (1980). "Disinhibitory Psychopathology: A New Perspective and a Model for Research." *Psychological Review*, 87, 301–315.

Newman, J. P., Gorenstein, E. E., and Kelsey, J. E. (1983). "Failure to Delay Gratification Following Septal Lesions in Rats: Implications for an Animal Model of Disinhibitory Psychopathology." *Personality and Individual Differences*, 4, 147–156.

13. Gilman, A. G., Rall, T. W., Nies, A. S., and Taylor, P. (Eds.). (1990). *Goodman and Gilman's the Pharmacological Basis of Therapeutics* (8th ed.). New York: Pergamon.

14. Brown, R. T., and Sexson, S. B. (1988). "A Controlled Trial of Methylphenidate in Black Adolescents." *Clinical Pediatrics*, 27, 74–81.

Pelham, W. E., Bender, M. E., Caddell, J., Booth, S., Moorer, S. H. (1985). "Methylphenidate and Children with Attention Deficit Disorder." *Archives of General Psychiatry*, 42, 948–952.

Pelham, W. E., Schnedler, R. W., Bologna, N. C., Contreras, J. A. (1990). "Behavioral and Stimulant Treatment of Hyperactive Children: A Therapy Study with Methylphenidate Probes in a Within-subject Design." *Journal of Applied Behavior Analysis*, 13, 221–236.

Rapport, M. D., Stoner, G., DuPaul, G. J., Kelly, K. L., Tucker, S. B., and Schoeler, T. (1988). "Attention Deficit Disorder and Methylphenidate: A Multilevel Analysis of Dose-response Effects on Children's Impulsivity Across Settings." *Child and Adolescent Psychiatry*, 27, 60–69.

Trommer, B. L., Hoeppner, J. B., and Zecker, S. G. (1991). "The Go-No Go Test in Attention Deficit Disorder Is Sensitive to Methylphenidate." *Journal of Child Neurology*, 6, s128-s131.

15. Rappoport, J. L., Buchsbaum, M. S., Zahn, T. P., Weingartner, H., Ludlow, C., and Mikkelsen, E. J. (1978). "Dextroamphetamine: Cognitive and Behavioral Effects in Normal Prepubertal Boys." *Science*, 199, 560–563.

Stewart, M. A. (1970, April). "Hyperactive Children." *Scientific American*, pp. 94–99.

16. Officers of Medical Economics Company. (1980). *Physician's Desk Reference* (34th ed.). Oradell, NJ: Medical Economics Company.

17. O'Leary, K. D. (1980). "Pills or Skills for Hyperactive Children." *Journal of Applied Behavior Analysis*, 13, 191–204.

18. Schweitzer, J. B., and Sulzer-Azaroff, B. (1988). "Self-control: Teaching Tolerance for Delay in Impulsive Children." *Journal of the Experimental Analysis of Behavior*, 50, 173–186.

19. Kendall, P. C. (1982). "Individual Versus Group Cognitive-behavioral Self-control Training: 1-year Follow-up." *Behavior Therapy*, 13, 241–247.

    Kendall, P. C., and Finch, A. J. (1979). "Developing Nonimpulsive Behavior in Children: Cognitive-behavioral Strategies for Self-control." In P. C. Kendall and S. D. Hollon (Ed.), *Cognitive-behavioral Interventions* (pp. 37–79). New York: Academic Press.

    Kendall, P. C., and Zupan, B. A. (1981). "Individual Versus Group Application of Cognitive-behavioral Self-control Procedures with Children." *Behavior Therapy*, 12, 344–359.

20. Abramowitz, A. J., and O'Leary, S. G. (1991). "Behavioral Interventions for the Classroom: Implications for Students with ADHD." *School Psychology Review*, 20, 220–2234.

    Carlson, C. L., Pelham, W. E., Milich, R., and Dixon, J. (1992). "Single and Combined Effects of Methylphenidate and Behavior Therapy on the Classroom Performance of Children with Attention-deficit Hyperactivity Disorder." *Journal of Abnormal Child Psychology*, 20, 213–232.

    Horn, W. F., Chatoor, I., and Conners, C. K. (1983). "Additive Effects of Dexedrine and Self-control Training: A Multiple Assessment." *Behavior Modification*, 7, 383–402.

    Horn, W. F., Ialongo, N. S., Pascoe, J. M., Greenberg, G., Packard, T., Lopez, M., Wagner, A., Puttler, L. (1991). "Additive Effects of Psychostimulants, Parent Training, and Self-control Therapy with ADHD Children." *Journal of the American Academy of Child and Adolescent Psychiatry*, 30, 233–240.

21. Mannuzza, S., Klein, R. G., Bonagura, N., Malloy, P., Giampino, T. L., and Addalli, K. A. (1991). "Hyperactive Boys Almost Grown Up." *Archives of General Psychiatry*, 48, 77–83.

22. McKeachie, *Teaching Tips*.

23. Becker, W. C. (1971). *Parents Are Teachers: A Child Management Program*. Champaign, IL: Research Press.

24. Boice, R. (1992). *The New Faculty Member: Supporting and Fostering Professional Development*. San Francisco: Jossey-Bass.

25. Ibid.

26. Ibid.

27. Ibid., p. 170.

28. Boice, *The New Faculty Member*.

29. Ibid.

    McKeachie, *Teaching Tips*.

30. Gould, S. J. (1989). *Wonderful Life: The Burgess Shale and the Nature of History*. New York: W. W. Norton, p. 245.

31. Forzano, L. B., and Logue, A. W. (in press). "Self-control in Adult Humans: Comparison of Qualitatively Different Reinforcers." *Learning and Motivation.*

Hyten, C., Field, D., Madden, G., Greenspoon, J., and Mistr, K. (1991, May). *Exchange Delays and Impulsive Choice in Humans.* Poster presented at the Association for Behavior Analysis, Atlanta, Georgia.

32. Elster, J. (1985). "Weakness of Will and the Free-rider Problem." *Economics and Philosophy*, 1, 231–265.

Lea, S. E. G., Tarpy, R. M., and Webley, P. (1987). *The Individual in the Economy: A Textbook of Economic Psychology.* Cambridge, England: Cambridge University Press.

Thaler, R. H., and Shefrin, H. M. (1981). "An Economic Theory of Self-control." *Journal of Political Economy*, 89, 392–406.

33. Lea, Tarpy, and Webley, *The Individual in the Economy.*

34. Kutner, L. (1991). *Parent and Child: Getting Through to Each Other.* New York: William Morrow and Company.

35. Shaklee, H. (1990, November). *Investment Decision Making: Short-term Interest and Long-Term Yield.* Paper presented at the Annual Meeting of the Psychonomic Society, New Orleans, LA.

36. Nasar, S. (1991, September 24). "Baby Boomers Fail as Born-again Savers." *The New York Times*, pp. A1, D5.

37. Hoch, S. J., and Loewenstein, G. F. (1991). "Time-inconsistent Preferences and Consumer Self-control." *Journal of Consumer Research*, 17, 492–507.

38. Goleman, D. (1991, July 17). "A Constant Urge to Buy: Battling Compulsion." *The New York Times*, pp. C1, C12.

39. Kaplan, M. (1992, September 14). "Frozen Assets." *New York*, p. 37.

40. Paulsen, K., Rimm, D. C., Woodburn, L. T., and Rimm, S. A. (1977). "Self-control Approach to Inefficient Spending." *Journal of Consulting and Clinical Psychology*, 45, 433–435.

41. "Instant Gratification and Sound Public Policy." (1991, October 2). *The Chronicle of Higher Education*, p. B2.

42. Rosovsky, H. (1990). *The University: An Owner's Manual.* New York: W. W. Norton.

43. Ibid.

44. Schuler, R. S., and Harris, D. L. (1992). *Managing Quality: The Primer for Middle Managers.* Reading, MA: Addison-Wesley Publishing Company.

45. Lea, Tarpy, and Webley, *The Individual in the Economy.*

46. "Betting On and Off the Track." (1992, November 30). *The New York Times*, p. B1.

47. American Psychiatric Association, *Diagnostic and Statistical Manual of Mental Disorders.*

48. Ibid., p. 324.

49. Lea, Tarpy, and Webley, *The Individual in the Economy.*

50. Mazur, J. E. (1989). "Theories of Probabilistic Reinforcement." *Journal of the Experimental Analysis of Behavior*, 51, 87–99.

Rachlin, H., Castrogiovanni, A., and Cross, D. (1987). "Probability and Delay in Commitment." *Journal of the Experimental Analysis of Behavior*, 48, 347–353.

Rachlin, H., Logue, A. W., Gibbon, J., and Frankel, M. (1986). "Cognition and Behavior in Studies of Choice." *Psychological Review*, 93, 33–45.

51. Rachlin, H. (1990). "Why Do People Gamble and Keep Gambling Despite Heavy Losses?" *Psychological Science*, 1, 294–297.

52. Lea, Tarpy, and Webley, *The Individual in the Economy*.

53. Gottfredson, M. R., and Hirschi, T. (1990). *A General Theory of Crime*. Stanford: Stanford University Press.

54. Wilson, J. Q., and Herrnstein, R. J. (1985). *Crime and Human Nature*. New York: Simon & Schuster.

55. Nurco, D. N., Hanlon, T. E., and Kinlock, T. W. (1991). "Recent Research on the Relationship Between Illicit Drug Use and Crime." *Behavioral Sciences and the Law*, 9, 221–242.

56. Gottfredson, and Hirschi, *A General Theory of Crime*.

57. Wilson, and Herrnstein, *Crime and Human Nature*.

58. Goleman, D. (1992, September 15). "New Storm Brews on Whether Crime Has Roots in Genes." *The New York Times*, pp. C1, C7.

10

Getting Along with Yourself and Others: Cooperation, Lying, Depression, Suicide, and Aggression

This chapter, the last in the book, discusses self-control with respect to how people (and other animals) interact with other people (or other animals), and how people feel about themselves. Thus this chapter completes the book's discussion of what the American Psychiatric Association defines as *impulse control disorders*, a general category that includes "failure to resist an impulse, drive, or temptation to perform some act that is harmful to the person or others."[1] The specific types of behavior to be discussed here include cooperation, lying, depression, suicide, and aggression—all examples of how people get along with others or feel about themselves. This chapter examines all of these types of behavior to show how a self-control analysis can help us understand why these behaviors do or do not occur, and how they might be changed.

COOPERATION

Cooperation exists whenever two or more people work together to obtain something that they value. It could be a single item that could not be obtained by someone working alone (for example, when members of a community work together to build a neighborhood swimming pool, or when corporate lawyers negotiate a complicated contract, or when countries agree to arms or environmental controls), or it could be a series of items, of which each person cooperating receives one (for example, when two children agree to take turns pushing each other on a swing). Doing someone a favor can also be a kind of cooperation because someone may only agree to do a favor with the expectation that he or she will receive a return favor sometime in the future.

In all of these cases, someone gives up a little something now (some time, money, effort) in return for almost certain receipt of a large something later (the pool, the contract, a safe and clean environment, a turn on the swing, a favor). Thus, all of these behaviors consist of self-control, choice of a larger, but more delayed, reward over a smaller, but less delayed, reward. Examined in this way, it is easy to see why cooperation can sometimes be so difficult for individuals, organizations, and countries. The positive consequences of co-operating are delayed and thus discounted, whereas the positive conse-quences of not cooperating, are more immediate. When people choose not to cooperate but instead choose the more immediate rewards of not cooperat-ing, they are said to be selfish or greedy. Sometimes, when the long-term con-sequences of noncooperation are destructive for a society, legislators enact laws designed to ensure that people cooperate and do not behave in a selfish, greedy manner.[2] For example, laws are enacted that ensure punishment if a contract is broken or if someone does not pay taxes.[3]

LYING

Lying consists of deliberate deceit—deliberately providing false infor-mation. Lying that is not easily detected has been described as a type of self-control, as providing false information in order to obtain something in the sometimes very distant future. A skilled, clever liar takes long-term conse-quences into account when going to the effort of creating the lie. It has been hypothesized that such an ability has evolved uniquely in humans.[4]

It may indeed be possible to classify effective lying as self-control, however, in many cases, lying should be classified as impulsiveness. Much lying is done in order to obtain some immediate reward, without consideration of the long-term consequences if the lying should be discovered (see Box 10.1). Examples of such

> Oh, what a tangled web we weave when first we practice to deceive.

Box 10.1

lying include a teenager who tells her parents that the beer cans in her car must have been put there by a stranger when the car was left on the street unlocked, or a bank teller who calls in sick when he wants a day off, or a researcher desperate for tenure who fabricates some data. In all of these cases, the liar obtains some im-mediate reward (avoidance of being punished, a day off, or tenure). However, should the lie be found out (and it often is), then people will be less likely to be-lieve the liar's representations of the truth in the future. People will not trust the liar, and this may make it much more difficult for the liar to obtain items of value in the future—the teenager's parents may limit her social activities, the bank may fire the teller, and the researcher may find it impossible to get a grant or any sort of research position.

In addition, if effective lying is described as behavior that misrepresents the truth and that results in positive long-term consequences, it may be misleading to state that effective lying has evolved uniquely in humans. Nonhuman animals frequently engage in deception that results in long-term positive consequences for the animal doing the deceiving. Consider, for example, scorpionflies. A female scorpionfly will only copulate with a male if the male first gives the female a dead insect. A male scorpionfly will sometimes pretend to be a female in order to obtain a dead insect from another male.[5] This deception not only makes it easier for the deceiving male scorpionfly subsequently to engage successfully in copulation, but it makes it harder for the deceived scorpionfly to so engage. The result is an increase in the deceiving scorpionfly's inclusive fitness (a valuable long-term consequence) and a decrease in the deceived scorpionfly's inclusive fitness.

DEPRESSION AND SUICIDE

Depression and Suicide as Impulsiveness and Self-Control

The American Psychiatric Association describes the symptoms of a *major depressive episode* as including "difficulty thinking or concentrating, and recurrent thoughts of death, or suicidal ideation or attempts. . . . loss of interest or pleasure. . . . The person may complain of memory difficulty and appear easily distracted."[6] What these symptoms suggest is that someone who is depressed may have difficulty showing self-control. In a depressed person, large, delayed rewards would not be so large due to the depressed person's inability to feel pleasure. Further, depressed people might have difficulty waiting for a delayed reward due to their inability to concentrate and the ease with which they are distracted by immediate stimuli. In other words, depressed people may be very sensitive to changes in reward delay, and not very sensitive to changes in reward amount.

Although some research has found no relationship between depression and self-control,[7] other research does indeed appear to suggest that depressed people tend to show less self-control than do nondepressed people.[8] Certainly, people suffering from the kind of depression called SAD (see Chapter 6) impulsively overeat. In addition, a great deal of indirect evidence suggests that depression should be correlated with impulsiveness. For example, among pigeons and children it has been repeatedly shown that self-control can be increased by doing enjoyable activities and thinking enjoyable thoughts, or even by presenting stimuli that have been previously associated with reward (see Chapter 5). Further, children demonstrate the most self-control when verbal instructions have been used to put them in a happy mood;

children show the least self-control when verbal instructions had been used to put them in a sad mood.[9] Finally, when dieters are in an unhappy mood, they are more likely to overeat (in other words, to be impulsive) than when they are not in an unhappy mood.[10]

In extreme cases, depression can result in suicide, which can often be defined as impulsiveness. Suicide is impulsive when it occurs in order to escape some current aversive stimuli, without regard for the loss of possible long-term positive stimuli. For example, a teenager may commit suicide due to a broken romance, even though, ten years later, if the suicide had not occurred, the teenager might be happily married with little or no memory of the former romantic interest. However, some cases of suicide should not be classified as impulsiveness but instead as self-control. For example, suppose someone is dying of an incurable disease and has six months to live. Suppose further that this person's daily treatments are extremely expensive and must be paid for by the patient's parents who are too old to work and who are very poor. Finally, suppose that this patient is in considerable pain that cannot be relieved by medication. In such a case, many people would define the patient's suicide as self-control (enduring some immediate aversive stimuli in order to avoid more aversive stimuli later).

Causes of Impulsive Depression and Suicide

There are a number of factors that may contribute to impulsive depressive behavior and suicide, some of which are related to increased impulsiveness. One such factor is drug abuse, particularly involving alcohol or cocaine. Suicide is more likely to occur when someone has been drinking or taking cocaine.[11] Alcohol and cocaine may increase the probability of suicide due to their decreasing the length of the drinker's time horizon, making long-term consequences of little or no consequence to the drinker[12] (see Chapter 7). A low level of serotonin may also contribute to depression and suicide. It has been repeatedly shown that cerebrospinal levels of this neurotransmitter are low in depressed people who commit suicide.[13] It has been hypothesized that serotonin is essential in animals' ability to tolerate delay—essentially that serotonin is involved in the suppression of impulsive behaviors[14] (see also the discussion in Chapter 6 of the role of serotonin in impulsive overeating of carbohydrates). In fact, self-control has been increased in rats by drugs that enhance serotonin functioning (for example, by blocking the reuptake into the neurons of released serotonin, so that the neurotransmitter effect of the serotonin lasts longer).[15]

Methods for Decreasing Impulsive Depression and Suicide

The preceding sections on the nature and causes of impulsive depression and suicide suggest some methods by which such impulsiveness can be decreased or prevented. For example, it might be possible to decrease impulsive depression and suicide by making the delayed, large rewards seem closer. One way that this might be accomplished is by having people suffering from depression and suicidal tendencies speak with recovered depressives to hear about the rewarding aspects of life that can follow a depression. Support groups can be helpful in this regard. Pharmacological treatments may also be useful. If there is a possibility that low levels of serotonin are a problem, drugs such as *Prozac* (a serotonin uptake blocker, also known as *fluoxetine*) may be helpful. Prozac is widely used as an antidepressant.[16] Finally, people who are depressed should use precommitment devices to avoid alcohol consumption and taking cocaine, thus avoiding increasing their risk of suicide.

AGGRESSION

Aggression as Impulsiveness and Self-Control

There is no one clear definition of aggression. However, one useful definition is the following: "Aggressive behaviors are behaviors intended to do physical or psychological damage to someone."[17] There are many types of such aggressive behaviors, including shouting, hitting, and, in some cases, simply staring. An analysis of the effects of aggression can help to show aggression's relationship with self-control.

In many cases, aggression results in the receipt of some immediate rewards. These rewards might include retrieval of some property (for example, when one child hits another child who took the first child's ball), or removal of some unpleasant stimulus (for example, when a man hits another man who is speaking lewdly to the first man's wife), or obtaining some sort of valuable item (for example, when a robber shoots a resisting victim). However, with all types of aggression, at the same time as the aggression is resulting in some immediate rewards, it is possible that the aggressor will damage someone's property, will hurt someone, or will do something that will make someone else hurt the original aggressor. Ultimately, the aggressor may lose his or her friends or job by such behaviors, or may even end up in jail or the morgue. Thus, although aggression may result in the receipt of some immediate reward, the long-term consequences are often not positive ones. Therefore aggression should frequently be classified as impulsiveness.

However, sometimes aggression can be classified as self-control. There are several types of situations in which this might be the case. First, someone may deliberately engage in aggression in order to decrease the size of a currently available, tempting, small reward. For example, if a married person is trying to avoid being seduced by an acquaintance, the potential seducee could start a fight with the potential seducer, thus eliminating the possibility

of the tempting seduction, and ensuring the possible long-term, large positive consequences of fidelity and a stable marriage[18] (consequences such as
the benefits of long-term mutual cooperation and division of labor, and of
gaining long-term assistance from the spouse's relatives).[19] Another type of
aggression which might be classified as self-control occurs in salamanders.
Before foraging for food, salamanders engage in territorial behaviors until
their territories are established.[20] Thus, the salamanders expend time and energy on a nonimmediate need, establishing a territory, in order that later they
will be able to forage for food relatively undisturbed in their own identified
areas. Similarly, among humans, professional boxers willingly endure some
immediate pain in order to ensure themselves adequate income later, a type
of self-control.

Melvin Konner has argued that many types of aggression are actually
adaptive in the long run (in other words, they represent self-control). According to Konner, although people who engage in fights have a higher probability of being killed, they also have a higher probability of winning fights.
In our evolutionary past, people who won fights were more likely to gain access to food and mates, and thus were more likely to survive or to have their
relatives survive. Thus, Konner argues, in our evolutionary past, aggressiveness increased inclusive fitness.[21] It is questionable, however, in these times
of laws and jails, whether aggressiveness is now the best way to maximize inclusive fitness.

When groups of people engage in aggression, as occurs in wars and
feuds, aggression can also be seen as impulsiveness or self-control, depending on the particular aspects of the environment that are present. For example, some wars—those in response to a real but conquerable threat—involve
giving up some immediate pleasure and experiencing the suffering caused
by war in order to obtain some long-term, large reward (a safe and independent country). Then war could be described as self-control. However, there
are other wars in which people engage even though they know they cannot
win; they engage in the war primarily for reasons of pride or honor. Many
people die, but even so, the war is lost. In such cases, although there is some
immediate reward in that pride and honor have been maintained, there are
no long-term large rewards—there is no one left to obtain them. Then war
could be described as impulsiveness. Throughout history, many stories and
songs have described all of these types of group conflicts, sometimes making
clear their impulsive nature (see Box 10.2).

Causes of Aggression

There are many factors that appear to increase the probability of aggressive behavior. This section describes some of those that are particularly
relevant to a self-control analysis of aggression.

Certain environmental conditions can greatly increase the probability
of aggressive behavior. Such conditions include, for example, removal of cur-

PRINCE:
This letter doth make good the friar's words,
Their course of love, the tidings of her death:
And here he writes that he did buy a poison
Of a poor 'pothecary, and therewithal
Came to this vault to die and lie with Juliet.
Where be these enemies? Capulet! Montague!
See, what a scourge is laid upon your hate,
That heaven finds means to kill your joys with love!
And I, for winking at your discords too,
Have lost a brace of kinsmen: all are punish'd. . . .
A glooming peace this morning with it brings;
    The sun for sorrow will not show his head:
Go hence, to have more talk of these sad things;
    Some shall be pardon'd and some punished:
For never was a story of more woe
Than this of Juliet and her Romeo.
[William Shakespeare[22]]

Box 10.2

rent rewards or prevention of receipt of expected rewards. Such situations cause anger and aggression. The aggression does not appear to be premeditated, and the aggressor seems unaware of the long-term consequences of the aggressive behavior.[23] Thus it is not surprising that under such circumstances, impulsive aggressive behavior would occur. Such was the case in the infamous Happy Land fire that occurred in the Bronx in New York City. Julio Gonzalez was visiting the Happy Land Social Club one night in 1990. His girlfriend worked there. They had a disagreement and a bouncer made Gonzalez leave. That same night, Gonzalez deliberately started a fire at the club, which had inadequate fire exits. As a result, eighty-seven people died, the largest mass murder in the history of the United States.[24]

Another way in which certain environmental conditions can increase the probability of aggressive behavior is if someone has been consuming alcohol. Some, but not necessarily all, of the increase in aggression due to alcohol consumption may be due to alcohol consumers' expectations concerning the effects of alcohol, rather than the actual physiological effects of the alcohol.[25] Alcohol may increase aggression in a person by decreasing that person's time horizon and thereby generally increasing the person's impulsiveness.[26]

There has also been a great deal of research to determine whether or not certain individuals might be more or less likely to show aggressive behavior, and what might be responsible for any such individual differences. One such line of research, mentioned earlier in this chapter, is the possibility that some individuals may be more likely to engage in impulsive behavior, including impulsive aggression as well as suicide, due to low levels of the neurotransmitter serotonin. The low levels of serotonin are hypothesized to result in a general tendency to show impulsiveness.[27] However, a great deal more research is needed before the relationship between aggressiveness and serotonin levels can be precisely characterized.

Another individual characteristic that appears to correlate with aggressive behavior is intelligence. Violent crimes are more likely to be committed by people of lower IQ than are nonviolent crimes. However, this correlation may be due, not to people of lower IQ being more violent than people of higher IQ, but to people of higher IQ avoiding committing violent crimes due to these crimes having a higher arrest rate. In addition, people with lower IQs may have shorter time horizons, committing crimes without much regard for the long-term consequences. Another possible reason for the correlation between violent crime and IQ could be that lower IQ children (who grow into lower IQ adults) are more likely to experience school failure than are higher IQ children, and these repeated failures ultimately cause the lower IQ children to engage in more asocial behavior, including violence. There are many possible reasons for the correlation between violent crime and IQ.[28]

Testosterone level has also been examined for its relationship with the tendency towards aggressive behavior. Much research in many species has shown that males tend to be more aggressive than females. For species that have a mating season, the higher aggressiveness among males appears to be strongest during that time. Further, aggressiveness seems to be lower among castrated than noncastrated males. All of these data suggest that the male hormone testosterone plays a role in the greater aggressiveness demonstrated by males as compared with females.[29] These data are consistent with the finding that among children who tend to be impulsive in the laboratory, the boys, but not the girls, are described as aggressive by their teachers and by the experimenters.[30] Perhaps exposure to prenatal testosterone during development results in a greater tendency towards impulsive aggressiveness in boys as opposed to girls. Chapter 4 reported some findings with adults similar to those described here for children. That chapter pointed out that people believe that men who are low in self-control tend to be assertive in a negative way; they try to overcontrol their environment (which would include by means of aggression). In contrast, people believe that women who are low in self-control tend to be yielding in a negative way, they do not try to control their environment enough.[31] However, as Chapter 4 also pointed out, in contrast to the results with children, it is not yet known whether or not these popularly held beliefs concerning personality differences between low self-control men and women are accurate descriptions of behavior.

There is a particular psychological disorder, known as either *intermittent explosive disorder* or *episodic dyscontrol*, which is characterized by aggression and which is believed to be caused by fairly specific brain disturbances.[32] The criteria for a diagnosis of intermittent explosive disorder include:

A. Several discrete episodes of loss of control of aggressive impulses resulting in serious assaultive acts or destruction of property.

B. The degree of aggressiveness expressed during the episodes is grossly out of proportion to any precipitating psychosocial stressors.

C. There are no signs of generalized impulsiveness or aggressiveness between the episodes.[33]

In other words, people with this disorder demonstrate occasional, not continuous, impulsive aggression, without sufficient environmental provocation to justify the aggression. In addition, people with this disorder may have inadequate social relationships due to other people avoiding them in order to avoid the repeated impulsive aggressive episodes.[34] Intermittent explosive disorder is thought to be due to disturbances in the limbic system[35] (which contains such structures as the septum) and/or to disturbances in the prefrontal cortex[36] (see also Chapters 3 and 7, including Figure 7.1). For example, stimulation of the septum calms behavior, but lesions of the septum result in increased aggressiveness.[37]

Perhaps because there appears to be some evidence that intermittent explosive disorder is due to a disturbance in a particular part of the brain, its diagnosis has been used successfully as a defense in United States courts (although people who successfully employ such a defense are usually committed for psychiatric treatment; they do not simply walk free).[38] The implication is that this type of impulsive aggression has a known origin in the brain and is therefore uncontrollable; sufferers are not responsible for their actions. However, all other types of impulsive aggression may also be caused by some as yet undiscovered disturbances in the brain and may be just as uncontrollable. Further, if, as most scientists believe, all behavior is a result of some combination of nature and nurture, no behavior is any more or less controllable by a person than is another behavior. Behavior is affected by the current and past environment, as well as by the genes; behavior is not caused by some freely acting, independent agent within the body. Thus the issue is not whether someone who commits a serious impulsive aggressive act could or could not control that behavior, but whether the aggressor and society are best served by a sentence of incarceration in a standard prison or in some sort of mental health facility.

Aggression in Children and Young Adults

Aggression of various sorts occurs frequently in children. Aggression obtains immediate attention and other immediate rewards for a child. The unpleasant consequences of aggression come only much later. Early during the school years, behaving aggressively may be one of the best ways to get the teacher's attention (see also Chapter 9) or to be first in line to go down the slide. It is only much later that aggressive children find themselves without friends and with poor grades.[39] Such examples of aggression are easily seen to be impulsive.

The rates of violent and other crimes are highest among the 15- to 19-year-old age group.[40] Alan Rogers has argued that this finding has an evolutionary basis. According to Rogers, it is adaptive for children of this age to discount the future greatly (in other words, to be very sensitive to the passage of time) due to the combined effects of their high reproductivity and low mortality at that age. As a result of this adaptation, delayed rewards have little impact on these children[41] (see Box 10.3, and see also Chapter 4).

> The young live as though there were no tomorrow.

Box 10.3

When children and young adults engage in repeated crime, they are often labeled delinquents. Research has shown that delinquents have significantly shorter time horizons than do nondelinquents;[42] delinquents' behavior is less likely to be affected by delayed consequences than is nondelinquents' behavior. However, the question remains as to why some children have shorter time horizons than other children, and why some children are delinquent and others are not. Some researchers think that being born at an abnormally low weight can result in a child having a relatively short time horizon and in being delinquent. Another hypothesis is that delinquent children have short time horizons because, during the delinquent children's development, their families did not set up and enforce clear contingencies between consequences and the children's behavior.[43]

Psychopaths

People suffering from what the American Psychiatric Association terms *antisocial personality disorder*,[44] people more commonly known as *psychopaths*, are described as people who display "an insensitivity to remote consequences of action."[45] They are depicted as behaving only so as to satisfy their immediate needs, however fleeting those needs may be. Researchers have argued that psychopaths are particularly likely to discount delayed aversive conse-

GETTING ALONG WITH YOURSELF AND OTHERS **165**

quences of their actions, and therefore psychopaths' behavior is little affected by the threat of delayed punishment. Thus, although psychopaths do not by definition necessarily engage in impulsive aggressive behavior, they are likely to do so.[46] In one group of Caucasian prisoners, those who were identified as psychopaths by means of their scores on the *MMPI* (the *Minnesota Multiphasic Personality Inventory*, a standard personality test) were first arrested at younger ages than were those prisoners whose scores did not identify them as psychopaths. In addition, those who were identified as psychopaths were less likely to choose a large, delayed over an immediate, small reward than were the nonpsychopaths.[47]

There have been a number of physiological explanations of impulsiveness in psychopaths, all related to other physiological explanations of impulsiveness described earlier in this book. For example, one explanation is that psychopaths have relatively low levels of the neurotransmitter serotonin.[48] Another possible explanation is that psychopaths suffer from disturbances in such areas of their brains as the septum and the hippocampus[49] (see Chapters 3 and 7 including Figure 7.1). However, there is as yet very little firm data on any of these possibilities.

Methods for Decreasing Impulsive Aggression

Many of the methods for decreasing impulsive aggression are similar to others previously mentioned in this book. People other than the aggressor, or the aggressor through use of precommitment techniques, can take steps to decrease the immediate rewards for aggression, and/or to increase the delayed rewards for nonaggression. For example, a teacher can punish a child who is aggressive in class without also giving the child attention by immediately sending an aggressive child to a separate, empty room. In addition, at a time when an aggressive child is not being punished, the teacher or older students can point out the many advantages of paying attention in class. Role playing may be useful in helping aggressive children to see the long-term consequences of their actions.[50] The perceived time to the negative consequences of aggression may be decreased by, for example, having an aggressive child become familiar with older aggressive children who have miserable lives as a result of their aggression. It may also be possible to decrease aggression by decreasing the perceived time to the rewards of nonaggression. One study showed that it was possible to increase self-control in young adult prisoners by having them observe peer models who held prestigious jobs within the prison, who were soon to be released, and who had a high tendency to delay rewards.[51] Other methods for decreasing aggressiveness as suggested by the material in this chapter include avoiding the consumption of alcohol, avoiding anger-causing situations, and using medication to increase serotonin levels. Parents may be able to raise less aggressive children by setting up and following through on specific reward consequences for their children, and by paying attention to their children when they behave well, not just when they are aggressive. In cases in which society feels it extremely important to ensure that someone cannot do harm to someone else, society may decide to incarcerate that person, possibly in solitary confinement, thus preventing the person from emitting an impulsive response.

CONCLUSION

This chapter has illustrated, perhaps more than any other, that whether or not a behavior is classified as impulsiveness or self-control is dependent on the characteristics of the particular situation. For example, aggression is sometimes an adaptive behavior that results in long-term, positive consequences for the aggressor (that is, aggression can be classified as self-control). On the other hand, sometimes aggression is nonadaptive, and results in long-term, negative consequences for the aggressor (that is, aggression can be classified as impulsiveness). Therefore, before making any decisions with regard to changing aggressive behavior (or cooperative, lying, or suicidal behavior), it is essential that a careful analysis be made of both the short- and long-term consequences of that behavior. Only then will it be possible to determine whether the aggressor would or would not be best served by a change in the aggressor's level of aggression. If a decision is made that the level of aggression should be decreased, and there are certainly many such situations in our current society, then there are a variety of methods available which may help to accomplish that decrease.

REFERENCES

1. American Psychiatric Association. (1987). *Diagnostic and Statistical Manual of Mental Disorders* (3rd ed. rev.). Washington, DC: Author, p. 321.
2. Elster, J. (1992). "Intertemporal Choice and Political Thought." In G. Loewenstein and J. Elster (Eds.), *Choice Over Time* (pp. 35–53). New York: Russell Sage Foundation.
3. Dinsmoor, J. A. (1992). "Setting the Record Straight: The Social Views of B. F. Skinner." *American Psychologist, 47,* 1454–1463.
4. Alexander, R. D. (1989). "Evolution of the Human Psyche." In P. Mellars and C. Stringer (Ed.), *The Human Revolution: Behavioural and Biological Perspectives on the Origins of Modern Humans* (pp. 455–513). Princeton: Princeton University Press.
5. Cheyney, D. L., and Seyfarth, R. M. (1991). "Truth and Deception in Animal Communication." In C. A. Ristau (Ed.), *Cognitive Ethology: The Minds of Other Animals* (pp. 127–151). Hillsdale, NJ: Erlbaum.
6. American Psychiatric Association. (1987). *Diagnostic and Statistical Manual of Mental Disorders.*

7. O'Hara, M. W., and Rehm, L. P. (1982). "Choice of Immediate Versus Delayed Reinforcement and Depression." *Psychological Reports*, 50, 925–926.

   Sohlberg, S., Norring, C., Holmgren, S., and Rosmark, B. (1989). "Impulsivity and Long-term Prognosis of Psychiatric Patients with Anorexia Nervosa/Bulimia Nervosa." *The Journal of Nervous and Mental Disease*, 177, 249–258.

8. Rehm, L. P. (1977). "A Self-control Model of Depression." *Behavior Therapy*, 8, 787–804.

   Rehm, L. P. (1984). "Self-management Therapy for Depression." *Advances in Behavior Research and Therapy*, 6, 83–98.

9. Moore, B. S., Clyburn, A., and Underwood, B. (1976). "The Role of Affect in Delay of Gratification." *Child Development*, 47, 273–276.

   Schwarz, J. C., and Pollack, P. R. (1977). "Affect and Delay of Gratification." *Journal of Research in Personality*, 11, 147–164.

10. Ruderman, A. J. (1986). "Dietary Restraint: A Theoretical and Empirical Review." *Psychological Bulletin*, 99, 247–262.

11. Hudson, P. (1978). "The Medical Examiner Looks at Drinking." In J. A. Ewing and B. A. Rouse (Eds.), *Drinking* (pp. 71–92). Chicago: Nelson-Hall.

    Marzuk, P. M., Tardiff, K., Leon, A. C., Stajic, M., Morgan, E. B., and Mann, J. J. (1992). "Prevalence of Cocaine Use Among Residents of New York City Who Committed Suicide During a One-year Period." *American Journal of Psychiatry*, 149, 371–375.

12. Wilson, J. Q., and Herrnstein, R. J. (1985). *Crime and Human Nature*. New York: Simon & Schuster.

13. Mann, J. J., and Stanley, M. (1986). *Psychobiology of Suicidal Behavior*. New York: New York Academy of Sciences.

    Soubrié, P. (1986). "Reconciling the Role of Central Serotonin Neurons in Human and Animal Behavior." *The Behavioral and Brain Sciences*, 9, 319–364.

14. Ibid.

15. Bizot, J. C., Thiébot, M. H., Le Bihan, C., Soubrié, P., and Simon, P. (1988). "Effects of Imipramine-like Drugs and Serotonin Uptake Blockers on Delay of Reward in Rats. Possible Implication in the Behavioral Mechanism of Action of Antidepressants." *The Journal of Pharmacology and Experimental Therapeutics*, 246, 1144–1151.

    Thiébot, M.-H., Le Bihan, C., Soubrié, P., and Simon, P. (1985). "Benzodiazepines Reduce the Tolerance to Reward Delay in Rats." *Psychopharmacology*, 86, 147–152.

16. Holloway, M. (1991, March). "Rx for Addiction." *Scientific American*, pp. 94–103.

17. Beck, R. C. (1990). *Motivation: Theories and Principles*. Englewood Cliffs, NJ: Prentice Hall.

18. Baron, J. (1988). *Thinking and Deciding*. New York: Cambridge University Press.

19. Buss, D. M., and Schmitt, D. P. (1993). "Sexual Strategies Theory: An Evolutionary Perspective on Human Mating." *Psychological Review*, 100, 204–232.

20. Jaeger, R. G., Joseph, R. G., and Barnard, D. E. (1981). "Foraging Tactics of a Terrestrial Salamander: Sustained Yield in Territories." *Animal Behaviour*, 29, 1100–1105.

21. Konner, M. (1987, May/June). "Why the Reckless Survive." *The Sciences*, pp. 2–4.

22. Shakespeare, W. (1936). "The Tragedy of Romeo and Juliet." In W. A. Wright (Ed.), *The Complete Works of William Shakespeare* (pp. 315–350). Garden City, NY: Garden City Books, p. 350.

23. Beck, *Motivation: Theories and Principles.*

24. Tomasson, R. E. (1991, July 9). "Shock Lingers, As Happy Land Trial Starts." *The New York Times*, pp. B1, B4.

25. Hull, J. G., and Bond, C. F. (1986). "Social and Behavioral Consequences of Alcohol Consumption and Expectancy: A Meta-analysis." *Psychological Bulletin*, 99, 347–360.

    Lang, A. R., Goeckner, D. J., Adesso, V. J., and Marlatt, G. A. (1975). "Effects of Alcohol on Aggression in Male Social Drinkers." *Journal of Abnormal Psychology*, 84, 508–518.

    Tinklenberg, J. R. (1973). "Alcohol and Violence." In P. G. Bourne (Ed.), *Alcoholism: Progress in Research and Treatment* (pp. 195–210). New York: Academic Press.

26. Wilson, and Herrnstein, *Crime and Human Nature.*

27. Soubrié, "Reconciling the Role of Central Serotonin Neurons." 319–364.

28. Wilson and Herrnstein, *Crime and Human Nature.*

29. Beck, *Motivation: Theories and Principles.*

30. Funder, D. C., Block, J. H., and Block, J. (1983). "Delay of Gratification: Some Longitudinal Personality Correlates." *Journal of Personality and Social Psychology*, 44, 1198–1213.

31. Shapiro, D. H. (1983). "Self-control: Refinement of a Construct." *Biofeedback and Self-Regulation*, 8, 443–460.

32. Restak, R. M. (1992, July/August). "See No Evil: The Neurological Defense Would Blame Violence on the Damaged Brain." *The Sciences*, pp. 16–21.

33. American Psychiatric Association, *Diagnostic and Statistical Manual of Mental Disorders*, p. 322.

34. American Psychiatric Association, *Diagnostic and Statistical Manual of Mental Disorders.*

35. Restak, "See No Evil." pp. 16–21.

36. Flekkoy, K. (1983). "The Neuropsychological Basis for the `Dopamine Hypothesis' in Schizophrenia." *Nordisk-Psychiatrisk-Tiddskrift*, 37, 283–289. (From *Psychological Abstracts*, 74, Abstract No. 25165.)

37. Beck, *Motivation: Theories and Principles.*

38. Restak, "See No Evil," pp. 16–21.

39. Kutner, L. (1991). *Parent and Child: Getting Through to Each Other*. New York: William Morrow and Company.

40. Wilson and Herrnstein, *Crime and Human Nature.*

41. Rogers, A. (in press). "The Evolution of Time Preference." *Behavioral and Brain Sciences.*

42. Siegman, A. W. (1961). "The Relationship Between Future Time Perspective, Time Estimation, and Impulse Control in a Group of Young Offenders and in a Control Group." *Journal of Consulting Psychology*, 25, 470–475.

43. Wilson, and Herrnstein, *Crime and Human Nature.*

44. American Psychiatric Association, *Diagnostic and Statistical Manual of Mental Disorders*.

45. Wilson and Herrnstein, *Crime and Human Nature*, p. 198.

46. American Psychiatric Association, *Diagnostic and Statistical Manual of Mental Disorders*.

    Wilson and Herrnstein, *Crime and Human Nature*.

47. Blanchard, E. B., Bassett, J. E., and Koshland, E. (1977). "Psychopathy and Delay of Gratification." *Criminal Justice and Behavior*, 4, 265–271.

48. Schalling, D. (1986). "The Involvement of Serotonergic Mechanisms in Anxiety and Impulsivity in Humans." *Behavioral and Brain Sciences*, 9, 343–344.

    Zuckerman, M. (1986). "Serotonin, Impulsivity, and Emotionality." *Behavioral and Brain Sciences*, 9, 3348–349.

49. Gorenstein, E. E., and Newman, J. P. (1980). "Disinhibitory Psychopathology: A New Perspective and a Model for Research." *Psychological Review*, 87, 301–315.

    Newman, J. P., Gorenstein, E. E., and Kelsey, J. E. (1983). "Failure to Delay Gratification Following Septal Lesions in Rats: Implications for an Animal Model of Disinhibitory Psychopathology." *Personality and Individual Differences*, 4, 147–156.

50. Pitkänen, L. (1974). "The Effect of Simulation Exercises on the Control of Aggressive Behaviour in Children." *Scandinavian Journal of Psychology*, 15, 169–177.

51. Stumphauzer, J. S. (1972). "Increased Delay of Gratification in Young Prison Inmates Through Imitation of High-delay Peer Models." *Journal of Personality and Social Psychology*, 21, 10–17.

Conclusion: Impulsiveness and Self-Control in our Current Environment

This book has presented many examples to demonstrate that humans and other animals must frequently choose between smaller rewards that they can have sooner (impulsive choices) and larger rewards that they can have later (self-control choices). Sometimes self-control is the most adaptive choice for an individual or for a group of individuals, and sometimes impulsiveness is the most adaptive choice.

Due to the uncertainties present in our previous environment, we evolved to discount delayed events and thus to show impulsiveness in many situations, a tendency that persists today. In our current environment, in which future events are much more certain, self-control, and not impulsiveness, is frequently the adaptive choice. Therefore, unfortunately, as a result of the mismatch between our evolution and our current environment, our behavior is frequently not very adaptive. The book described such nonadaptive behavior. It also described some of the many possible mechanisms responsible for this nonadaptive behavior. Finally, the book described ways in which self-control behavior can be increased or decreased. Some of these methods are useful only for very specific situations, and others are of more general use.

The strategies described here for increasing self-control and decreasing impulsiveness can be placed into two categories. First, we can take steps to make the choices available in our environment more similar to those available in the environment in which we evolved, so that even though we continue to make choices in the same way, those choices will be adaptive. One example of such a strategy would be to precommit to eat only at home and to never buy sweet or salty foods. Then the only food choices available would be among a group of foods much more similar to those present when humans were evolving. With these restricted food choices, high blood pressure, diabetes, and obesity would be less likely. Our innate preferences for sweet and salty foods would once more be adaptive, and not impulsive.

The other category of strategies for increasing self-control and decreasing impulsiveness consists of psychological techniques used to change our behavior so that we make choices that are adaptive within our current environment, choices that take into account the long-term consequences in effect within that environment. For example, the long-term consequences of excess salt consumption could be made to seem larger and more imminent by giving someone graphic descriptions of or actual exposure to people who are ill with hypertension caused or aggravated by excess salt consumption. The person who is educated in this way may subsequently be less likely to consume large amounts of salt, despite its availability.

However, whatever is done, or needs to be done, to remove or prevent the negative consequences of our evolved tendency to discount delayed consequences, we should try not to cast blame on those who show nonadaptive impulsiveness. Such people are simply revealing their evolutionary heritage. Instead of casting blame, we need to apply our energies to helping impulsive people to do what is best for them in the near and distant future.

Further Information and Self-Help Organizations

This is a partial list; it is not meant to be complete.

ALCOHOL ABUSE

Alcoholics Anonymous
15 E. 26th Street
New York, NY 10010
(212) 683-3900

New York State Council on Alcoholism
Information Hotline
(800) 252-2557

COMPULSIVE SPENDING

Debtors Anonymous
250 W. 57th Street
New York, NY 10019
(212) 642-8220

National Hotline:
(212) 642-8222

DRUG ABUSE

Drug Abuse Information Hotline
(800) 522-5353

Narcotics Anonymous
5790 Broadway
Bronx, NY 10063
(718) 601-5817

EATING DISORDERS

American Anorexia/Bulimia Association
133 Cedar Lane
Teaneck, NJ 07666
(201) 836-1800

BASH Treatment and Research Center
for Eating and Mood Disorders
6125 Clayton Avenue, Suite 215
St. Louis, MO 63139
(800) 762-3334 or (314) 768-3794

Overeaters Anonymous
World Service Office
4025 Spencer Street, Suite 203
Torrance, CA 90503
(213) 542-8363

SUICIDE PREVENTION

Suicide Prevention Hotline
(718) 389-9608

VIOLENCE AND AGGRESSION

Child Abuse and Maltreatment Reporting Center
40 N. Pearl Street
Albany, NY 12243
(800) 342-3720

New York State Domestic Violence Hotline
(800) 942-6906

Author Index

A

Abarca, N., 98
Abel, E. L., 119
Abramowitz, A. J., 152
Addalli, K. A., 152
Addesso, V. J., 168
Ader, R., 133
Adornetto, M., 39, 54, 56, 74, 151
Agras, W. S., 102
Ainslie, G. W., 5, 17, 31–32, 54, 69, 71, 74–76, 119
Albert, J., 17
Alexander, R. D., 26, 32, 166
Allan, L., 32, 53
Altura, B. M., 122
Altura, B. T., 122
Anderson, G. H., 101–102
Anderson, J. R., 32
Anderson, K., 75
Anderson, M. E., 98
Anderson, W. H., 77
Antelman, S. M., 93, 102

B

Baer, J. S., 122
Baker, N., 76

Bandura, A., 75
Banks, R. K., 119
Barash, D. P., 31
Barker, J., 53
Barnard, D. E., 167
Barndt, D. C., 122
Baron, J., 76, 167
Barr, H. M., 119
Bassett, J. E., 169
Bates, K. L., 57
Battalio, R. C., 99
Baum, A., 133
Beall, P. C., 57
Beasty, A., 55
Beatty, W. W., 100
Beck, R. C., 132, 167–68
Becker, W. C., 152
Bemis, K. M., 102
Bender, M. E., 151
Beneke, W. M., 150
Benowitz, N., 121
Bentall, R. P., 55–56, 77
Bernstein, D. J., 98
Berry, S. L., 100
Bigelow, G. E., 121
Bizot, J. C., 167
Björntorp, P., 99
Black, J. L., 122

Subject Index

*An asterisk indicates a page where a definition of the relevant term appears.